OFFICE OF POPULATION CENSUSES AND SURVEYS
SOCIAL SURVEY DIVISION

The Youth Service and similar provision for Young People

by Margaret Bone
Assisted by Elizabeth Ross

*An enquiry carried out
on behalf of the
Department of Education
and Science*

LONDON
HER MAJESTY'S STATIONERY OFFICE
1972

SBN 11 700128 7

THE YOUTH SERVICE AND SIMILAR PROVISION
FOR YOUNG PEOPLE

TABLE OF CONTENTS

LIST OF TABLES

vi

LIST OF DIAGRAMS

ACKNOWLEDGEMENTS

I should like to thank the many people who contributed to this enquiry, including those in the Youth Service, and other organisations, whose views and advice were invaluable. In particular I am grateful to members of H.M.I. and the Research Consultative Group, Mr. G. Bourne, Professor S. J. Eggleston and Mr. S. Rowe, Mr. J. D. Ridge and Mr. A. Griffiths for their practical help and suggestions. I would also like to express my appreciation to Christine Frost, Neale Pharoah and Malcolm Lomas who helped at various stages of the enquiry, and especially to Evelyn Scott-Jupp for her indispensable assistance. Above all I am indebted to the many young people and their parents who gave so much time and thought to the interviews.

Finally, although it is the names of the research workers which appear on this Report, the execution of any enquiry of this kind is the work of a team, and only made possible by the contributions to the research effort of the Sampling, Field, Coding, Computing and Administrative Sections of the Social Survey Division.

Margaret Bone

SUMMARY OF MAIN FINDINGS

Chapter 2 – Attachment to the Youth Service and allied activities

Most young people of 14 to 20 years (65%) go to a club, team, society or similar group and nearly all (93%) pass through such groups before the age of 21. Evidence from earlier studies suggests that the prevalence of attachment amongst young people has not changed markedly since at least the late 1940's. Only a minority (26%) of the age group attend what they call 'Youth Clubs', (a definition which excludes some Youth Service organisations), but most (68%) pass through 'Youth Clubs' before the age of 21.

Current use of clubs of all kinds varies with the social and demographic characteristics of the young people. The least likely to use clubs are those who intend to leave or left school at the minimum age of 15, (referred to as 'early school leavers'), girls, the older teenagers, those at work and working class children. The older girl early school leavers who are mostly from working class homes make less use of clubs than any other group. But only a small proportion of any group have never done so by the age of 20.

Current use of Youth Clubs varies less with social characteristics, but more with age: a much higher proportion of the 14 to 16 year olds use Youth Clubs than of the 17 to 20 year olds.

Fewer parents than young people are currently attending clubs of some kind, (only 35% of the mothers interviewed), but parental use is related to the young person's use, so that the children of parents who attend clubs are more likely to attend clubs themselves. This relationship is itself associated with the general tendency for the most socially and educationally privileged of all ages to participate most in voluntary organisations.

Chapter 3 – Degree of attachment

Most (87%) of the young people who used clubs, (termed the 'attached'), went at least once a month, and 62% attended once a week or more. Attendances were rather more frequent in late autumn than summer.

60% of the attached attended more than one club, and it was the later school leavers who were most likely to hold multiple memberships: 67% of the later school leavers and 42% of the early leavers went to more than one club.

11% of the attached had founded one of the clubs they used, 20% were office holders, including 10% who held influential positions such as chairman, team captain or secretary. Amongst those who used clubs, late school leavers were twice as likely as early leavers to play these active roles.

Chapter 4 – Types of club and their attractions

60% of the young people in full-time education or employment said there was a club of some kind available to them at work or school or college. And of this 60%, a little over half made use of the facility. Clubs were more often available in educational than employing establishments, but where they were available, those in full-time education were most likely to use them. Amongst those still at school, the early leavers were less likely than late leavers to use school linked clubs, although these facilities were more or less equally available to both groups.

Sports Clubs were patronised more frequently than any other kind, and they were followed in order of utilisation by Youth Clubs, Social Clubs and Cultural Groups, like folk clubs, or drama societies. Youth Clubs were the organisations most frequented by early school leavers and Sports Clubs by later leavers, who were also much more likely to use Interest-Centred Clubs (e.g. cultural groups, clubs for academic subjects, and political and debating societies) than were those who left school at the minimum age.

Each of the four main types of club, as used, provided a characteristic pattern of activities. Sports Clubs were typically used for active sport, drinking and chatting; Youth Clubs for indoor sport, entertainment, dancing and chatting; Social Clubs for the same activities, but with less emphasis on indoor sport, and with the addition of drinking; whilst Interest-Centred Clubs typically provided interest centred activities like active drama and music and instruction through, for example, discussions and talks.

The main reason given for joining a club was the influence of other people, and 87% of the young people first went to a club in the company of others. The early school leavers were more likely to cite this reason than later leavers and were also more likely to say they first went for lack of anything else to do. More of those who left or intended to leave school after the minimum age, on the other hand, said they first went because of an interest in the activity provided. There was a relationship between the reason given for joining and the type of club joined, but the relationship between school leaving groups and reason for joining persisted when each type of club was considered separately. For example, although all young people were more likely to say they joined Youth rather than other clubs for lack of anything to do, more of the early than late school leavers said they had joined Youth Clubs for this reason.

2

People most commonly left clubs because they no longer found them attractive. The second most frequent reason was the unavailability of the club, followed by lack of time and lastly by the absence of friends to go with or meet there.

On the whole Youth Clubs had a favourable image both with the young people and their parents. But the majority of 17 to 20 year olds expected to find too many younger people in them.

Chapter 5 – Ideal Clubs – what young people want from clubs

The pattern of activities young people claimed they would like in an ideal club was similar to that provided in actual Youth Clubs. But they asked for more interest-centred activities, and in particular, for two new categories of these; domestic and motorised pursuits. The former were particularly favoured by the older girl early school leavers, the typical unattached. In general the provision of interests was considered to be a very important function of clubs by a majority of every group.

Up to the age of 17, young people tended to prefer clubs which included people older than those who used the clubs they actually attended. But the 18 to 20 year olds seldom wanted to mix with children younger than 16 and most commonly favoured groups aged from 17 or 18 up to between 21 and 25.

A third of the young people said they preferred commercial provision, (like dance-halls, coffee bars and night clubs), to organisations of the Youth Club type. It was the older early leavers who were most likely to favour commercial places, although a majority of no group opted unequivocally for them. Commercial places appeared to be preferred for their professional organisation and the absence of supervision, whilst non-commercial clubs were chosen for the freedom of choice they offered and the opportunity to influence provision, as well as for their greater friendliness.

Chapter 6 – Voluntary Community Service and Residential Courses

A little over a third of the young people had undertaken voluntary work at some time. Approaching two thirds of these had assisted old people in some way and a quarter had helped to raise funds, whilst smaller proportions had worked with children, sick or handicapped people and in various other ways.

More of the girls than the boys had been involved and it was the later school leavers and the attached who had most often done voluntary work. This seemed to be because the opportunity to take part was most often presented through school and, to a lesser extent, through Youth organisations. Amongst those still at school, the late leavers were no more likely to be involved than early leavers.

3

Rather more than a quarter of the 14 to 20 year olds had been on a non-vocational residential course at some time. Boys, the late school leavers and the attached were the most likely to have done so.

Although schools played the dominant role in channelling young people into such courses, this did not explain the different experience of the two educational groups. For, even amongst those still at school, the later leavers were almost twice as likely to have been on a residential course as the early leavers.

The most common activity provided by residential courses was sport, followed in frequency by orienteering, sightseeing and field studies.

Chapter 7 – Leisure activities of the young people

Social activities were the most frequently mentioned pastime, followed by watching television, entertainment and sport, mainly of the outdoor non-competitive kind like walking, cycling and fishing.

Late school leavers were more active than early leavers, and the attached more than the unattached. In particular the attached were more likely to participate in sport, to see their friends more often and to do things with their friends, to read, study and act or make music, as well as to be receiving part-time education. That is to say, within each social and demographic group, the attached appeared to be more physically, socially and intellectually active than the unattached.

Over half (57%) the young people wanted to do something in their spare time which they said was currently impossible. The most frequently desired of these unavailable activities were sports; mainly indoor sports or outdoor pursuits. More outdoor team games were rarely wanted. The second commonest demand was for more facilities for meeting and mixing with other people.

Chapter 8 – Other differences between the attached and unattached and members of different types of club

The attached differed from the unattached young people in their approach towards the world beyond their immediate experience, in their relationships with their contemporaries and in their sense of well being, but not in their relationships with the older generation. Although differences between school leaving groups were sometimes greater, within each social and demographic group the attached were more socially confident and more adventurous, (i.e. more enthusiastic about varied experiences, more socially enterprising and more interested in the wider world), than the unattached. They were also less inclined to complain of boredom and, with the exception of the older girl early leavers and older boy late leavers, more likely to be very happy than the unattached.

Amongst those who were attached, there were differences in these areas according to the type of club used. Youth Club members were inclined to be less adventurous, to perceive their parents as more restrictive, to be more hostile towards older people and to worry their parents more about possible antisocial behaviour than members of other types of club. They were also more likely to complain of boredom.

On the grounds that adventurousness is shown to be related to absence of boredom, and closer social relationships to happiness, it is suggested that organisations which promote adventurousness and good social relationships may contribute to their members' sense of well being through meeting these needs. But because a single cross sectional survey cannot determine even whether the young peoples' attitudes in each area precede or follow attachment, the causal nature of the relationship remains in doubt.

Chapter 9 – Differences within the main school leaving groups

Amongst those giving a school leaving age of 15, fewer of the children of semi-skilled, unskilled and unemployed urban workers were attached (46%) than of early school leavers in general (51%). The difference was entirely due to the lower prevalence of attachment amongst the younger girls and older boys in the first group. The lower prevalence amongst the younger girls was the result of their more transitory attachments, and amongst the older boys to their tendency to drop out earlier than the equivalent group of early school leavers as a whole.

Overall the children of the least skilled urban workers were no less likely to be attached at some time before the age of 21 than early school leavers in general, and they were more likely to pass through a Youth Club than any other kind of club.

In thinking of ideal clubs the girls amongst this least privileged group favoured rather more instructive, cultural and domestic activities, as well as more sport, socialising and entertainment than the attached amongst them experienced in actual clubs. The older boys wanted more cultural and motorised pursuits. And, at a more general level, the children of the least skilled urban workers were as enthusiastic about the provision of interests by clubs as any other group. In addition more of the younger girls than of any other group attributed great importance to club facilities for help and advice about their problems.

Amongst the early leavers the children of the least skilled urban workers were the least adventurous in the sense of pre-

5

ferring the company of known people to new contacts, and being the least interested in the wider world. They were the most likely to find it difficult to mix with others and were the least integrated with their families, whilst their parents were the most likely to be anxious about their behaviour. Most, but not all, of each difference was due to differences between the boys. That is to say, fewer of the sons of the least skilled were more adventurous in the two ways mentioned, or had good social relationships, than of boy early leavers as a whole. Although there was no difference overall between the children of the least skilled and early leavers in general, in the proportions who expressed boredom or happiness, the older boys in the first group were more likely to be bored and less likely to say they were very happy than older boy early leavers as a whole.

NOTES

1. Illustrative tables are interspersed with the text because they were thought necessary to comprehension. Fuller reference tables, the number of which is preceded by the letter 'R', are given at the end of each chapter. The appropriate reference table number is indicated in the margin of the text.

2. Percentages do not always add up to 100 because they have been rounded to the nearest whole number.

CHAPTER 1

PURPOSE AND METHOD

1.1 Aims

The two broad aims of this enquiry which was commissioned by
the Department of Education and Science were to describe the
use made of Youth Service and allied facilities and to assess how
far they met the needs of the young people for whom they were
provided. It was therefore designed to yield a description of
the prevalence and style of use, and the differences between
those young people who were involved and those who were not.
This design has made it possible to show who uses what facilities,
how they are used and with less certainty, why people do or do
not use them and what advantages are enjoyed by those who do.

1.2 Method

A single national cross sectional survey of the potential clientele
of the Youth Service was selected as an appropriate method of
investigation for these purposes. It is a method suited to
describing a situation at one point in time, but less effective in
suggesting why the situation is as it is, and whether and how it
is changing. This means that the first aim of the enquiry was
more satisfactorily fulfilled than the second.

Information was collected by personal interviews using the
structured schedules reproduced in Appendix 1. These were
developed by pilot work which began with focussed but initially
loosely structured interviews with individual young people, groups
and individual parents. The object was to find out the ways in
which young people viewed their free time and use of leisure
provision, and the aspects of both which were important to them
and at the same time relevent to the aims of the enquiry. The
results provided a framework for the interview schedules which
were then tested on about 100 young people and 100 parents before
the final fieldwork which took place in 1969.

The fieldwork was carried out in two stages. The first half
of the sample was interviewed in the early summer (May-July)
when the evenings were light and the second in late autumn
(October-December) when the evenings were dark. This was
because it seemed likely that leisure activities and interests,
and in particular use of Youth Service type facilities would
vary with the season of the year.

We attempted to interview the young person alone, and this
proved possible for 73% of the informants.

1.3 The Samples

Two samples were selected for interview. Young people aged
14 to 20 years inclusive and living in England or Wales, and
one parent of each young person (normally the mother), unless
the young person was married or living away from home. The
sample of approximately 3, 800 young people was designed to be
representative of all people of that age group living in the Country.
The parents, who were selected primarily because of their
relationship to the sampled young people, were also representative of parents of 14 to 20 year olds, except of those whose
parents were purposely excluded.

The Youth Service at present provides for the 14 to 20 year
old age range, and one of the more specific questions to be
examined was whether this range corresponds with the way in
which young people prefer to associate. Ideally we should have
drawn a sample of people from a broader range, because it is
possible that preferred groupings violate the boundaries of the
statutory range. But it was clear at an early stage that it would
be difficult to devise a standard interview which would be equally
meaningful to 14 and 20 year olds, and it was thought that any
extension of the range would both reduce the response rate and
the validity of the responses. Accordingly we opted for a
universe of all 14 to 20 year olds living in England or Wales in
1969.

The target sample size of 3, 500 was determined by the
number of principle variables thought necessary for the analysis;
these are discussed in Section 5 of this chapter.

Because of the absence of any national list of Youth Service,
and Youth Service type facilities, no attempt was made to relate
the sample to local provision. The sample was spread over
100 randomly selected Local Authority areas in England and
Wales giving an average of under 40 young people in each area.

No national sampling frame for 14 to 20 year olds exists
and to locate a sample of the required size, a probability sample
of 18, 400 addresses was drawn from the Electoral Registers.
A postal questionnaire was sent to each selected address asking
for the name, date of birth and sex of each occupant aged
between 10 and 25 years if any. Interviewers then visited each
address containing one or more 14 to 20 year olds and interviewed as far as possible all those eligible for inclusion, and
one parent for each child where appropriate.

A full account of the sample, design and procedure is given
in Appendix 2, but the table opposite summarises the results
of the search for the sample.

Because of the very small proportion of people living in truly
rural areas, the quota of such areas was deliberately doubled
to provide larger numbers of people for analysis. This is only

Table 1.1 Young people found by postal enquiry sent to 18,400 addresses, and number of young people and parents interviewed

	Young People		Parents	
	Number	%	Number	%
Eligible young people from postal enquiry	4,692			
Found eligible by interviewers	4,566	100	3,118	100
refusals	394	9	285	9
non contacts	230	5	97	3
Interviews	3,942	86	2,736	88

important when rural areas are being compared with others, and for most of the analysis presented in this Report the totals have been weighted down to give the true distribution of people living in each kind of area, giving numbers as follows:

Young people – 3,849
Parents – 2,592

The achieved sample size was greater than the target size largely because of the unexpectedly high response rate to the postal enquiry.

The Parents

One parent of each selected young person was also interviewed, except in cases where the young person was married or living away from home permanently. Parents of young people away from home for training purposes (i.e. at boarding school, college, nurses hostel, etc.,) were included. Wherever possible the mother or the mother substitute was interviewed, in a few cases where there was no mother or it was impossible to interview her for some reason, the father was interviewed.

Table 1.2 Percentage of parents interviewed

	%
No parent interviewed	10
Natural mother interviewed	85
Mother substitute interviewed	1
Natural father interviewed	3
Some other person interviewed	1
	100
Weighted Base	3,849 young people

11

1.4 The Design of the Analysis

The main aim of the analysis was to differentiate the young
people involved in Youth Service and similar facilities from
those who were not. There were two phases to this analysis.
In the first we were concerned with the characteristics of the
young people which almost certainly influenced use rather than
being influenced by it. These are the mainly social and demographic characteristics described as main variables in Section
1.5 below. They were used to classify young people into groups
so that the extent and manner of use of facilities by each group
could be examined and compared. They were selected because
they were known from other studies to be related to people's
behaviour and attitudes and appeared to be relevant to the present
enquiry.

In the second phase we were interested in how attitudes and
behaviour varied according to use of the facilities. In this case
use seemed as likely to influence behaviour and attitudes as to
be a consequence of them, and for this reason use and type of
facility used are treated as the independent variables. The
construction of these variables is described in the main body
of the Report and is not covered in Section 1.5.

1.5 Main Variables and Composition of the Sample

(a) Age and sex

In a study of teenagers, age and sex are certain to be of great
importance as it is unlikely that a 14 year old will enjoy the
same sorts of activities as a 20 year old, or that an activity
will be equally popular with boys and girls alike.

The sample was distributed approximately equally between
the sexes and over the seven ages, 14 to 20.

Table 1.3 Sex and age distribution of the sample

Qs. (iv) & (v) Age	M	F	T
14	287.5	280	567.5
15	294	308	602
16	274.5	304.5	579
17	271	294	565
18	247	256.5	503.5
19	261	251.5	512.5
20	276.5	243	519.5
T	1911.5	1937.5	3849

Note: The figures include fractions because they are weighted.

In chapters 2 and 3, which are concerned with the prevalence
and degree of use of clubs, the full age distribution is given,

12

but in later chapters the sample is grouped into 14 to 16 year olds and 17 to 20 year olds, for reasons which become apparent in chapter 2.

(b) School Leaving Age

The young people were asked either at what age they had left school or, for those still at school, when they intended to leave. For most of the analysis the sample has been divided into those who left or intended to leave at the minimum age of 15 years or under, and those who stayed or intended to stay on after the minimum school leaving age.

Table
R1.16

Table 1.4 Percentage of the sample specifying each school leaving age

School leaving age	*%*
15	42
16	27
17	11
18 or over	19
Over 15 but exact age not known	1
	100

42% of the sample left or intended to leave at 15 or under, but if young people of each age are considered separately a continuous increase over the years in the proportion remaining at school beyond the minimum leaving age is evident (Table 1.5). This is in line with the national figures published by the Department of Education and Science (1970), although a higher proportion of the sample than the total population reported that they had remained at school after 15.

Table 1.5 Percentages of young people in each age group who left or intended to leave at 15

Qs. (v) & 4

Age	*% leaving at 15*
14	31
15	38
16	38
17	47
18	44
19	46
20	52
Total leaving at 15	42

There was little difference in school leaving age between the sexes, 43% of the girls gave a school leaving age of 15, compared with 40% of the boys.

(c) Type of school

Table R1.17 The variable, type of school, refers to the present school or last school attended by the young person. The schools were defined as schools which took children of under 15 years of age, to ensure that further educational establishments, such as a technical college, were not included.

54% of the total sample went to Secondary Modern schools, 15% to Comprehensive schools and 20% to Grammar schools. (The remainder went to other types of school such as Direct Grant, Independent and Technical schools). As expected type of school was closely related to age of leaving school. If the sample is split into those giving the minimum school leaving age and others, it becomes apparent that the great majority of early leavers come from Secondary Modern schools, but only a third of the later leavers.

Table 1.6 Type of school, by age of leaving school

Qs. 2 & 4 Type of school	School leaving age = 15	School leaving age = 16 or over	Total
	%	%	%
Secondary Modern	83	33	54
Comprehensive	12	18	15
Grammar	3	32	20
Technical	1	4	3
Independent/Direct Grant	1	10	6
Other types	1	3	2
Total percentages	100	100	100
Weighted Base: All young people	(1615.5)	(2233.5)	(3849)

Looking at this table the other way around, 35% of those at Secondary Modern schools gave a school leaving age above the minimum, 68% at Comprehensive schools and 95% of those at Grammar schools.

(d) Social Class

The social class of each young person was based on his or her parent's occupation whenever this was known, (94% of the young people).

Table R1.18 The occupations were classified according to the Registrar General's five social class groupings, and the third group was subdivided into manual and non-manual occupations, giving six groups in all.

14

Table 1.7 Percentages of young people belonging to each of the Registrar General's Social Classes

Parents	Social Class		%
Q. (xiii)	Non-manual:	I professional	4
		II managerial and technical	14
		III clerical and miner supervisery	15
		Total Non-manual	**33**
	Manual:	III skilled manual	41
		IV semi-skilled manual	16
		V unskilled	4
		Total Manual	**61**
	Other*		6

*Includes 109.5 head of households who were not working (e.g. housewives) and 141 who gave an inadequate description of their jobs.

33% of the young people had parents whose occupations fell into the top three classes (i.e. non-manual work). There was a close relationship between social class and age of leaving school as can be seen from the table below.

Table 1.8 Age of leaving school, by social class

Q.4	Parents Q. (xiii)			Social Class			
	Non-manual			Manual			Other
Age of leaving school	I Professional	II Managerial & Technical	III Clerical & minor supervisory	III Skilled manual	IV Semi-skilled manual	V Unskilled manual	
	%	%	%	%	%	%	%
15	3	21	27	49	55	64	61
Over 15	97	79	73	51	45	36	39
Total percentages	100	100	100	100	100	100	100
Weighted Base: All young people	165.5	547.5	564	1570.5	596.5	154.5	250.5

The children of non-manual workers were far more likely to stay on at school after the minimum school leaving age than the children of manual workers. Given the relationship of both social class and type of school to school leaving age, it was to be expected that both the former would be related to one another.

School leaving age was considered a more useful variable than class, it is for example, as shown in chapter 2, more closely related to attachment than is class. It is therefore used as a main variable throughout this Report, whilst class is rarely

Table 1.9 Type of school, by social class

Q.2	Parents Q. (xiii) Social Class						
Type of school	Non Manual			Manual			Other
	I	II	III	III	IV	V	
	%	%	%	%	%	%	%
Secondary Modern	17	36	43	60	65	77	62
Comprehensive	14	13	16	16	16	15	14
Grammar	32	29	30	17	13	4	13
Technical school	3	2	3	3	2	1	3
Independent/Direct Grant	33	18	7	2	1	1	4
Other schools	1	2	1	2	3	2	3
Total percentages	100	100	100	100	100	100	100
Weighted base:							
All young people	165.5	547.5	564	1570.5	596.5	154.5	250.5

used except in chapters 2 & 9. However it should be noted that
although class and school-leaving age are related, half of the
later school leavers are the children of manual workers simply
because manual workers form the majority of the population.

(e) Occupational Status

Table
R1.19 Another variable which is closely related to age of leaving school
and to actual age is occupational status at the time of the interview which is divided into three groups, those in a job (full-time
employment), those in full-time education (at school, college,
university, etc.) and those who were unemployed for any reason
(e.g. out of work, between jobs, housewives).

49% of the young people were employed, and 44% in full-time
education. Obviously younger age-groups were more likely to
be in full-time education than in a job, but the following table
shows that by the age of 17 two-thirds of the young people were
in full-time employment and by the age of twenty this had risen
to nearly three quarters. The percentages who were unemployed
increased steadily with age, amongst the girls.

Table 1.10 Percentages of each sex and age group in a job, full-time education and unemployed

Q.1	Male							Female							Total
Present Occupation	Age at time of interview														
	14	15	16	17	18	19	20	14	15	16	17	18	19	20	
	%	%	%	%	%	%	%	%	%	%	%	%	%	%	%
Job	-	23	47	65	73	79	80	1	24	40	64	74	72	64	49
Full-time education	99	75	48	32	22	17	16	99	73	54	29	14	14	14	44
Other	1	2	5	3	5	4	4	-	3	6	7	12	14	22	7
Total percentages	100	100	100	100	100	100	100	100	100	100	100	100	100	100	100
Weighted Base:															
All young people	286.5	294	275.5	271	247	261	276.5	280	308	304.5	294	256.5	251.5	243	3,849

16

Occupational status was closely related to age of leaving school, presumably in part because school leaving age was likely to affect whether or not a young person had the opportunity to go on to full-time further education after school. Those who stayed on at school after 15 were less likely to be in a job at the time of the interview. As Table 1.11 shows it was rare to find early school leavers who were in full-time education of any kind after the age of 15. On the other hand, late school leavers were more likely to be in full-time education than a job until the age of 18 when the reverse became true. But even amongst 20 year old late leavers, almost a third were still in full-time education.

Table 1.11 Percentages of each age and school leaving age group in a job, full-time education and unemployed

Q.1	School leaving Age = 15							School leaving age = 16 or over						
Present Occupation	Age at time of interview													
	14	15	16	17	18	19	20	14	15	16	17	18	19	20
	%	%	%	%	%	%	%	%	%	%	%	%	%	%
Job	0.5	62	84	90	88	86	84	-	-	18	42	61	67	60
Full-time education	99	31	9	3	3	2	1	100	100	77	54	31	27	30
Other	0.5	7	7	7	9	12	15	-	-	5	4	8	6	10
Total percentages	100	100	100	100	100	100	100	100	100	100	100	100	100	100
Weighted Base: All young people	174.5	227.5	220.5	264	222.5	236	270.5	392	374.5	359.5	301	281	276.5	249

The rise in unemployment with age, especially amongst girls and early leavers was due very largely to the fact that, as will be shown later, female early leavers were more likely to be married than any other group. 40% of all those unemployed were married and 53% of all girls who were unemployed. 60% of the girls who were unemployed, were in fact looking after their houses and in some cases children.

(f) Marital Status

As expected the great majority of young people were single (89%), 7% were engaged and 4% married.

There was however a considerable difference between the sexes. 94% of the boys were still single, only 4% were engaged and 2% married. Amongst the girls however, 84% were single, 9% engaged and 7% were married.

Table R1.20

Obviously marital status was also connected with age. Amongst the twenty year olds 16% were married, whereas less than 1% of the 16 year olds were married.

Marital status also varied with school leaving age. In the earlier age groups, at least, age of leaving school is likely to affect marital status simply because at present school children rarely marry and only occasionally get engaged. However even by the age of 20, there was a higher percentage of early school

17

leavers who were married (21%) than late leavers (11%) although the same percentage were engaged (18%). The difference between school leaving groups was mainly due to the relatively high proportion of early leaving girls who were married. Of those who were married nearly half (47%) had at least one child, about 2% of the total sample.

Table 1.12 Percentages of young people in each age group, by school leaving age who are married, engaged or single

Q. (viii)	School leaving age = 15							School leaving age = 16 or over							Total
Marital Status	Age at time of interview														
	14	15	16	17	18	19	20	14	15	16	17	18	19	20	
	%	%	%	%	%	%	%	%	%	%	%	%	%	%	%
Single	100	100	96	87	79	68	61	99	100	99	97	89	85	71	89
Engaged	-	-	1	9	11	19	18	1	-	1	2	9	10	18	7
Married	-	-	3	4	10	13	21	-	-	-	1	2	5	11	4
Total percentages	100	100	100	100	100	100	100	100	100	100	100	100	100	100	100
Weighted Base: All young people	174.5	227.5	220.5	264	222.5	236	270.5	392	374.5	359.5	301	281	276.5	249	3,849

(g) Area and Region

The local authority areas in the sample were classified by two criteria, first of all by type of area, that is conurbation, urban, semi-rural and truly rural, and secondly by the Registrar General's regional classification which divides England and Wales into ten large regions.

The proportion of young people giving the minimum school leaving age varied little by type of area, but considerably by region.

Table 1.13 Percentages of young people in each region leaving school at 15 and at over 15

	North	Yorkshire & Humber	North-West	East Midlands	West Midlands	East Anglia	London & Sth.-East	South-West	South Wales	Rest of Wales
	%	%	%	%	%	%	%	%	%	%
Left at 15	45	48	47	52	46	51	35	38	45	29
Left at over 15	55	52	53	48	54	49	65	62	55	71
Total percentages	100	100	100	100	100	100	100	100	100	100
Weighted Base: All young people	256.5	373	543	256	426	120.5	1,322	337.5	161	53.5

This seemed to be related to the class distribution over the regions, rather than to the type of schools attended in each region.

Table 1.14 Percentages of young people in each region who attended each type of school

Type of school	North	Yorkshire & Humber	North-West	East Midlands	West Midlands	East Anglia	London & Sth.-East	South-West	South Wales	Rest of Wales
	%	%	%	%	%	%	%	%	%	%
Secondary modern	53	53	53	48	60	57	55	54	44	22
Comprehensive	16	17	10	27	14	12	13	9	26	65
Grammar	18	23	23	18	20	15	18	25	24	6
Technical	3	1	3	2	1	-	3	4	1	2
Independent	10	2	7	3	4	15	8	6	5	1
Other	-	4	3	2	1	2	3	2	1	5
Total percentages	100	100	100	100	100	100	100	100	100	100
Weighted Base: All young people	256.5	373	543	256	426	120.5	1,322	337.5	161	53.5

Table 1.15 Percentages of young people in each region whose parents had manual and non-manual occupations

Parent's occupation	North	Yorkshire & Humber	North-West	East Midlands	West Midlands	East Anglia	London & Sth. East	South-West	South Wales	Rest of Wales
	%	%	%	%	%	%	%	%	%	%
Non-manual	33	27	34	23	31	28	37	35	30	44
Manual	57	66	59	71	64	64	57	59	63	48
Other*	10	7	8	6	5	8	6	5	7	8
Total percentages	100	100	100	100	100	100	100	100	100	100
Weighted Base: All young people	256.5	373	543	256	426	120.5	1,322	337.5	161	53.5

*This includes 109.5 parents who were not working and 141 who gave an inadequate description.

(h) Colour

It was of some interest to know whether coloured young people were able to use Youth Service facilities to the same extent as others, but because the main target of the enquiry was all young people of 14 to 20, it was not possible to design the sample to include disproportionate numbers of coloured people. In the event only 39 of the informants (just over 1%) were coloured, and apart from a brief reference in Chapter 2, this characteristic is not used for analytical purposes.

1.6 The Plan of the Report

The Report is presented in ten chapters, of which the last is a discussion of conclusions. Chapters 2 to 4 deal with use of the Youth Service and allied provision; chapters 2 and 3 cover prevalence and intensity of use and chapter 4 is concerned with the manner in which facilities are used, including reasons for joining and leaving.

Chapters 5 to 8 concern differences in behaviour and attitudes between those who use the facilities and those who do not, and, where appropriate, differences between young people who use different kinds of facilities.

Chapter 5 is about the kind of clubs young people think they would like, and mainly about the sort of things they would like to be able to do there. The aim here is to see how far ideal clubs differ from actual provision.

Chapter 6 describes involvement in voluntary community service and residential courses, both of which may be provided through the Youth Service, but which are considered here as possible alternatives to club membership. In other words our main concern is with whether they were used most by those who used clubs or those who did not.

In chapter 7 we examine the total pattern of leisure activities to see whether the club members differed from others in the way they spent their leisure time. And in chapter 8 we attempt an assessment of the extent to which the Youth Service meets certain needs of young people. This is distinct from the assessment in chapter 5 of the extent to which existing clubs are consistent with young people's ideal clubs.

Chapter 9 concerns many of the attitudes and experiences covered by the earlier chapters but relates these to social or educational groups within each of the two main groups of school leavers.

Table R1.16 Age by age of leaving school and sex

Q. (v) Age	School leaving age 15			School leaving age 16 and over			Total		
	Male	Female	Total	Male	Female	Total	Male	Female	Total
	%	%	%	%	%	%	%	%	%
14	11	11	11	18	17	18	15	14	15
15	14	14	14	17	17	17	15	16	16
16	15	12	14	14	18	16	14	16	15
17	15	18	16	14	13	13	14	15	15
18	13	15	14	13	12	13	13	13	13
19	15	15	15	13	12	12	14	13	13
20	18	16	17	12	10	11	14	13	14
Total percentages	100	100	100	100	100	100	100	100	100
Weighted base: all young people	(777.5)	(838)	(1615.5)	(1,134)	(1099.5)	(2233.5)	(1911.5)	(1937.5)	(3,849)

Table R1.17 Type of school, by age of leaving school

Q.2 Type of school	School leaving age 15	School leaving age 16 and over	Total		
			Male	Female	Total
	%	%	%	%	%
Secondary modern	83	33	54	54	54
Comprehensive	12	18	15	15	15
Grammar	3	32	19	20	20
Technical	1	4	3	2	3
Independent	1	10	7	6	6
Abroad	-	-	-	-	-
Other	1	3	2	2	2
Total percentages	100	100	100	100	100
Weighted base: all young people	(1615.5)	(2233.5)	(1911.5)	(1937.5)	(3,849)

Table R1.18 Social class, by age of leaving school and sex

Social Class	School leaving age 15			School leaving age 16 and over			Total		
Parents Q. (xiii)	Male	Female	Total	Male	Female	Total	Male	Female	Total
	%	%	%	%	%	%	%	%	%
I	-	-	-	8	7	7	5	4	4
II	8	6	7	19	20	19	15	14	14
III non manual	8	11	9	18	18	18	14	15	15
III manual	50	45	47	37	35	36	42	39	41
IV	19	21	20	11	13	12	15	17	15
V	5	7	6	2	2	2	4	4	4
Not working	4	4	4	2	2	2	3	3	3
N.A./inadequate description	4	6	5	2	3	3	3	4	4
Total percentages	100	100	100	100	100	100	100	100	100
Weighted base: All young people	(777.5)	(838)	(1615.5)	(1,134)	(1099.5)	(2233.5)	(1911.5)	(1937.5)	(3849)

Table R1.19 Occupational status, by school leaving age and sex

Q.1	School leaving age 15			School leaving age 16 and over			Total		
Occupational Status	Male	Female	Total	Male	Female	Total	Male	Female	Total
In a job	%	%	%	%	%	%	%	%	%
In a job	78	70	74	33	30	31	51	47	49
Full-time education	16	17	17	62	65	63	43	44	44
Other	6	13	10	6	5	6	6	9	7
Total percentages	100	100	100	100	100	100	100	100	100
Weighted base: all young people	(777.5)	(838)	(1615.5)	(1,134)	(1099.5)	(2233.5)	(1911.5)	(1937.5)	(3849)

Table R1.20 Marital status, by age of leaving school and sex

Q. (vii)	School leaving age 15			School leaving age 16 and over			Total		
Marital Status	Male	Female	Total	Male	Female	Total	Male	Female	Total
	%	%	%	%	%	%	%	%	%
Married	3	12	8	1	3	2	2	7	4
Engaged	5	13	9	3	6	5	4	9	7
Single	92	75	83	95	90	93	94	84	89
Total percentages	100	100	100	100	100	100	100	100	100
Weighted base: all young people	(777.5)	(838)	(1615.5)	(1134)	(1099.5)	(2233.5)	(1911.5)	(1937.5)	(3849)

ATTACHMENT TO THE YOUTH SERVICE

AND ALLIED ACTIVITIES

2.1 The Prevalence of Participation

(a) Earlier evidence

At various times estimates of the proportion of young people involved in the Youth Service have been given. As can be seen from Table 2.1, the figures available for such estimates have varied considerably, but because of the different age groups covered and the different way in which the question has been posed, it has been difficult to discern either changes over time or which figures, if any (other than those for 1969), represented the true picture of *Youth Service* participation. However, the figures suggest some decline in attachment with increasing age as well as a lower membership amongst girls than boys.

Table 2.1 Percentage of young people who belong to a Youth Club or club of any kind as shown by various surveys

Age Group	Males						Females					
	1947[1]	1950[2]	1959[3]	1965[4]	1966[5]	1969[6]	1947[1]	1950[2]	1959[3]	1965[4]	1966[5]	1969[6]
14-15	77						73					
13-16					45*						44*	
15-18			65(41*)	55(27*)		36*			47(26*)	43(21*)		25*
15-19		65				(14-20)		58				(14-20)
18½-20½					38†						18†	
19-22				62(14*)						48(12*)		

*Youth clubs only   †'social clubs or youth clubs'

[1] Ward (1948)   [4] Sillitoe (1969)
[2] Wilkins (1951)   [5] Morton-Williams & Finch (1968)
[3] Harris (1959)   [6] H.M.S.O. (1969)

(b) Current Participation

It would be satisfying and appropriate if we could now present the precise figures for young people involved in the Youth Service in 1969. However, it was early found that at a national level this is impossible, firstly because young people do not know whether the organisation to which they are attached is part of the Youth Service, secondly because they do not always know the correct name of the organisation, and thirdly because even if they did, there exists no national list of all the groups and activities which are part of the official Youth Service. Thus it would only be feasible at the local level to match accurately the groups attended by young people with bodies receiving Youth Service funds.

Instead we looked firstly at attachment to all groups of the kind provided under the Youth Service, and secondly at involvement in what the young people themselves considered to be youth clubs. Lastly in chapter 6 we examine participation in other activities which could be part of the Youth Service such as residential courses and voluntary community service activities.

By 'attachment' we mean 'attending', that is we asked about 'going to' an organisation rather than membership. And the groups we enquired about were specified in a series of questions as clubs, societies, or other groups, as well as places attached to school, college or work which were used for social activities including students unions etc. For the sake of brevity, all these places will be referred to as 'clubs' throughout this Report.

Table 2.2 shows attachment to clubs in the broad sense defined above.

Table 2.2 **Percentages of young people attached to clubs, in 1969** (Based on Table R2.12)

Age	M	F	Total
14	79	71	75
15	75	67	71
16	72	60	66
17	76	53	64
18	71	51	61
19	70	53	62
20	64	45	55
Total Attached	72	58	65

Not only are these figures rather higher than most of those produced by previous enquiries, but they are in striking contrast to the official estimates given for the proportion of young people attracted by the Youth Service. The Albermarle Report (H.M.S.O. 1961) quoted 'one in three', and the 1969 Y.S.D.C. Report mentioned 29% (H.M.S.O. 1969).

The first difference (between the present figures and those from earlier studies) is probably largely explained firstly by the definition of attachment which we used, and secondly by our definition of groups which was probably rather more comprehensive than any used in earlier enquiries. However it is clear that there is no evidence of a decline in attachment to clubs since 1947 and it is probable that some of the apparent fluctuation in attachment over the years is attributable to the different ways in which attachment has been defined by the questions asked.

The second difference (between the present figures and estimates of Youth Service attachment) is certainly due to the fact that we asked about attachment to all sorts of organisations of a Youth Service kind and did not, for reasons already given, confine questions to Youth Service membership. Interestingly enough the proportion of 14-20 year olds in the present enquiry who said they went to a group they would call a 'Youth Club' was 26%, a very similar figure to that quoted in the 1969 Y.S.D.C. report of 29% (H.M.S.O. 1969, P 16). However, there is evidence that the young people's definition of 'youth clubs' excludes some Youth Service organisations, as the following examples show.

Some examples of organisations which some young people did not call 'Youth Clubs'

Boys Brigade*
Welfare and Sports club (for all ages)
Fishing club+ (for 12-15 year olds)
Works football club (for 16-45 year olds)
Cine Club+ (for 15-16 year olds)
A.T.C.*

*Youth Service organisations
+Might qualify for Local Authority Youth Service funds

A check of a small random sample of 70 of the interview schedules for young people who said they were attached to clubs they did not regard as Youth Clubs, showed that 10% definitely went to Youth Service organisations, and a further 33% went to the sort of clubs which might qualify for Youth Service funds. Over all, what the young people said they would call youth clubs were over-whelmingly made up of groups entitled 'Youth Clubs'. Thus the more unusually named Youth Service organisations are likely to be omitted.

From an administrative point of view it would clearly be valuable to know the exact proportion of 14-20 year olds involved in the Youth Service. But for those concerned with the interests of young people it is at least of equal importance to know that only about one third were unattached to any club and in this report we shall concentrate on attachment in this wider sense. Tables for attachment to what the young people regarded as 'Youth Clubs' will also be given, where appropriate, but the above examples show that these are not identical with Youth Service organisations.

(c) Participation at any time

Whilst almost two thirds of 14-20 year olds were currently attached to clubs in 1969, 93% were then or had previously been attached, and in comparison with the 26% currently attached to a 'Youth Club', 68% went or had been to a 'Youth Club' in the past. Thus only 7% had never been attached to any club which catered for the leisure of young people, and only 32% had never been to a 'Youth Club'.

2.2 Differences between the attached and unattached young people

In this section we shall be concerned with differences in the demographic, socio-economic and educational characteristics of the attached and unattached. These are treated as the independent variables in the sense that they are more likely to influence participation in clubs than they are likely to be influenced by it, the paradigm being age. In chapter 8 we shall discuss other differences between the attached and unattached, which might loosely be termed aspects of social integration. In the latter case it is of course well nigh impossible to determine the nature or direction of the causal relationship by the survey method of investigation.

It should be remembered that throughout this report 'attachment' is used to mean attending a group. In chapter 3 we shall examine the nature of attachment, but in no place does it have any connotations of social or psychological adjustment.

Earlier evidence shows that it is boys, the more educated and (less consistently) the younger members of the age range who are most likely to go to voluntary social organisations, and the present evidence supports these findings.

Table R2.12

(a) Age and Sex

Table 2.3 shows that at all ages a higher proportion of boys than girls went to groups so that in all 72% of boys currently went to a club but only 58% of girls. Almost consistently, attachment varied directly with age, but the fall off was rather gradual. The decline was greater for girls than boys, 26% less of the 20 than of the 14 year old girls went to voluntary organisations, but only 15% less of the 20 than 14 year old boys.

Table 2.3 Percentage of young people attached to what they called a Youth Club, in 1969

Q23(a) Age	M		F		Total	
	Clubs of any kind	Youth Clubs	Clubs of any kind	Youth Clubs	Clubs of any kind	Youth Clubs
14	79	35	71	38	75	37
15	75	42	67	37	71	39
16	72	41	60	33	66	37
17	76	38	53	23	64	30
18	71	22	51	8	61	15
19	70	16	53	11	62	14
20	64	13	45	5	55	9
Total	72	30	58	23	65	26

Looked at from the point of view of attachment to any club the picture as far as age and sex are concerned is much less gloomy than the Albermarle and 1969 Reports believed. On the other hand attachment to 'Youth Clubs' bears out their findings (Table 2.3). But as has already been suggested, this definition is likely to exclude some groups which in fact are part of the Youth Service. There is a steep decline in this case for both boys and girls between 16 and 18. This is not, as will be shown later, because 'Youth Clubs' are especially likely to have an upper age limit of 17 or 18.

A higher proportion of girls than boys had never been to any group. And presumably because of their longer exposure to the chance of going to a club and so on, the oldest of the group were slightly more likely to have been attached at some time than were the younger children. Unexpectedly, girls were more likely than boys to have been to a 'Youth Club' at sometime.

The influence of age and sex on participation are confounded by at least three other factors, which in turn depend in part on age; namely, education, occupational status and marital status. For example, a 20 year old is less likely to be in full-time education than a 14 year old and a girl aged 20 is more likely to be married than a boy, and so on.

(b) Age, sex, and educational experience

Those who left or were planning to leave school at 15 were less likely on the whole, whatever their age or sex, to be attached to an organisation than those who stayed on or were planning to stay on at school until after the minimum leaving age. The early school leavers were also rather less likely ever to have been attached to a club. In other words, school leaving age was rather more closely related to participation than either sex or

Table 2.4 Percentage of 14–20 year olds currently attached to clubs by school leaving age, age and sex

Q.16 (c) Age	Left school at 15 years or under			Left school at over 15 years			Total
	M	F	T	M	F	T	
14	67	64	66	84	74	79	75
15	58	52	55	84	76	80	71
16	55	37	47	85	72	78	66
17	64	37	49	84	68	76	64
18	66	38	50	76	63	70	61
19	59	38	48	78	67	73	62
20	58	33	46	70	60	66	55
T	61	42	51	81	70	75	65

26

age, although the sex differences and age trends persisted within all but one group of leavers. Thus, the 19-20 year old girl late school leavers were more likely to be attached than 14-15 year old boy early leavers, although less likely than 19-20 year old boy *late* leavers.

The steepest decline in attachment occurred for girl early leavers. In this case only about half as many of the 20 year olds as of the 14 year olds were attached. For all early leavers the biggest drop in attachment occurred between the ages of 14 and 16, evidently at the time the children left school. But whereas this was followed, for boys (exceptionally), by an increase in participation at the age of 17, for girls attachment remained at the new low level throughout the subsequent ages.

The pattern of attachment to 'Youth Clubs' was rather different. Firstly there was much less difference between the sexes and little difference between the school leaving groups within each sex especially after the age of 17 or 18. Secondly, the steepest decline in attachment occurred from 16 or 17, although girl early leavers first began dropping out in considerable numbers from at least 14 years.

Table R2.13

Table 2.5 Percentage of 14-20 year olds currently attached to what they call a 'Youth Club' by school leaving age, age and sex

Age	Left school at 15 years or under			Left school at over 15 years			Total
	M	F	T	M	F	T	
14	35	40	38	35	37	36	37
15	42	31	36	41	39	40	39
16	37	24	31	44	36	40	37
17	32	22	27	42	22	32	30
18	22	6	13	22	10	16	15
19	15	13	14	17	8	13	14
20	12	5	8	14	6	10	9
T	27	19	23	32	26	29	26

Around a third of each group had never been to what they called a Youth Club. And unlike attachment to clubs of any kind, it was the later school leavers who were slightly less likely ever to have been to a 'Youth Club'.

So far we have implicitly assumed that the crucial difference is between those who leave school as soon as they legally can and those who leave later. But in fact attachment varied directly with actual or intended age of leaving school over the whole range of possible leaving ages. More importantly the percentage drop in attachment was as great between those who gave a school leaving age of 17 and those who specified 16, as it was between the 16 year leavers and the earliest school leavers. Ideally, if the sample were large enough, we should further sub-divide school leaving age into the three groups; 15, 16 and 17 and over. But in practice, besides adding to the complexity of the analysis, this would often leave too small numbers in each cell for the last group when other important characteristics, such as age, were also considered. In chapter 8 we shall return to this question.

Table 2.6 Percentage of 14-20 year olds currently attached by school leaving age

School leaving age	M	F	Total
15	61	42	51
16	73	58	65
17	85	75	80
18	90	83	87
15+ but exact age not known	75	84	80

(c) Occupational Status

Table R2.14 It was shown above that the steepest decline in attachment for early school leavers occurs around school leaving age. In fact what difference does being in full time education, as distinct from being at school, make to whether or not a young person goes to a club and so on?

For the early school leavers the evidence is inconclusive because so few early leavers were in further full time education. But the effect of leaving school itself was not, as might be supposed, immediate. Thus 58% of the early leavers aged 15 and still at school were attached, compared with 54% of those who were already working at this age.

For the later school leavers there was a clear relationship between being in full time education and being attached, so that, for example, over 90% of the eighteen pluses in full time education went to a voluntary social group, compared with around 60% of those in a job. But attachment was always higher amongst the late leavers who were working than amongst the early leavers in a job.

Tables R2.14 & R2.15 However, from the point of view of occupational status, the outstanding feature is the lower proportion (40%) of those who were 'unemployed' i.e. neither in full time education nor employment, who were attached. This was particularly marked amongst females, and early school leavers. Although this group (the 'unemployed') was relatively small (around 6% of the total sample) it is perhaps worth emphasising, that in addition to being uninvolved with the wider society through the formal

28

organisations of employment and education, a high proportion of its members did not participate in the secondary network of clubs.

Table 2.7 Percentage of 14-20 year olds attached to a Club by occupational status and age

Age	Leaving/left school at 15 years			Leaving/left school at over 15 years			Total
	In a job	In full-time education	Neither	In a job	In full-time education	Neither	
14	–	66		–	79		75
15	54	58		–	80		71
16	48	*		61	82		66
17	51	*	30	61	88	56	64
18	50	*		59	90		61
19	50	*		67	93		62
20	49	*		57	92		55
T	50	63	30	61	83	56	65

Note: *Bases are too small for percentages to be meaningful

(d) Class

There is a well-documented relationship between socio-economic class and age of leaving school which is illustrated in Table 1.8 in Chapter 1. Not unexpectedly therefore class is directly related to attachment but within each class, school leaving age is related to whether or not a young person goes to a voluntary social group. For example 55% of early school leavers who were the children of managerial workers were attached compared with 75% of the late school leavers of the same class, but only 44% of early school leavers who were the children of semi skilled workers and 67% of the late leavers. School leaving age appears to be more closely related to attachment than does class, but since class and school leaving age are also closely related, in the real world the relationship with class is close. To see the effects of the length of education alone, we shall have to await the raising of the school leaving age in 1973.

Tables R2.16 & R2.17

Table 2.8 Percentage of 14-20 year olds attached to a Club by school leaving age, socio-economic class and sex

Registrar General's Socio-economic Class	Leaving/left school at 15 yrs			Leaving/left school at over 15 yrs			Total
	M	F	T	M	F	T	
I professional	–	–	–	86	86	86	85
II managerial	61	46	55	83	72	75	73
III skilled non-manual	61	43	50	83	74	78	71
III skilled manual	62	43	52	81	67	74	64
IV semi skilled	53	36	44	73	63	67	55
V unskilled	62	40	50	68	67	67	56

One other feature worth comment is that the higher the social class the less the difference between the sexes in attachment, so that in class I, 85% of both sexes were attached, but in class V 64% of the boys compared with only 48% of the girls went to clubs. But the size of these sex differences was also related to the different educational experience of each social class.

(e) Marital status

Table R2.18 Naturally enough, only a small minority of the 14-20 year olds were married or engaged. 11% were either one or the other, that is 6% of boys and 15% of girls. Because marriage is related both to age and within the 14-20 year age group, to age of leaving school, any conclusions about the relationship between marital status on the one hand, and participation on the other must be tentative. But the indications are that being married, and to a lesser extent being engaged, reduced the likelihood that a young person went to a club. The decline in attachment was particularly marked for the girls, so that over 60% of the single girls were attached compared with 34% of the married girls. Of course these figures do not indicate whether unattachment is related to marriage, to the early years of marriage or to the kind of people who marry young.

Table 2.9 Percentage of 14-20 year olds attached to a Club by age of leaving school and marital status

Age of leaving school	Single	Engaged	Married	Total
15 or under	52	43	40	51
Over 15	77	62	36	75
Total	67	50	39	65

(f) Colour

Table R2.19 Only 39 young people, or 1% of the sample, met the criterion coloured as assessed by the interviewer and therefore any conclusions about their attachment are open to doubt. For what it is worth 'coloured' young people appeared less likely to be attached than their 'white' peers regardless of school leaving age. But clearly any informative account of the difference in patterns of attachment between immigrants (however defined) and others must await studies devoted to this specific problem.

(g) Type of area and Region

Table R2.20 The type of area (broadly urban or rural) in which the young people lived had no clear relationship with attachment, although there is an interesting hint that the difference in attachment between boys and girls is much greater in truly rural areas than elsewhere. This again could only be verified by special studies in rural areas since those living there formed only 3% of the total unweighted sample.

The Regions in which the 14-20 year olds lived were associated with some differences in attachment and such differences as appeared seemed to be partly dependent upon the differing proportions of young people leaving school at various ages. Thus, in the East Midlands where 52% of the sample specified a school leaving age of 15 or under and only 19% gave an age of 17+ years, 62% were attached, whilst in Wales II, where less than a third gave a school leaving age of 15 or under and 52% had left or intended to leave at 17 or later, 73% were attached. Table R2.21

(h) Seasonal variations in attachment

The first stage of interviewing took place in early summer and the second stage in autumn and early winter. The sample was split in this way because it was thought that attachment would reach a peak in the autumn and decline over the year. In fact a higher proportion of young people were attached in the autumn than in the summer but the difference was small, (67% compared with 62%). Table R2.22

2.3 Relationship between young people's and adults' attachment

It has already been shown that the least privileged socially and educationally of the 14-20 year olds (i.e. the working class girl early school leavers) were least likely to be attached to voluntary social groups. This pattern, however, is not limited to the young. Sillitoe (1969) and Horton (1967), amongst others, have shown the same phenomenon holds for adults; more specifically that men, the middle classes and the most educated are most likely to participate in voluntary organisations and that women, the working classes and the least educated are least likely to participate.

The same relationships held for the parents of the young people in this sample, and therefore, as might be expected, there was a relationship between parent's and their children's attachment, (see Tables 2.10 and 2.11). Table R2.23

In the case of 'Youth Clubs', the children of parents who said they had attended a 'Youth Club' themselves in their youth, were rather more likely to go to a 'Youth Club'; 31% of the children of parents who said they had been attached to 'Youth Clubs', compared with 25% of the children of parents who had not attended. Similarly 31% of the children of parents who claimed any contact with possible Youth Service organisations or workers were attached to 'Youth Clubs', but only 21% of those whose Table R2.24

31

Table 2.10 Percentage of parents who go to clubs by parent's age of leaving school

Age of leaving school	'Mothers' *	'Fathers' *
14	30	35
15	35	42
16	50	52
17	50	56
18+	72	61
T	35+	40+

*'mothers' = informant, 'fathers' = spouse. In a small proportion of cases the informant was the father, and the spouse therefore the mother.

+The reason that the difference between males and females is not as great as shown by Sillitoe or Horton, is probably due to the fact that 'fathers' attachment was reported by the informant, which would almost certainly have resulted in an underestimate: i.e. the true figure for 'fathers' would be higher than given here.

Table 2.11 Percentage of 14-20 year olds attached or unattached by attachment of parents

Young person's attachment	Parent's attachment	
	attached	unattached
	%	%
attached	74	60
unattached	26	40
Total percentage	100	100
Weighted base: All parents	(1646)	(1831)

parents denied such contacts. In all, 44% of the parents inter-viewed said that they or their spouse had been attached to a 'Youth Club' when they were younger, and 69% claimed some past contact with putative Youth Service groups or personnel. The fact that a smaller proportion of parents than children said they had ever been to a youth club may well be due to forgetfulness rather than genuine generational change, a possibility which casts some doubt on the level of the relation-ship between past parental and present child attachment.

This suggests traditions of attachment or non-attachment amongst particular groups which operate for the young and adults alike. For those who see value in increasing attachment amongst the under privileged young people this may appear to present a problem. However, what is interesting is firstly that apparently, at least since 1947, attachment of any kind amongst the 14-15 year olds has been high for all groups, and secondly that, at least in 1969, the proportion of any group who had *never* been attached was very low. Thus by far the great majority of young people (93%) are evidently attached at some time before adult- hood, and most, (68%), go or have been to 'Youth Clubs', so that the problem must be seen as one of retaining attachment amongst particular groups rather than of attracting people in the first place.

Table R2.12 Attachment to clubs, by age of leaving school, age and sex

Qs. 16c & 19

Attachment	Age of leaving school															
	15								Over 15							
	14	15	16	17	18	19	20	Total	14	15	16	17	18	19	20	Total
	%	%	%	%	%	%	%	%	%	%	%	%	%	%	%	%
BOYS																
Never attached	13	8	10	3	6	5	6	7	3	4	7	4	5	2	4	4
Past attachment	20	34	35	32	28	36	36	32	13	11	8	12	19	20	25	15
Present attachment	67	58	55	64	66	59	58	61	84	84	85	84	76	78	70	81
Total percentages	100	100	100	100	100	100	100	100	100	100	100	100	100	100	100	100
Weighted base: All boys	(84.5)	(106)	(116)	(117)	(100)	(113.5)	(140.5)	(777.5)	(202)	(188)	(159.5)	(154)	(147)	(147.5)	(136)	(1134)
GIRLS																
Never attached	12	17	14	13	16	13	9	13	6	5	5	6	3	5	3	5
Past attachment	24	31	48	50	46	49	57	45	20	19	24	26	34	28	38	26
Present attachment	64	52	37	37	38	38	33	42	74	76	72	68	63	67	60	70
Total percentages	100	100	100	100	100	100	100	100	100	100	100	100	100	100	100	100
Weighted base: All girls	(90)	(121.5)	(104.5)	(147)	(122.5)	(122.5)	(130)	(838)	(190)	(186.5)	(200)	(147)	(134)	(129)	(113)	(1099.5)
TOTAL																
Never attached	12	13	12	8	12	9	7	10	5	4	6	5	4	4	4	5
Past attachment	22	32	41	42	38	43	46	39	16	15	17	19	26	24	31	20
Present attachment	66	55	47	49	50	48	46	51	79	80	78	76	70	73	66	75
Total percentages	100	100	100	100	100	100	100	100	100	100	100	100	100	100	100	100
Weighted base: All young people	(174.5)	(227.5)	(220.5)	(264)	(222.5)	(236)	(270.5)	(1615.5)	(392)	(374.5)	(359.5)	(301)	(281)	(276.5)	(249)	(2233.5)

Table R2.13 Youth Club attachment, by age of leaving school, age and sex

Q.23	Age of leaving school																
Youth Club attachment	15								Over 15								Total
	14	15	16	17	18	19	20	Total	14	15	16	17	18	19	20	Total	Total
	%	%	%	%	%	%	%	%	%	%	%	%	%	%	%	%	%
BOYS																	
Never attached	42	22	34	22	20	33	31	29	46	38	33	24	31	35	40	36	36
Past attachment	22	35	29	46	57	52	57	44	19	21	23	34	46	48	46	32	32
Present attachment	35	42	37	32	22	15	12	27	35	41	44	42	22	17	14	32	32
Total percentages	100	98*	100	98*	100	100	100	100	100	100	100	100	100	98*	100	100	100
Weighted base: All boys	(84.5)	(121.5)	(116)	(117)	(100)	(113.5)	(140.5)	(777.5)	(202)	(188)	(159.5)	(154)	(147)	(147.5)	(136)	(1134)	(1134)
GIRLS																	
Never attached	33	30	36	24	29	32	29	30	39	35	25	29	26	30	34	31	31
Past attachment	26	37	40	52	65	56	66	50	24	24	38	49	64	60	60	43	43
Present attachment	40	31	24	22	6	13	5	19	37	39	36	22	10	8	6	26	26
Total percentages	100	98*	100	98*	100	100	100	98*	100	98*	100	100	100	98*	100	100	100
Weighted base: All girls	(90)	(121.5)	(104.5)	(147)	(122.5)	(122.5)	(130)	(838)	(190)	(186.5)	(200)	(147)	(134)	(129)	(113)	(1099.5)	(1099.5)
TOTAL																	
Never attached	37	26	35	24	25	32	30	30	43	36	28	26	29	32	37	33	33
Past attachment	24	36	34	49	61	54	62	47	22	23	31	41	55	54	52	38	38
Present attachment	38	36	31	27	13	14	8	23	36	40	40	32	16	13	10	29	29
Total percentages	100	98*	100	98*	100	100	100	98*	100	98*	100	100	100	98*	100	100	100
Weighted base: All young people	(174.5)	(227.5)	(220.5)	(264)	(222.5)	(236)	(270.5)	(1615.5)	(392)	(374.5)	(359.5)	(301)	(281)	(276.5)	(249)	(2233.5)	(2233.5)

*No answer accounts for rest

Table R2.14 Attachment to clubs, by occupational status, age and age of leaving school

Qs.16c & 19 Attachment	In full-time employment							In full-time education							In neither full-time employment nor education
	14	15	16	17	18	19	20	14	15	16	17	18	19	20	
	%	%	%	%	%	%	%	%	%	%	%	%	%	%	%
AGE OF LEAVING SCHOOL 15															
Never attached	-	11	11	9	12	8	7	12	16	13	-	(1)	-	-	12
Past attachment	-	35	41	39	38	41	44	22	26	32	(4)	(1)	-	(1)	57
Present attachment	-	54	48	51	50	50	49	66	58	55	(5)	(3)	(4.5)	(2)	30
Total percentages	-	100	100	100	100	100	100	100	100	100	(9)*	(5.5)*	(4.5)*	(3)*	100
Weighted base: All who left/will leave school at 15	-	(142)	(185)	(237.5)	(196)	(202)	(227.5)	(173.5)	(71.5)	(19)					(139.5)
AGE OF LEAVING SCHOOL OVER 15															
Never attached	-	-	5	10	4	4	4	5	4	6	1	1	3	1	9
Past attachment	-	-	34	29	37	28	39	16	15	12	11	8	4	7	36
Present attachment	-	-	61	61	59	67	57	79	80	82	88	90	93	92	56
Total percentages	-	-	100	100	100	100	100	100	100	100	100	100	100	100	100
Weighted base: All who left/will leave school over 15	-	-	(63.5)	(126.5)	(172)	(185.5)	(149)	(391)	(374.5)	(278)	(163.5)	(86)	(75.5)	(75.5)	(93)

*percentages for individual ages are unreliable because of the small numbers in each group. For this reason actual numbers are shown in brackets.

36

Table R2.15 Attachment to clubs, by occupational status, age and sex

Qs.16c & 19 Attachment	In full-time employment							In full-time education							In neither full-time employment nor education
	14	15	16	17	18	19	20	14	15	16	17	18	19	20	
	%	%	%	%	%	%	%	%	%	%	%	%	%	%	%
BOYS															
Never attached	-	6	10	5	6	4	6	6	6	7	1	4	-	2	3
Past attachment	-	34	30	26	28	31	34	14	15	8	9	7	7	9	36
Present attachment	-	60	60	69	66	65	60	80	79	86	90	87	93	89	61
Total percentages	-	100	100	100	100	100	100	100	100	100	100	98*	100	100	100
Weighted base: All boys	-	(68)	(128)	(175)	(179.5)	(206)	(220)	(285.5)	(221)	(133.5)	(88)	(55.5)	(45)	(45.5)	(61)
GIRLS															
Never attached	-	16	8	14	11	8	6	8	7	6	1	-	6	-	14
Past attachment	-	36	48	45	47	40	52	21	19	18	16	10	-	6	53
Present attachment	-	48	43	42	42	52	41	71	74	76	83	90	94	94	33
Total percentages	-	100	100	100	100	100	100	100	100	100	100	100	100	100	100
Weighted base: All girls	-	(74)	(120.5)	(189)	(188.5)	(181.5)	(156.5)	(279)	(225)	(163.5)	(84.5)	(36)	(35)	(33)	(171.5)
TOTAL															
Never attached	-	11	9	9	8	6	6	7	6	6	1	2	2	1	11
Past attachment	-	35	39	36	38	35	42	18	17	14	12	8	4	8	49
Present attachment	-	54	52	55	54	59	52	75	77	80	86	88	94	91	40
Total percentages	-	100	100	100	100	100	100	100	100	100	100	98*	100	100	100
Weighted base: All young people	-	(142)	(248.5)	(364)	(368)	(387.5)	(376.5)	(564.5)	(446)	(297)	(172.5)	(91.5)	(80)	(78.5)	(232.5)

*No answer accounts for rest

37

Table R2.16 Attachment to clubs, by social class and sex

Qs. 16c & 19	Social Class							
Attachment	I Profes- sional	II Managerial & technical	III Clerical & minor supervisory	III Skilled manual	IV Semi- skilled manual	V Unskilled manual	Not working	Unclassi- fiable
	%	%	%	%	%	%	%	%
BOYS								
Never attached	3	3	4	5	9	12	–	8
Past attachment	12	19	18	23	29	23	31	16
Present attachment	85	78	78	72	62	64	69	75
Total percentages	100	100	100	100	100	100	100	100
Weighted base: All boys	(89)	(283)	(269)	(813.5)	(274)	(73)	(51.5)	(58.5)
GIRLS								
Never attached	4	6	7	9	10	14	7	11
Past attachment	11	27	29	36	41	38	44	36
Present attachment	85	67	64	55	48	48	49	53
Total percentages	100	100	100	100	100	100	100	100
Weighted base: All girls	(76.5)	(264.5)	(295)	(757)	(322.5)	(81.5)	(58)	(82.5)
TOTAL								
Never attached	4	4	5	7	10	13	4	10
Past attachment	12	23	24	29	35	31	38	28
Present attachment	85	73	71	64	55	56	58	62
Total percentages	100	100	100	100	100	100	100	100
Weighted base: All young people	(165.5)	(547.5)	(564)	(1570.5)	(596.5)	(154.5)	(109.5)	(141)

Table R2.17 Attachment to clubs, by age of leaving school, social class and sex

Qs. 16c & 19

	Age of leaving school															
	15								Over 15							
Attachment	I Profes-sional	II Mana-gerial & tech-nical	III Clerical & minor super-visory	III Skilled manual	IV Semi-skilled manual	V Un-skilled manual	Not working	Un-classi-fiable	I Profes-sional	II Mana-gerial & tech-nical	III Clerical & minor super-visory	III Skilled manual	IV Semi-skilled manual	V Un-skilled manual	Not working	Un-classi-fiable
	%	%	%	%	%	%	%	%	%	%	%	%	%	%	%	%
BOYS																
Never attached	-	6	7	7	9	10	-	12	4	2	3	4	9	(5)	-	(1)
Past attachment	(1.5)	33	31	32	37	29	36	15	10	15	14	15	18	(5)	(4)	(4.5)
Present attachment	(2)	61	61	62	54	62	64	72	86	83	83	81	73	21	14	(20.5)
Total percentages Weighted base: All boys	(3.5)*	100 (63.5)	100 (62)	100 (391.5)	100 (149.5)	100 (42)	100 (33.5)	100 (32.5)	100 (85.5)	100 (219.5)	100 (207)	100 (422)	100 (124.5)	(31)*	(18)*	(26)*
GIRLS																
Never attached	-	13	13	13	14	16	7	14	4	4	4	5	6	(2)	(1.5)	(2)
Past attachment	(1)	41	43	44	50	44	47	39	10	24	22	28	31	(6)	(9)	(9.5)
Present attachment	-	46	43	43	36	40	46	47	86	72	74	67	63	16	(12.5)	20
Total percentages Weighted base: All girls	(1)*	100 (50)	100 (92)	100 (375)	100 (177)	100 (57.5)	100 (35)	100 (51)	100 (75.5)	100 (214.5)	100 (203)	100 (382)	100 (145.5)	(24)*	(23)*	(31.5)*
TOTAL																
Never attached	-	9	10	10	12	14	4	13	4	3	3	4	7	13	4	5
Past attachment	(2.5)	37	38	38	44	37	42	30	10	19	18	21	25	20	32	24
Present attachment	(2)	55	51	52	44	49	55	57	86	78	78	74	68	67	65	70
Total percentages Weighted base: All young people	(4.5)*	100 (113.5)	100 (154)	100 (766.5)	100 (326.5)	100 (99.5)	100 (68.5)	100 (83.5)	100 (161)	100 (434)	100 (410)	100 (804)	100 (270)	100 (55)	100 (41)	100 (57.5)

*Percentages are unreliable because of the small numbers in each group. For this reason actual numbers are shown in brackets.

Table R2.18 Attachment to clubs, by marital status

Qs. 16c & 19 Attachment	Single	Engaged	Married	Total
	%	%	%	%
Never attached	7	8	9	7
Past attachment	26	41	52	28
Present attachment	67	50	39	65
Total percentages	100	100	100	100
Weighted base: All young people	(3421)	(253.5)	(174.5)	(3849)

Table R2.19 Attachment to clubs, by colour

Qs. 16c & 19 Attachment	White	Coloured	Total
	%	%	%
Never attached	7	33	7
Past attachment	28	15	28
Present attachment	65	51	65
Total percentages	100	100	100
Weighted base: All young people	(3805)	(39)	(3849)

Table R2.20 Attachment to clubs, by type of area and sex

Qs. 16c & 19 Attachment	BOYS				GIRLS				TOTAL			
	Conur-bation	Urban	Semi-Rural	Rural	Conur-bation	Urban	Semi-Rural	Rural	Conur-bation	Urban	Semi-Rural	Rural
	%	%	%	%	%	%	%	%	%	%	%	%
Never attached	5	6	6	2	8	9	8	2	6	7	7	9
Past attachment	24	22	19	14	33	34	34	34	29	28	26	25
Present attach-ment	71	73	74	84	59	57	58	51	65	65	66	66
Total percentages	100	100	100	100	100	100	100	100	100	100	100	100
Unweighted base: All young people	(637)	(887)	(356)	(63)	(692)	(875)	(335)	(71)	(1329)	(1762)	(691)	(134)

Table R2.21 Attachment to clubs, by region

Qs. 16c & 19 Attachment	Region										Total
	North	York-shire & Humber-side	North West	East Mid-lands	West Mid-lands	East Anglia	Greater London & South East	South West	South East Wales	Rest of Wales	
	%	%	%	%	%	%	%	%	%	%	%
Never attached	5	8	7	9	6	9	7	7	4	12	7
Past attachment	28	28	26	29	27	22	29	28	30	15	28
Present attachment	67	64	67	62	68	69	63	64	65	73	65
Total percentages	100	100	100	100	100	100	100	100	100	100	100
Weighted base: All young people	(256.5)	(373)	(543)	(256)	(426)	(120.5)	(1322)	(337.5)	(161)	(53.5)	(3849)

Table R2.22 Attachment to clubs, by time of year interviewed

Qs. 16c & 19 Attachment	Early Summer	Winter/Autumn	Total
	%	%	%
Not attached at present	37	33	35
Present attachment	62	67	64
Total percentages	100	100	100
Weighted base: All young people	(1990)	(1859)	(3849)

Table R2.23 Parental club attachment, by social class

Parents Q.30	Social Class							
Parental club attachment	I Profes-sional	II Mana-gerial & tech-nical	III Clerical & minor super-visory	III Skilled manual	IV Semi-skilled manual	V Unskilled manual	Not working	Unclassi-fiable
	%	%	%	%	%	%	%	%
MOTHERS*								
Attached	63	48	41	30	26	29	25	31
Unattached	37	52	59	69	74	70	75	60
Total percentages	100	100	100	100	100	100	100	91†
Weighted base: All mothers	(117)	(382)	(406.5)	(1081)	(401.5)	(98)	(82)	(24)
FATHERS*								
Attached	60	53	42	36	32	25	-	(7)
Unattached	40	46	58	63	68	73	(4)	(7)
Total percentages	100	100	100	100	100	98†	-	-
Weighted base: All fathers	(116)	(366)	(359.5)	(1044.5)	(362)	(79)	(4)‡	(16)†‡

*Mothers = informant, fathers = spouse. In a small proportion of cases the informant was the father, and the spouse therefore the mother.
†No answer accounts for rest.
‡Percentages are unreliable because of the small numbers in each group. For this reason actual numbers are shown in brackets.

Table R2.24 Youth Club attachment, by parental Youth Club attachment

Qs. 16c & 19 Youth club attachment	Q. 7(d) Parental youth club attachment		
	Went to youth club	Never went to youth club	Not known
	%	%	%
Never attached	30	34	28
Past attachment	38	41	60
Present attachment	31	25	12
Total percentages	100	100	100
Weighted base: All young people	(1528)	(1950)	(371)

41

CHAPTER 3

DEGREES OF ATTACHMENT

3.1 Frequency and recency of visits

So far we have taken attachment to mean *going* to a club. We chose this wide definition because it was pointed out to us that limiting it to formal membership might exclude many young people who were in fact involved in the Youth Service and allied activities. This is because some organisations do not demand formal membership. It may be thought that such a wide definition would mean that many who were classified as attached would have only the most tenuous contact with clubs. In fact this was not the case. The majority of the attached visited organisations rather frequently.

Thus about 66% of the attached said they had been to a club during the week before interview and nearly 90% had been within the preceding 4 weeks. It seems therefore that on the whole a young person's claim that he goes to a club or group can reasonably be taken to mean that he goes at least once a month, and very probably more frequently. And the figures for attachment presented in the last chapter are therefore not misleading. In fact, looked at in another way, 58% of all the 14-20 year olds interviewed had been to a club or group during the month before interview, and about 44% had been during the past week. Table R3.6

Although this result shows that the definition of 'attachment' used here is meaningful in at least one sense, it is also of importance to consider how frequency of attendance varies with age, sex and so on, and whether the infrequent attenders are more like the frequent attenders or more like the unattached.

(a) The characteristics of frequent and infrequent attenders

In order to measure frequency of attendance in the most realistic way possible from reported information, the answers to questions on frequency and last visit were combined so that, for instance, a young person who went to any of up to three groups during the week before interview and claimed he went there once a week was placed in a higher category than either one who went only once a month or than someone who had not been in the preceding week although he claimed a weekly attendance. Examples of the reasons for such discrepancies will help to explain the need for this composite measure. In the first case, someone who visits a club only once a month, may well have paid his monthly visit in the week preceding interview. In the second case, we found that someone who belonged, for example

43

to a sports club, might say he went once a week, but because it was not the season for that sport at the time of interview had in fact not attended for a month or so.

62% of the attached were currently visiting a club at least once a week, and only 13% went less than once a month or had not been for a month or more. Those aged 17 and over went less frequently than children of 14 to 16. Differences were very small, but the least frequent visitors shared some of the characteristics of the unattached and the most frequent, the characteristics of all the attached, so that the older girl early school leavers were the most likely of any group to go less than once a month, and the younger boy late leavers were the most likely to go once a week or more. This suggests that a decline in frequency of attendance may sometimes be a first step towards unattachment. On the other hand, and with the exception of the younger boys, the late school leavers were a little less likely than the early leavers to visit a club as frequently as once a week. Since the late leavers are most likely to remain attached, the lower frequency of attendance in this case may be a means of maintaining attachment whilst concurrently devoting time to other interests, or it may be a result of attending clubs which are less often available.

Table 3.1 Frequency of attendance of the attached, by school leaving age, age and sex

School leaving age	Age	M			F			Total		
		Attends once a week or more	At least once a month but less than once a week	Less than once a month	Attends once a week or more	At least once a month but less than once a week	Less than once a month	Attends once a week or more	At least once a month but less than once a week	Less than once a month
15	14-16	68	21	10	69	22	9	68	22	10
	17-20	63	22	13	55	21	22	60	22	17
16 or over	14-16	70	21	8	61	29	10	65	25	13
	17-20	61	24	13	49	31	19	55	27	16
Total		66	22	11	57	27	15	62	25	13

Those at work went rather less frequently than young people in full time education and this is partly related to the fact that those at work were on average older. The least frequent attenders, however, were those who were neither in a job nor full time education. This group, as was shown in chapter 2, was also least likely to be attached at all.

Table R3.7   *(b) Seasonal variation in attendance*

It has already been shown that there were rather more young people attached in the winter than in the summer, although the difference was slight. The difference in frequency of attendance, however is more considerable. In the summer months 56% of the attached went to a group once a week or more, compared

Table 3.2 Frequency of attendance by occupational status, age and sex

Occupational status	Age	M			F			Total		
		Attends once a week or more	At least once a month but less than once a week	Less than once a month	Attends once a week or more	At least once a month but less than once a week	Less than once a month	Attends once a week or more	At least once a month but less than once a week	Less than once a month
In a job	14-16	65	24	13	62	26	12	64	25	11
	17-20	62	24	10	51	27	20	58	25	16
	T	63	24	13	54	27	18	59	25	15
In full-time education	14-16	70	21	8	63	27	9	66	24	9
	17-20	62	25	12	52	27	21	57	26	15
	T	68	22	11	59	27	12	64	24	10
Neither	14-20	65	11	22	49	28	21	55	21	21

with 67% in the winter. But the differences between the seasons for those who went less than once a month or had not been for more than a month was less; 15% in the summer compared with 11% in the winter. The difference in attendance may be partly due to the rival attractions of other activities in the summer months and partly to the non-availability of some of the groups during at least part of the summer.

3.2 Multiple Attachments

Nearly 60% of the attached went to more than one club, in fact one boy said he attended 17 different clubs. However, the same group who were most likely to be attached in the first place, were also most likely, amongst the attached, to go to more than one club. Specifically, it was the boys giving a school leaving age of 16 or over who most often went to more than one group, and the girl early leavers, particularly the older ones who least often went to more than one.

Table R3.8

Table 3.3 Percentage of the attached 14-20 year olds who went to more than one club by sex, school leaving age and age

Age	Leaving/left school at 15 years			Leaving/left school at 16 years or over		
	M	F	T	M	F	T
14-16	47	40	42	70	67	68
17-20	48	35	42	68	60	65
Total	48	37	42	69	65	67

3.3 Degree of involvement

The number of attachments provides some measure of the relative attraction of organised groups for a young person, just as frequency of visiting may be taken as some indication of the relative attraction of a particular group for him. This last also suggests one aspect of the limits within which the organisation can hope to have any influence upon the young person. Thus most young people are exposed to the influences of their school or place of employment for 5 days a week, but only 43% of the attached claimed to go to a club more than once a week, although the effect of an influence must depend on much more than the length of time during which a person is exposed to it. However, given such a relatively tenuous and voluntary relationship, it may be that a young person will be able to use the organisation for his own purposes as easily as he can be influenced by it. He may use it, for example, primarily to meet friends, or to pursue an interest. However he may more effectively shape the organisation to his own requirements, either by forming it in the first place or by gaining office within the group.

(a) *People who founded clubs*

11% of the attached young people had founded or helped to found at least one of the groups they went to. The later school leavers were twice as likely as the early leavers to have been involved in such an initiative. Age and sex were not important.

Table 3.4 **Percentage of attached 14–20 year olds who had helped to form a club by sex and school leaving age**

School leaving age	M	F	Total
15	7	6	7
16 or over	15	12	14
T	12	10	11

(b) *Office holding*

The extent to which office holding confers real power on the office holder may vary from one organisation to another. Important decisions may be taken outside the organisation, or influence may be exerted by individuals or groups within the organisation who do not hold office. But other things being equal, an office holder is usually in a better position to wield influence than a non-office holder.

20% of the attached said they held a position of responsibility
Table R3.9
in the groups they went to, and again it was the later leavers who were most prone to be office holders and the early leavers who were least so. Sex differences were small. The same pattern was evident for those who held the most influential positions, such as chairman, secretary, team captain and so on. In this case 10% of the attached were involved. For both categories of office holding, later school leavers were about

twice as likely as the early leavers to occupy positions. Boys rather more often held office when they were younger, but girls, by contrast, more often held office as they grew older, (see table R3.9).

Table 3.5 Percentage of attached 14-20 year olds who held office by sex and school leaving age

School leaving age	All office holders			Influential office holders		
	M	F	T	M	F	T
15	13	10	12	6	5	6
16 or over	25	22	24	13	12	13
T	21	18	20	11	10	10

In summary, it appears that whatever measure of attachment is used, with the possible exception of frequency of attendance, the early school leavers, and particularly the girls are least able or willing to make use of the facilities available.

Table R3.6 Last visit to a club and reported frequency of visits
       (a) as percent of all those attached
       (b) as percent of total sample

Q. 17(b) (viii) Last visit to a club	(a) All attached	(b) All 14-20 year olds
	%	%
None	-	35
Last went: a week ago or less	67	44
a month ago or less	22	14
more than a month ago	11	7
Total percentages	100	100
Weighted bases	(2502.5)	(3849)
Q. 17(b) (vi) Reported frequency of visits		
None	-	35
More than once a week	43	28
About once a week	37	24
Less than once a week but at least once a month	13	9
Or less than once a month	6	4
Total percentages	100	100
Weighted bases:	(2502.5)	(3849)

Table R3.7 Frequency of visiting clubs, by time of year interviewed

Qs. 17(b) (vi) & (viii) Frequency of visiting	Early Summer	Winter/Autumn	Total
	%	%	%
Goes once a week or more and has been within last week	36	45	40
Goes less than once a week but at least once a month and has been within last month	17	15	16
Goes less frequently than once a month, or has not been within last month	9	7	8
No present attachment	37	33	35
Total percentages	100	100	100
Weighted base: All young people	(1990)	(1859)	(3849)

Table R3.8 Number of attachments to clubs, by age of leaving school, age and sex

Q. 16(c)

Number of attachments	Age of leaving school															
	15								Over 15							
	14	15	16	17	18	19	20	Total	14	15	16	17	18	19	20	Total
	%	%	%	%	%	%	%	%	%	%	%	%	%	%	%	%
BOYS																
No attachments	32	42	46	36	34	41	42	39	16	16	15	16	24	22	30	19
One	33	32	30	39	30	28	31	32	29	28	18	28	26	25	19	25
Two	15	14	14	16	22	20	14	16	15	20	26	16	13	16	12	17
Three	9	8	7	6	4	5	9	6	15	16	16	16	8	12	16	14
Four or more	11	3	3	3	10	5	5	7	24	20	26	24	29	25	24	24
Total percentages	100	100	100	100	100	100	100	100	100	100	100	100	100	100	100	100
Weighted base: All boys	(84.5)	(106)	(116)	(117)	(100)	(113.5)	(140.5)	(777.5)	(202)	(188)	(159.5)	(154)	(147)	(147.5)	(136)	(1134)
GIRLS																
No attachments	36	48	63	63	62	62	67	58	26	24	29	32	27	33	40	30
One	34	33	24	23	28	24	21	26	28	22	22	26	25	28	20	25
Two	16	9	6	8	8	9	8	9	22	27	24	15	9	14	12	18
Three	11	7	5	5	1	3	2	5	11	13	14	11	9	8	9	11
Four or more	3	4	3	1	1	2	2	2	13	15	12	16	20	17	19	16
Total percentages	100	100	100	100	100	100	100	100	100	100	100	100	100	100	100	100
Weighted base: All girls	(90)	(121.5)	(104.5)	(147)	(122.5)	(122.5)	(130)	(838)	(190)	(186.5)	(200)	(147)	(134)	(129)	(113)	(1099.5)
TOTAL																
No attachments	34	45	54	51	49	52	54	49	21	20	22	25	30	27	35	25
One	34	33	27	30	29	26	26	29	29	25	20	27	26	26	19	25
Two	15	11	10	12	14	14	11	12	19	23	25	15	11	15	12	18
Three	10	7	6	5	2	4	6	6	13	14	15	13	8	10	13	13
Four or more	7	3	3	2	5	3	4	4	19	17	18	20	25	22	22	20
Total percentages	100	100	100	100	100	100	100	100	100	100	100	100	100	100	100	100
Weighted base: All young people	(174.5)	(227.5)	(220.5)	(264)	(222.5)	(236)	(270.5)	(1615.5)	(392)	(374.5)	(359.5)	(301)	(281)	(276.5)	(249)	(2233.5)

49

Table R3.9 Young people holding office in the organisations they go to, by age of leaving school, age and sex
ONLY THOSE ATTACHED TO A CLUB

Q. 18

Whether holds office	Age of leaving school															
	15								Over 15							
	14	15	16	17	18	19	20	Total	14	15	16	17	18	19	20	Total
	%	%	%	%	%	%	%	%	%	%	%	%	%	%	%	%
BOYS																
No office held †	90	84	86	87	91	88	83	87	73	72	75	72	75	80	77	75
Holds office	10	16	14	13	9	12	17	13	27	28	25	28	25	20	23	25
(Holds influential office*)	5	12	11	4	3	3	6	6	17	14	13	13	14	10	10	13
Total percentages	100	100	100	100	100	100	100	100	100	100	100	100	100	100	100	100
Weighted base: All boys who were attached	(57.5)	(61)	(63)	(75.5)	(65.5)	(66.5)	(82)	(471)	(169.5)	(158.5)	(136)	(129)	(111)	(115)	(95.5)	(914.5)
GIRLS																
No office held †	95	91	90	87	87	85	95	90	82	81	81	70	74	76	75	78
Holds office	5	9	10	13	13	15	5	10	18	19	19	30	26	24	25	22
(Holds influential office*)	4	3	3	9	6	8	5	5	12	13	7	14	14	10	16	12
Total percentages	100	100	100	100	100	100	100	100	100	100	100	100	100	100	100	100
Weighted base: All girls who were attached	(57.5)	(63.5)	(39)	(54.5)	(46.5)	(47)	(43)	(351)	(141)	(142)	(143)	(100)	(85)	(86.5)	(67.5)	(765)
TOTAL																
No office held †	93	87	87	87	89	87	87	88	77	76	78	71	74	78	76	76
Holds office	7	13	13	13	11	13	13	12	23	24	22	29	26	22	24	24
(Holds influential office*)	4	7	8	6	4	5	6	6	15	14	10	14	14	10	13	13
Total percentages	100	100	100	100	100	100	100	100	100	100	100	100	100	100	100	100
Weighted base: All young people who were attached	(115)	(124.5)	(102)	(130)	(112)	(113.5)	(125)	(822)	(310.5)	(300.5)	(279)	(229)	(196)	(201.5)	(163)	(1679.5)

*Influential office means President/Chairman, Secretary/Treasurer, Leader in a uniformed organisation or a Captain/Vice captain of a sports team – these are also included in the 'Holds office' category.
†No office held includes the 1% of the attached for whom no information was known.

50

CHAPTER 4

TYPES OF CLUB AND THEIR ATTRACTIONS

It is clear that different groups of young people are more or less attracted to voluntary social organisations, but it seems reasonable to suppose that as well as the influences which are peculiar to each group, the characteristics of the organisations themselves will also act so as to attract, retain or repel members. The particular characteristics which are examined here are the organisation's connection with an educational or employing establishment, the type of club as indicated by its name or description and the activities provided, as well as the age range and sex composition of its members. Clearly these are not the only club-centred influences on its attractions; it seems likely, for instance, that its structure would be important, but a survey of actual and potential members is not a suitable method for determining this.

4.1 School and work based clubs

Fifty-seven per cent of the young people, or just over 60% of those at work or in full-time education, said that there was a club or similar facility attached to their school, college or place of employment, and of these, 54% actually went to one (or 33% of all those at work or in full time education).

It was shown in Chapter 2 that young people in full-time education were more likely to be attached than those who were not. One possible explanation is that voluntary social groups were more readily available to those in educational establishments since 88% of those at school or college said there was a linked group they could go to if they wished, compared with only 36% of those at work. But where the facility *was* provided 60% of the children in full-time education went, compared with only 41% of those at work. Obviously it is not the ready availability of a club and so on which alone influences attachment to it.

Table R4.15

Further evidence of the lack of any simple relationship between availability and use is provided by the young people still at school. Although the early school leavers still at school were a little less likely to claim that a club was available to them, the big difference lay in the extent to which they, in comparison with the later leavers, actually made use of the available facilities. Thus only 38% of the early leavers who went to schools which provided clubs, went to them, compared with 59% of the later school leavers of the same age. This means that school linked clubs and similar facilities, like clubs of all

Table R4.16

51

kinds, were less attractive to the early leavers than to the late leavers. But there is no evidence that the school linked clubs were peculiarly unpopular with the first group, for in both cases about 6 or 7 early leavers were attached for every 10 later leavers.

Table 4.1 Attachment to school, college and work linked clubs

Occupational Status	% having a group available			% of those for whom group was available, who went		
	M	F	T	M	F	T
In a job	39	32	36	43	40	41
In full-time education	89	88	88	68	59	60
At school:						
School leaving age 15	83	81	82	46	40	38
School leaving age 16 or over	88	86	89	66	53	59

4.2 Types of club

By 'type' is meant the name or description of the group according to the young person. Such names are by no means ideal for classificatory purposes, since some categories must refer to what seems to be the main activity provided by the organisation, for example 'sports clubs', whilst others are determined by other sorts of characteristics, like 'youth clubs' or 'uniformed organisations'.

The largest single group of attached young people went to sports groups (42%), next in popularity were youth clubs* (36%) followed by social clubs (22%), and cultural groups (18%). No other type of club was mentioned by as many as 10% of the attached, but academic and uniformed organisations, and students unions (including school councils) were each used by about 8% of the attached.

Table R4.17 Unlike the boys, the girls more often patronised youth clubs than sports clubs and were more likely than boys to go to social, cultural and religious groups. Apart from the preference of boys for sports clubs, however, the greatest differences were between the early and later school leavers and the younger and older children. Looked at in this way, some types of club, mentioned by only a small proportion of all the attached, are seen to be rather well patronised by specific groups.

---

*i.e. organisation entitled 'youth clubs'. These are not synonymous with what the young people said they would call youth clubs, because some people included other groups, such as uniformed organisations as youth clubs in the latter definition. Throughout this and the following chapter the term is used in the first sense to mean clubs entitled 'Youth Clubs'.

Table 4.2 Percentage of attached going to different types of club by school leaving age, sex and age (all clubs attended)

Type of club	School leaving age – 15 years						School leaving age – 16 or over					
	M		F		T		M		F		T	
	Age at time of interview											
	14-16	17-20	14-16	17-20	14-16	17-20	14-16	17-20	14-16	17-20	14-16	17-20
Sports clubs and teams	43	44	25	24	35	36	54	52	34	37	44	46
Youth clubs	61	31	55	23	58	28	39	29	48	16	43	23
Social clubs	9	38	23	42	16	40	6	28	16	23	11	26
Cultural groups	2	4	8	6	5	5	19	22	27	33	23	27
Students union etc.	3	2	2	2	2	2	4	18	6	23	5	20
Uniformed	8	4	2	5	6	4	18	5	12	3	15	4
Academic clubs	-	1	1	-	-	-	14	13	9	12	12	13
Common rooms etc.	3	3	3	3	3	3	5	12	4	15	5	14
Religious groups	3	2	6	4	5	3	6	5	12	12	9	8
Debating, current affairs etc.	1	-	2	-	1	-	8	7	7	6	7	7
Film clubs	2	-	1	-	1	-	8	8	5	10	7	9

The most obvious difference is that what appear to be interest centred organisations (e.g. sports, cultural, academic and religious groups) were used most by the late school leavers, as also were predominantly educationally linked facilities, like students unions (including school councils) and common rooms, although the latter included similar work linked provision. The early leavers, on the other hand, more often frequented the less differentiated groups like youth clubs and social clubs. The girl early leavers in particular made more use of social clubs.

Some examples of the kind of organisation included in each category are given in Appendix 3, but it must be mentioned here that social clubs, and to a lesser extent sports clubs, present a special problem. Over a third of the social clubs were almost certainly commercially provided in the sense that they were run for profit. Overwhelmingly these places were dancing clubs and discotheques. A third of the social clubs were almost certainly not commercial, for example 'school discotheque', 'church social club'. 20% could not be classified and about 10% were working men's clubs, which do not necessarily fall clearly into the commercial category. Amongst sports clubs, none were definitely commercial, although some of the very few golf and snooker clubs may have been.

Ideally, the commercial organisations should be examined separately, but except in a few cases, the difficulty of identification is insurmountable in an enquiry of this kind, and since both types of organisation function as providers of leisure facilities for young people, no attempt has been made to do so. However it should be borne in mind that between a third and a half of the social clubs or up to about 10% of all the groups to which the young people were attached, were probably commercially provided. This does not lower the figure for overall attachment to non-commercial organisations by as much as 10%, because some of those going to commercial groups also went to non-commercial groups.

4.3 What young people do in Clubs

(a) By type of club

Table R4.18 The name of the club provides a rough guide to the kind of activities it makes available to the young people who go to it, and indeed it is obvious that most people who go to sports clubs will play games, just as most people who go to cultural clubs will take part in musical or dramatic activities and so on (see Fig. 4.1).

In youth clubs the predominant activity was indoor sport, followed by dancing, talking and chatting, listening to music and outdoor team games. This makes them very similar to sports-and-social clubs, the main difference being the greater opportunity at the latter for drinking. Church linked youth clubs provided a similar diet of activities but evidently placed more emphasis on discussion (which included Bible study). Students Unions, too bore some resemblance to Youth clubs, in that dancing and chatting were mentioned more often than average, but in this case organising events and discussion were also important and sports, indoor or outdoor, did not receive above average mention.

The activities in interest centred organisations (i.e. cultural groups, academic clubs, current affairs and film clubs) naturally varied with the interest concerned, but it is worth noting that the most frequently mentioned activities in these cases were always of an interest centred kind and that the social activities appeared to be subordinate to them. The uniformed organisations, as might be expected resembled the interest centred groups rather than the Youth clubs in that the most popular activities there were interested-centred as opposed to social.

Since it is clear that some types of club bear a close resemblance to others, similar types will be grouped together for the remainder of this report. The groupings are as follows:

Sports club – all sports clubs
Social – social clubs and sports-and-social clubs
Interest-centred – debating/current affairs societies, cultural groups, academic clubs, creative craft clubs, hobby clubs, film societies, chess/bridge clubs
Youth Clubs – all youth clubs

This grouping of course excludes some clubs which did not easily fit into these categories.

(b) By characteristics of the young people who go

In order to simplify the discussion, club activities will also be grouped in this section into broader categories than hitherto, but where necessary we shall mention important features of the

composition of categories. The groupings used are shown on
Fig. 4.1, each column represents one category, but 'outings' and
'other' are excluded from the table 4.3

FIG. 4.1.

Selected types of clubs, showing activities receiving above average mention (10% or more)

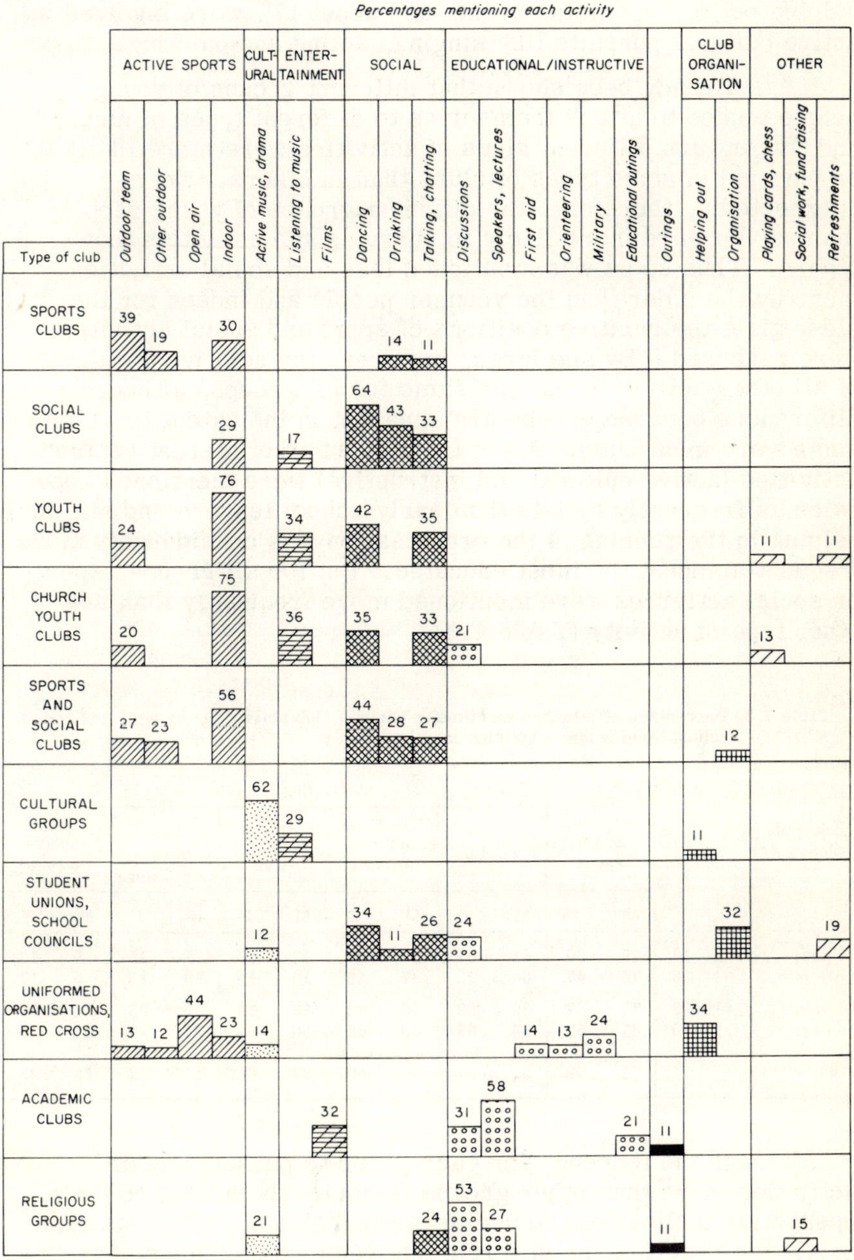

Percentages mentioning each activity

Type of club	ACTIVE SPORTS				CULTURAL	ENTERTAINMENT		SOCIAL			EDUCATIONAL/INSTRUCTIVE						CLUB ORGANISATION			OTHER		
	Outdoor team	Other outdoor	Open air	Indoor	Active music, drama	Listening to music	Films	Dancing	Drinking	Talking, chatting	Discussions	Speakers, lectures	First aid	Orienteering	Military	Educational outings	Outings	Helping out	Organisation	Playing cards, chess	Social work, fund raising	Refreshments
SPORTS CLUBS	39	19		30				14	11													
SOCIAL CLUBS				29		17		64	43	33												
YOUTH CLUBS	24			76		34		42	35											11		11
CHURCH YOUTH CLUBS	20			75		36		35	33		21									13		
SPORTS AND SOCIAL CLUBS	27	23		56				44	28	27									12			
CULTURAL GROUPS					62	29													11			
STUDENT UNIONS, SCHOOL COUNCILS					12			34	11	26	24								32			19
UNIFORMED ORGANISATIONS, RED CROSS	13	12	44	23	14								14	13	24			34				
ACADEMIC CLUBS							32				31	58				21	11					
RELIGIOUS GROUPS					21					24	53	27					11				15	

55

By far the most frequently mentioned activities were sports (mainly indoor sports) quoted by over two-thirds of the attached, and social pursuits, such as chatting, dancing and drinking (57%). Over a third mentioned entertainment, mainly listening to records, but also including visiting the theatre and watching films, and over a quarter took part in instructive activities like discussions, debates, orienteering, tests and educational outings. Twenty per cent said they spent some of their time helping out or organising events and about 17% were involved in active cultural pursuits like singing, acting and painting.

It has already been shown that different groups of young people tended to attach themselves to different types of clubs, and that in turn different kinds of activities were more likely to be pursued in some types of clubs than in others. Not unexpectedly, therefore, the different groups of young people themselves were more likely to pursue some activities than

Table R4.19

others. Thus sport was mentioned less and social activities more by the older than the younger people and indeed for the older girls the relative positions of sport and social activities were reversed. By and large, however, the relative popularity of all other activities was the same for all groups, although differences between groups are apparent in the extent to which some were mentioned. Apart from sport, the interest centred activities (active cultural and instructive) were mentioned about twice as frequently by late than early school leavers and similarly helping in the running of the organisation was considerably more frequent amongst the most educated. But for all groups, sport or social activities were mentioned more frequently than any other type of activity (Table 4.3).

Table 4.3 Percentage of attached mentioning various club activities, by age, sex and school leaving age – 1st club mentioned only

School leaving age	Age	Activities											
		active sport		social		enter-tainment		instruc-tive		club organ-isation		active cultural	
		M	F	M	F	M	F	M	F	M	F	M	F
15 years	14–16	85	69	41	69	34	37	17	17	9	15	9	13
	17–20	76	47	64	73	27	36	13	14	14	15	5	12
16 years or over	14–16	77	67	35	59	36	42	36	34	16	23	16	27
	17–20	67	50	64	63	40	42	30	34	25	29	15	29
Total		75	59	51	64	35	40	27	28	18	22	13	23

Although the tendency for each group to pursue certain activities more than other groups is obviously related to their respective inclinations to use different types of club, it is also

Table R4.20

partly the result of the different use each group makes of the same type of club. So that within each of the major categories

(Sports, Social, Interest-centred and Youth Clubs), the later school leavers were more likely than early leavers to take part in interest centred and organisational activities. Of course, it is not possible to determine from an enquiry of this kind whether the two groups used the same clubs differently, or whether they each used different clubs in the same broad category, which conceals a shifting spectrum of possible activities.

4.4 Age Range

The young people went to clubs catering for many different age ranges and in fact a few of them claimed to attend clubs having an age range which excluded their own. However, there was a tendency for each age group to cluster in clubs with particular age ranges although this was more marked for the 14 and 15 year olds and the 18-20 year olds than for the middle group, aged 16 and 17 (Table 4.4).

Table 4.4 Percentage of attached attending clubs of various age ranges – 1st club mentioned only

Age Range	Age						
	14	15	16	17	18	19	20
between 14-16	42	17	5	1	1		
14-18	21	26	16	11	2		
14-20	11	14	11	14	5	5	1
14- more than 20	12	11	13	11	10	10	6
15-20		12	14	12	4	1	-
15- more than 20		4	7	10	7	8	10
16-20			11	9	3	2	-
16- more than 20			8	10	16	12	14
17 or 18-20				3	3	1	1
17 or 18-30				5	16	22	26
17 or 18- more than 30				6	19	18	20

A curious feature of this distribution is that considerably more of the younger teenagers (both as percentages and absolute numbers) said they went to clubs having members aged up to between 16 and 20 years than people aged from 16-20 said they went to them. This suggests either that, at least within the 14-20 year age group, people seldom remained in a club until they reached the upper age limit, and that the older members were in the minority, or that the younger children sometimes exaggerated the age of older members because they liked to think they belonged to a group which included young adults.

There does appear to be a change between the ages of 16 and 17 so that more of the people above this age went to groups having a lower age limit of 17 or 18 than went to clubs taking younger people, *unless* in the latter case, the upper limit was over 20 years. In fact, about a third of those aged 17 and over went to groups whose youngest members were not yet 17 or 18, but whose oldest members were over 20.

Table R4.21 Generally speaking, the early school leavers more often went to groups having a wider age range than did the later leavers and the explanation lies in the relationship between the type of club and the age range covered (see Fig. 4.2). Put simply, the youth clubs and the social clubs, which were more often patronised by early than late school leavers, catered for broader age ranges than did other types of club. Interest centred clubs in particular were confined to the narrowest age ranges. For example, the youth clubs attended by 14 year olds typically covered age ranges of 14-18, 14-20 and 14 to over 20 years, but 14 year olds going to other kinds of club most commonly quoted an age range of 14 to 15 or 16. At the other end of the scale, the few 18-20 year olds who attended youth clubs continued to use those for 14 to 20 or over 20 year olds, whilst those who went to social clubs gave a modal age range of 17 or 18 to over 30 years. But the interest-centred clubs used by the older group were normally limited to a range of from 17 or 18 to between 21 and 25. Sports clubs, on the other hand, covered both restricted and extended age ranges with almost equal frequency; a pattern which may reflect the variety of sport involved.

This analysis suggests that it may be meaningless to consider age range in isolation and that at least the type of club concerned should be taken into consideration. At the same time, it is not possible to say from the data provided whether the existing relationships represent a uniquely viable pattern or whether they are the result of circumstances largely irrelevant to the success of a club. For example, some of the interest-centred groups were linked to schools and may only have been available to pupils in specific forms, irrespective of whether others might have been interested. Similarly the age range for youth clubs is presumably largely influenced by the recognised youth service age range of 14 to 20 years, which was first proposed over thirty years ago for reasons which may be irrelevant to the current success of a club. All that can be said with certainty is that different types of club tend to have different kinds of age ranges, and that these are compatible with their continuing existence, although youth clubs in particular are more successful in attracting people at one end of the age band covered than at the other.

58

FIG. 4.2
Age ranges covered by the four major types of club, by age of those attending

Percentages

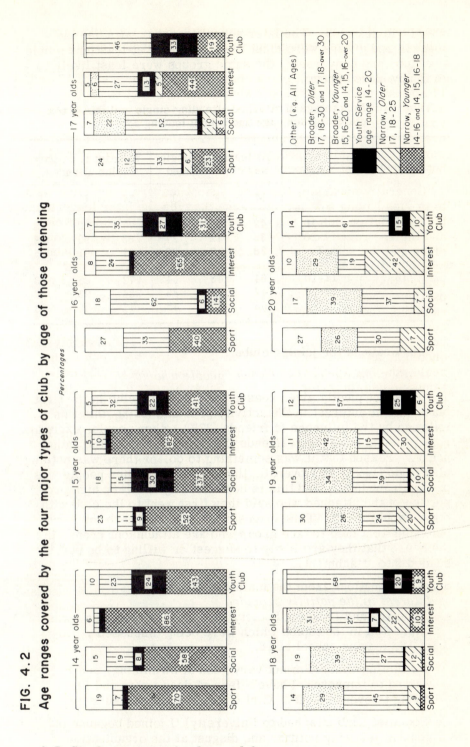

4.5 Single versus mixed sex clubs

Eighty-three per cent of the attached went to at least one mixed club (of up to three first mentioned), and 40% went to at least one single sex club. The later school leavers, boys and the younger age groups were most likely to attend at least one single sex club, and conversely, the same groups were least likely to go to any mixed group.

Table 4.5 **Percentage of attached attending single and mixed sex clubs, by sex, age and school leaving age**

School leaving age	Age	At least one single sex club attended			At least one mixed club attended		
		M	F	T	M	F	T
15	14–16	42	23	33	77	90	83
	17–20	35	12	27	83	92	86
	T	38	17	29	81	91	85
16	14–16	64	43	54	72	85	78
	17–20	42	25	35	84	92	87
	T	53	35	45	77	89	83

4.6 Reasons for joining clubs

(a) By characteristics of young people who go

Table R4.23

Table R4.24

The most frequently given reason for going to a club in the first place was an interest in the activity provided (31%), this was followed by the influence of friends (27%), other people, excluding relatives and boy or girl friends (17%) and finally by the rather negative reason that it was something to do, or there was nothing else to do (14%). But overall, the influence of other people was predominant (53%), and this is confirmed by the very high proportion of the attached who said they first went to the club with other people (87%). This suggests the importance to joining of belonging to a face to face group who are attachment prone, in the sense that they are likely to suggest or willing to be persuaded into attachment.

Some illustrations from the main categories are:
Interest in the activity provided
(Literary and Debating Society) 'I went along because I was interested in the topics which were being discussed'. Boy of 16, leaving school at 18.

(Swimming Club) 'I'm not very good at swimming, and I wanted to improve – I have a fear of deep water and I'm trying to overcome it'. Girl of 15, leaving school at 18.

(Socialist Club attached to University) 'I joined because of general left wing politics and disgust at the organisation of the university'. Girl of 20, who left school at 18.

(Drama Club) 'Because I wanted not to be afraid to speak in front of people'. Girl of 14, leaving school at 15.

Influence of other people
(Youth Club) 'Well, it's next door to me and my friends went, so when I was the right age I went to see if I'd like it'. Girl of 16, leaving school at 16.

(Social Club) 'That's where my mates went, so I went with them'. Girl of 17, left school at 15.

(Working Men's Club) 'My Dad goes, so I thought it must be something good, so I went'. Boy of 19, left school at 15.

(Youth Club) 'One of my friends told me it was a smashing club'. Boy of 14, leaving school at 18.

Something to do
(Youth Club) 'Mainly because there was nothing else to do — going for walks was getting boring — somewhere we could be at night instead of just doing nothing'. Girl of 15, leaving school at 15.

(Youth Club) 'I don't like lazing about the streets at night — you get bored with the same thing every night. I was too young at first and used to laze about the streets, then my mates went — I suppose it's like sheep'. Boy of 15, leaving school at 15.

(Youth Club) 'Just to meet people and have something to do in the evening instead of watching TV.' Boy of 14, leaving school at 18.

The early school leavers again differed from the later leavers in that they more often cited both the influence of other people and lack of anything better to do for first going along to a club. They, and particularly the girls amongst them, were least likely to have first gone to the club on their own. The later leavers, by contrast, more often mentioned an interest in the activity available. Their relatively greater concern with what the club could provide even extended to the purely social side, for although this was rather rarely mentioned, it was the later leavers who slightly more often said they had first gone to a club to meet new people or as a place to meet their existing friends.

Table 4.6 **Percentage of attached stating various reasons for first going to club – 1st club mentioned only**

School leaving age	Age	Influence of other people			Interest in activity			Something to do/nearby			To meet friends			Other		
		M	F	T	M	F	T	M	F	T	M	F	T	M	F	T
15	14-16	62	62	62	22	20	21	22	24	23	1	8	5	15	18	17
	17-20	53	64	57	25	15	21	19	22	20	5	7	6	26	19	23
	T	56	63	59	24	18	21	20	23	21	4	7	5	22	19	21
16 or over	14-16	52	56	54	41	33	37	12	14	13	3	6	5	23	22	23
	17-20	46	44	45	33	33	33	14	12	13	7	11	9	22	27	25
	T	49	51	50	37	33	35	13	13	13	5	8	7	23	24	24

(b) By characteristics of the club

The reasons given for first going to a club were related to the type of club involved. Thus the sports and other interest centred clubs, those for example concerned with culture, politics and current affairs, were most often first visited because of an interest in the activity provided. But the two most frequently given reasons for going to a social or youth club were the influence of other people or lack of anything better to do. And an interest in the activity was mentioned less for youth clubs than for any other type of club, just as negative reasons were given more frequently.

Table R4.25

The relationship between type of club and reasons for first going held whichever school leaving group was concerned, but for each type of club involved, the later school leavers were rather more likely to say they went because of an interest in the activity and less likely to say it was because there was little else to do, or (with the single exception of youth clubs), that they had been influenced by other people.

Table 4.7 **Percentage of attached stating various reasons for first going to club, by type of club, and school leaving age – 1st club mentioned only**

Type of club	Other people			Interest in activity			Something to do			To meet friends			Other		
	S.L.A.			S.L.A.			S.L.A.			S.L.A.			S.L.A.		
	15	16+	T	15	16+	T	15	16+	T	15	16+	T	15	16+	T
Sports	53	46	48	43	52	49	8	8	8	3	4	4	17	18	17
Social /Sports and social	66	57	61	13	13	13	23	21	22	6	14	10	28	22	25
Interest centred	(48)	42	43	(53)	56	55	(11)	7	7	(-)	4	3	(20)	24	24
Youth Clubs	63	66	65	5	8	7	36	27	30	7	9	8	16	22	19

Figures in brackets are percentages based on less than 50 cases.

4.7 Reasons for leaving clubs

(a) By the characteristics of the people who left

The most frequently cited reason for leaving a club was that it was no longer congenial (43%). Most of the complaints here were of boredom, the youth of other members, or unattractive activities rather than of more dramatic experiences like rigid discipline, officiousness and fighting. But 17% said they had stopped going because they had no friends to go with, or to meet there. Nearly 30% had stopped going because the organisation was no longer available to them; for example, they had moved, reached the upper age limit, or the club concerned had closed down. Twenty per cent had left because of lack of time or, in other words, because they gave priority to other activities such as work, study, courting or other leisure pursuits.

Some examples of the kind of reason classified as 'club uncongenial' are:

(Youth Club) 'I feel a bit as though I've grown out of it now,
the others are a bit on the young side'. Boy of 20, left
school at 18, unattached.

(Youth Club) 'There wasn't much going on – just had to talk
to friends. At one time they used to do things – but they
just play records now, or drink coffee'. Girl of 17, left
school at 15, unattached.

(Church Youth Club) 'Because it was boring, they weren't
doing anything at all, everybody just used to sit about and
there wasn't anything to do'. Girl of 19, left school at 15,
unattached.

(Church Youth Club) 'My mates stopped going – got fed up –
same thing every week – play table tennis, snooker every
week, and that was it'. Boy of 15, leaving school at 15,
attached.

And illustrations of 'lack of friends':

(Social Club) 'My friend got married – three of us went
round together – then one got married, then the other one
got married, so there was no one else to go with'. Girl of
19, left school at 15 – attached.

(Youth Club) 'Change of boy friend – I stopped going with
this particular boy and he still went to the Youth Club and
I didn't wish to see him again, so I stopped going'. Girl
of 20, left school at 15, unattached.

(Social Club) 'I fell out with the girl I used to go with'.
Girl of 17, left school at 15, unattached.

(Youth Club) 'Because everybody else did''. Girl of 15,
leaving school at 18, attached.

Table 4.8 Percentage of those who had left a club giving various reasons for
leaving, by age, sex and school leaving age

School leaving age	Age	Club unavailable			Lack of time			Club uncongenial*			Lack of friends*		
		M	F	T	M	F	T	M	F	T	M	F	T
15	14-16	23	33	28	16	11	13	51	46	49	17	25	21
	17-20	26	26	26	22	25	22	42	37	39	14	20	17
	T	25	29	27	20	20	20	45	40	43	15	22	19
16 and over	14-16	30	28	29	19	18	19	45	49	47	16	17	16
	17-20	35	32	34	20	23	22	40	41	40	15	18	17
	T	32	30	31	20	21	20	42	45	43	15	18	17

*These items overlap; unfriendliness of other club members is included in both.

Dislike of the club was the most frequently mentioned reason for leaving by every group, and the only difference that appears worth noting is the more frequent mention of lack of time by the older age group.

As far as could be ascertained, those who were no longer attached to any club, had no different reasons for leaving the last club attended, than did the young people who still went to at least one club, although they had abandoned one of their earlier attachments.

(b) By type of club

Again the reasons given for leaving varied according to the type of club abandoned. Sports and interest centred clubs were most often left because of their non-availability or because of lack of time. Social clubs were most likely to be abandoned because they were uncongenial or for social reasons (ie no friends to go with, or the people there were unfriendly). But it was defections from Youth Clubs which were most frequently attributed to dislike of the club, and more often than average to social reasons. In this case, again, there were no considerable consistent differences between early and late school leavers in the reasons each gave for leaving the *same* type of club.

Table 4.9 Percentage of those who had left a club giving various reasons for leaving, by type of club and school leaving age

Type of club	Club unavailable			Lack of time			Club uncongenial*			Lack of friends*		
	S.L.A.		T	S.L.A.		T	S.L.A.		T	S.L.A.		T
	15	16+		15	16+		15	16+		15	16+	
Sports	26	33	31	22	29	27	31	30	30	14	16	15
Social/Sports and social	32	29	31	14	22	17	40	37	38	18	26	21
Interest-centred	(37)	36	36	(16)	22	21	(26)	32	31	(12)	10	10
Youth Clubs	25	29	27	20	16	18	47	53	50	21	22	21

*These items overlap; unfriendliness of other club members is included in both.
Percentages in brackets are based on less than 50 cases.

4.8 The young people's views on Youth Clubs

As can be seen from the evidence presented in chapter 2, most young people pass through Youth Clubs. We shall later argue in more detail that Youth Clubs are consequently in a key position to influence young people's views on the value of belonging to clubs and in anticipation of our conclusions, it is worth considering the way in which young people regard Youth Clubs.

It should be said first of all that our informants in general held overwhelmingly favourable views on Youth Clubs in that, with few exceptions, a majority of every group agreed with favourable statements and disagreed with unfavourable statements about Youth Clubs, their members, and youth workers. The most frequently endorsed (presumably) unfavourable beliefs were that 'you feel obliged to go regularly', 'you will find too many younger people there', and that 'the people who go to Youth Clubs follow the crowd rather than think for themselves'. These were the only pejorative statements to receive the agreement of the majority of any group.

The greatest differences between early and late school leavers were that the former were considerably more likely to agree that they would feel obliged to go regularly and disagree that Youth leaders were sympathetic people. More of them also saw Youth Clubs as rough or violent places, and considered Youth leaders to be dull. On the other hand they were more inclined to think that Youth Clubs would provide lots of interesting things to do.

Table 4.10 Percentage of young people who agreed with various statements about Youth Clubs, by age, school leaving age and attachment (to any club)

At Youth Clubs you will:	Attachment	School leaving age = 15			School leaving age = 16 or over		
		14-16	17-20	Total	14-16	17-20	Total
Find people friendly	attached	81	79	80	82	78	80
	unattached	72	79	77	80	79	79
	total	77	79	78	81	78	80
See fights and violence	attached	32	36	34	27	28	27
	unattached	42	36	38	26	29	28
	total	36	36	36	27	28	27
Be bored	attached	16	31	24	20	31	26
	unattached	23	32	29	22	36	30
	total	19	31	26	21	33	27
Please yourself what you do	attached	65	61	63	67	58	63
	unattached	64	63	64	71	60	65
	total	65	62	63	68	59	63
Be bossed around	attached	14	17	16	14	17	15
	unattached	21	18	19	17	17	17
	total	17	17	17	15	17	16
Have lots of interesting things to do	attached	75	63	68	67	49	59
	unattached	68	60	63	69	52	59
	total	72	61	65	68	50	59
Feel obliged to go regularly	attached	69	45	55	43	32	38
	unattached	57	46	50	50	34	41
	total	63	45	52	45	32	39
Find too many young people	attached	29	58	46	28	58	42
	unattached	34	62	52	31	62	49
	total	31	60	49	29	59	44
Be treated as an adult	attached	71	59	64	63	50	57
	unattached	58	52	54	62	53	57
	total	65	55	59	63	51	57
Feel lonely and out of it	attached	6	14	11	9	15	12
	unattached	14	15	15	13	16	15
	total	10	15	13	10	16	13
Weighted bases: All young people	attached	(341.5)	(480.5)	(822)	(889)	(790.5)	(1679.5)
	unattached	(281)	(512.5)	(793.5)	(237)	(317)	(554)
	total	(622.5)	(993)	(1615.5)	(1126)	(1107.5)	(2233.5)

Table 4.11 Percentage of young people who agreed with various ways of describing 'people who go to Youth Clubs', by age, school leaving age and attachment (to any club)

People who go to Youth Clubs are:	Attachment	School leaving age = 15			School leaving age = 16 or over		
		14-16	17-20	Total	14-16	17-20	Total
Rough	attached	18	15	16	15	10	12
	unattached	26	15	19	14	10	12
	total	22	15	18	15	10	12
Sensible	attached	61	54	57	54	48	51
	unattached	50	53	52	53	52	52
	total	56	53	55	54	49	51
Childish	attached	13	22	18	12	21	16
	unattached	21	21	21	14	23	19
	total	17	21	20	12	22	17
Lively	attached	84	68	75	80	66	73
	unattached	74	69	71	70	65	67
	total	80	68	73	78	65	72
People who think for themselves	attached	34	29	31	30	20	25
	unattached	33	27	29	26	19	22
	total	33	28	30	29	29	29
Lonely	attached	10	16	13	9	16	12
	unattached	16	19	18	14	18	16
	total	12	17	16	10	16	13
Behind the times	attached	5	14	10	4	11	7
	unattached	11	11	11	9	13	11
	total	7	12	11	5	11	8
Friendly	attached	77	68	72	73	66	70
	unattached	62	66	65	70	62	65
	total	71	67	68	73	65	69
Weighted bases: All young people	attached	(341.5)	(480.5)	(822)	(889)	(790.5)	(1679.5)
	unattached	(281)	(512.5)	(793.5)	(237)	(317)	(554)
	total	(622.5)	(993)	(1615.5)	(1126)	(1107.5)	(2233.5)

On the whole the differences between the 14 to 16 year olds and the 17 to 20 year olds were more marked than differences between school leaving groups, particularly in their expectations of the clubs. Not surprisingly more of the older group expected to find too many young people in the club but they also were less likely to expect to find lots of interesting things to do or to be treated as an adult, and more of them thought they would be bored, and fewer supposed that people who went to Youth Clubs were lively. On the other hand the younger group were much more likely to think they would feel obliged to go regularly.

The attached (to any kind of club) and the unattached were compared to see whether there were any perceived characteristics of Youth Clubs which were particularly unattractive to those who currently went to no club at all. Since it is already clear that Youth Clubs in their present form appeal little to the 17 to 20 year olds, apparently largely because they are seen as more appropriate to a younger group, it is worth considering only the younger children. Moreover since unattachment is rare amongst the younger late school leavers, we shall concentrate only on the early leavers aged 14 to 16 years.

In almost every way the unattached amongst this group were less favourably disposed towards Youth Clubs than the attached, the only exception being that fewer of them thought they would feel obliged to go regularly. In particular more of the unattached disagreed that they would be treated as adults, and expected fighting and violence. They were less inclined to see them as friendly places, and although their views on Youth leaders generally differed little from those of the attached, rather more of them thought that people who ran Youth Clubs were trying 'to push their ideas on to you'. It is therefore difficult to distinguish any specific features of Youth Clubs which repel the unattached, particularly because, although less well disposed than the attached, the majority were still more favourable than hostile to Youth Clubs.

The items used to examine views of Youth Clubs were derived from early pilot interviews, but it is always possible that the most relevant material was ignored, and the aspects selected

Table 4.12 Percentage of young people who agreed with various ways of describing 'people who run clubs for young people', by age, school leaving age and attachment (to any club)

People who run clubs for young people are:	Attachment	School leaving age = 15			School leaving age = 16 or over		
		14-16	17-20	Total	14-16	17-20	Total
Dull	attached	19	22	20	13	14	13
	unattached	23	24	24	16	18	17
	total	21	23	22	13	15	14
Sympathetic	attached	52	56	54	61	73	67
	unattached	50	52	52	55	63	60
	total	51	54	53	60	70	65
Interested in young people's ideas	attached	88	84	86	90	89	90
	unattached	84	83	84	84	84	84
	total	86	84	85	89	88	88
Bossy	attached	24	28	27	22	22	22
	unattached	27	27	27	18	27	23
	total	26	28	27	21	23	22
Full of good sense	attached	71	78	72	71	69	70
	unattached	69	69	69	69	64	66
	total	70	71	70	71	68	69
Trying to push their ideas	attached	30	44	38	30	32	31
	unattached	38	35	36	28	37	33
	total	33	39	37	30	34	32
Young	attached	50	44	46	45	42	44
	unattached	49	42	45	47	38	42
	total	49	43	45	45	41	43
Behind the times	attached	21	25	23	16	19	18
	unattached	19	26	23	20	24	22
	total	20	25	23	17	21	19
Weighted base: All young people	attached	(341.5)	(480.5)	(822)	(889)	(790.5)	(1679.5)
	unattached	(281)	(512.5)	(793.5)	(237)	(317)	(554)
	total	(622.5)	(993)	(1615.5)	(1126)	(1107.5)	(2233.5)

were not those which most concerned the young people. However, we would suggest that a more likely explanation is that in general young people feel it is right to approve of the idea of Youth Clubs in the same way as it is right to approve of education or democracy and that in order to find out exactly what it is that becomes inappropriate about Youth Clubs as the children reach their middle teens, it would be necessary to compare reactions to similar statements related to different kinds of clubs and ways of spending leisure periods. In the absence of any more precise evidence, it appears that one of the major reasons why Youth Clubs fail to retain members after the age of 16 years, is that they attempt to cater for too wide an age range.

It is of some interest that parents' views of Youth Clubs were also overwhelmingly favourable, but that working class parents, particularly the semi-skilled, unskilled and unemployed, were especially prepared to endorse favourable statements, and to reject unfavourable ones. The only exception was that rather more of the least skilled group, than any other, expected violence

Table 4.13 Percentage of parents who agreed with various statements about Youth Clubs, by Registrar General's Socio-economic Class

| Parent agreed that: | Socio – economic Class | | | | | | Total |
	I & II	III non-manual	All non-manual	III manual	IV, V & un-employed	All manual	
Youth Clubs are good for helping young people to find new interests	92	91	92	96	95	95	94
Y.Cs. are full of the wrong type of people	5	9	7	7	7	7	7
Fights and violence are common in Y.Cs.	13	15	14	13	19	15	15
Y.Cs. are good for the shy young person	85	86	85	91	94	92	90
Y.Cs. have nothing for the young person with serious interests	30	35	32	29	26	28	29
Parents know their children are safe when they are at a Y.C.	55	55	55	66	71	68	63
Y.Cs. are good for helping young people to make the right kind of friends	57	65	61	72	77	73	69
Only young people who don't know what to do with themselves go to Y.Cs.	17	20	19	20	21	21	20
A useful thing about Y.Cs. is that they keep young people off the streets	93	93	93	94	96	95	94
Weighted base: All parents	(499)	(406.5)	(905.5)	(1081)	(581.5)	(1662.5)	(2592*)

*The total includes 24 parents who gave an inadequate description of their work.

in Youth Clubs. The same group, however, were also more likely to regard Youth Clubs as 'respectable' places, in which their children would meet the right kind of friends and where they felt they were safe. And it therefore appears that the relatively low prevalence of current Youth Club membership cannot be attributed to parental hostility. On the other hand, of the 29% of parents who said there were specific places in their area they would not like their children to visit, 27% (i.e. about 8% of the total sample) mentioned a particular Youth Club, about the same proportion as specified pubs. The commonest reason for being against a Youth Club was that the wrong type of people went there (52% of those specifying a Youth Club) followed by a belief that there were fights and violence at the club (35%). Similar reasons were most commonly given for rejecting dance halls and discotheques. But the most frequent reason for hostility to pubs was the drinking that went on there.

Table R4.28

Table 4.14 Places specified by parents not wanting their child(ren) to visit local places available for young people, by Registrar General's Socio-economic Class

Place parent would not like child to visit	Socio-economic Class						Total
	I & II	III non-manual	All non-manual	III manual	IV, V & un-employed	All manual	
Public house(s)	22	21	22	27	39	31	28
Youth Club(s)	27	25	26	31	23	28	27
Dance hall/discotheques	24	25	25	21	21	21	22
Sports club	9	17	13	7	7	7	9
Other club(s)	10	10	10	11	10	11	11
Coffee bar(s)	10	5	7	7	6	6	7
Bingo/gambling club	11	6	9	4	5	4	6
Other place(s)	9	9	9	8	6	7	8
Weighted base: Parents not wanting their child(ren) to visit certain local places	(141.5)	(137.5)	(279)	(301)	(166.5)	(467.5)	(756.5)*

*The total includes 10 parents who gave an inadequate description of their work.

It seems, therefore, that it is not the 'image' of the Youth Service which accounts for the relatively low membership. For the image is generally favourable, but like the experience, undifferentiated. Most young people have passed through Youth Clubs and know what at least one is like, and it seems to be the experience which fails to grip young people once they reach their mid-teens. Since they generally view Youth Clubs benignly and, as will be shown in the next chapter, tend to cast their ideal club in a similar mould, it must be supposed that most of them enjoy the experience for a time, but at some point find it no longer relevant to their interests and pleasures.

4.9 Some Interpretations

In this chapter we have been concerned with how and why young people use and leave clubs. But the reasons why people make

69

use of, or lapse from a service are immensely complex questions which may involve many aspects of their social and psychological circumstances, as well as the quality and availability of the service concerned. The reasons people actually give, their conscious and admitted motivations, are only a partial explanation of their behaviour. In this connection it should be recalled that only about 4 out of 10 of the girl early school leavers were attached, and not more than 2 out of 10 were attached to sports or other interest centred clubs. Since members of each group are likely to mix mainly with other people in the same groups, this means that most of the early girl leavers, particularly those over 16, will have few or no friends who are attached, and very few of them indeed will have friends who go to interest centred clubs. Nor, as has been shown, will most of them have parents who go to voluntary social organisations. By contrast, 8 out of 10 boy late school leavers were attached and most of these went to at least one sports or other interest centred club. Their parents were also more likely than not to belong to a club of some kind. These considerations suggest that, whereas a member of the first group would feel it was quite natural not to belong to a club, particularly of the interest centred kind, a boy late leaver who did not go might well feel he was missing something, that he was not sharing at least one field of experience with his contemporaries, nor probably with his parents. Moreover, since the majority of young people first visited clubs with friends, it is clear that joining is not usually the action of isolated individuals.

This possible explanation of what happens within groups to influence attachment touches on the area of norms 'the person to person sharing of opinions and attitudes', an area largely beyond the scope of the present investigation. But where whole social groups tend to behave in characteristic ways, and there is no reason to suppose that these are determined by their physical or material circumstances, there are grounds for suspecting that such norms constitute at least one factor influencing what the people in each group do. This is an important problem and worth research in the present context because it has a bearing on the way in which behaviour can be changed. If decisions to join or leave clubs are either joint decisions amongst circles of friends or acquaintances, or are individual decisions based on what is currently considered 'the thing to do' by most members of such circles, then it seems likely that attempts to persuade people to join or remain in clubs will be more successful if directed to face to face groups rather than to their members as individuals.

The reasons the young people gave for joining, the type of club they went to and their reasons for leaving, although insufficient alone to explain the different patterns of attachment, reveal another aspect of the problem. The different and characteristic styles of use suggest that the late school leavers more often perceive clubs as a means of pursuing interests, usually of a kind which demand some degree of physical, intellectual or aesthetic skill, or at least effort. On the other hand the early leavers appear typically to see them only as places of entertainment and social gatherings. If this interpretation is correct, it would suggest another explanation for the characteristically ephemeral attachment of the least privileged group, and that is that their requirements can be satisfied outside organised social groups in a way which is not so true for those who for example want to play football, to act or debate.

There are also hints, from both their style of use, and their minimum involvement in organisational activities, that the early school leavers receive what clubs provide in a passive way, and leave when the provision loses its appeal. Whilst the later leavers on the other hand appear more aware of the way in which clubs can be of value to them and the means by which they can be shaped to meet their requirements.

These interpretations, if correct, would suggest that, if attachment amongst early school leavers is to be prolonged, their engagement in interest centred activities may be important, and secondly that it might be valuable to help them to learn how to use clubs as malleable organisations rather than finished products.

Table R4.15 Clubs available and attended at work and school/college, by occupational status, age and sex

Q. 16(a) Clubs available and attended	In full-time employment									In full-time education								
	14-16 years			17-20 years			Total			14-16 years			17-20 years			Total		
	Boys	Girls	Total	Boys	Girls	Total	Boys	Girls	Total	Boys	Girls	Total	Boys	Girls	Total	Boys	Girls	Total
	%	%	%	%	%	%	%	%	%	%	%	%	%	%	%	%	%	%
No clubs available	74	78	76	57	64	60	60	67	64	12	15	13	9	3	6	11	12	12
Clubs available:																		
and goes	7	5	6	21	15	18	18	13	15	56	45	50	74	77	75	61	52	56
and does not go	19	16	18	21	20	21	21	19	20	32	41	37	17	19	18	28	36	32
Not known	-	1	1	1	1	1	1	1	1	-	-	-	-	-	-	-	-	-
Total percentages	100	100	100	100	100	100	100	100	100	100	100	100	100	100	100	100	100	100
Weighted base: All young people in a job or full-time education	(196)	(194.5)	(390.5)	(780.5)	(715.5)	(1496)	(976.5)	(910)	(1886.5)	(640)	(667.5)	(1307.5)	(234)	(188.5)	(422.5)	(874)	(856)	(1730)

Table R4.16 Clubs available and attended at school, by age of leaving school, age and sex

Q.16(a)

	Age of leaving school																	
	15									Over 15								
	14-16 years			17-20 years			Total			14-16 years			17-20 years			Total		
Clubs available at school	Boys	Girls	Total	Boys	Girls	Total	Boys	Girls	Total	Boys	Girls	Total	Boys	Girls	Total	Boys	Girls	Total
	%	%	%	%	%	%	%	%	%	%	%	%	%	%	%	%	%	%
No clubs available	17	19	18				17	19	18	10	13	12	8	5	7	10	12	11
Clubs available:																		
and goes	38	32	35				38	32	35	60	48	54	77	69	73	62	51	57
and does not go	45	49	47				45	49	47	30	38	34	16	26	20	27	37	32
Total percentages	100	100	100				100	100	100	100	100	100	100	100	100	100	100	100
Weighted base: Those at school only	(115)	(125.5)	(240.5)				(115)	(125.5)	(240.5)	(500.5)	(520)	(1020.5)	(90)	(77)	(167)	(590.5)	(597)	(1187.5)

Table R.4.17 Type of club, by age of leaving school, age and sex

THOSE ATTACHED

Q.16 (a) & (b)

Age of leaving school (%)

Type of club	15									Over 15								
	14-16 years			17-20 years			Total			14-16 years			17-20 years			Total		
	Boys	Girls	Total	Boys	Girls	Total	Boys	Girls	Total	Boys	Girls	Total	Boys	Girls	Total	Boys	Girls	Total
Sports club	43	25	35	44	24	36	44	25	36	54	34	44	52	37	46	53	35	45
Social club	9	23	16	38	42	40	27	33	30	6	16	11	28	23	26	17	19	18
Sports and social club	2	3	2	8	6	7	5	5	5	2	1	1	6	5	5	4	3	3
Debating/current affairs society	1	2	1	-	-	-	-	1	-	8	7	7	7	6	7	7	7	7
Political societies	1	1	1	2	4	3	2	3	2	1	1	1	6	5	6	4	3	3
Cultural club	2	8	5	4	6	5	3	7	5	19	27	23	22	33	27	21	30	25
Club to do with academic subjects	-	1	1	1	-	-	-	-	-	14	9	12	13	12	13	13	10	12
Clubs for creative crafts	1	-	-	-	-	-	-	-	-	3	1	2	-	-	-	2	1	1
Hobbies not included elsewhere e.g. stamp collecting club, gardening club, travel club, etc.	3	2	2	1	-	1	2	1	1	8	2	5	4	1	3	6	1	4
Film society	2	1	1	-	-	-	1	-	1	8	5	7	8	10	9	8	7	8
Religious society	3	6	5	2	4	3	2	5	4	6	12	9	5	12	8	6	12	9
Uniformed Organizations	8	2	6	4	5	4	6	4	5	18	12	15	5	3	4	12	8	10
Red Cross/St. John's Ambulance Brigade	-	3	2	-	2	1	-	2	1	1	2	2	-	1	1	1	2	1
Youth Clubs of any kind	61	55	58	31	23	28	43	38	40	39	48	43	29	16	23	34	34	34
Chess/Bridge club	1	-	-	-	-	-	-	-	-	10	1	5	2	-	1	6	1	4
Common room/Library	3	3	3	3	3	3	3	3	3	5	4	5	12	15	14	9	9	9

(continued)

74

Table R.4.17 (continued)

THOSE ATTACHED

Q.16 (a) & (b)	Age of leaving school																	
	15									Over 15								
	14-16 years			17-20 years			Total			14-16 years			17-20 years			Total		
Type of club	Boys	Girls	Total	Boys	Girls	Total	Boys	Girls	Total	Boys	Girls	Total	Boys	Girls	Total	Boys	Girls	Total
	%	%	%	%	%	%	%	%	%	%	%	%	%	%	%	%	%	%
Students Union/Association	3	2	2	2	2	2	2	2	2	4	6	5	18	23	20	11	14	12
Young Farmers club	1	1	1	1	1	1	1	1	1	1	-	1	1	1	1	1	1	1
Community Centre	2	3	3	-	2	1	1	2	2	1	1	1	1	1	1	1	1	1
Other clubs not included elsewhere	3	4	4	5	6	5	4	5	5	5	5	5	11	10	10	8	7	8
Clubs for voluntary work/charities	-	-	-	1	1	1	1	-	1	1	3	2	1	5	3	1	4	2
Duke of Edinburgh Award Scheme	-	-	-	-	-	-	-	-	-	1	2	1	-	-	-	1	1	1
Total percentages	149	145	147	147	131	141	147	137	144	215	199	206	231	219	228	226	210	218
Weighted base: All young people attached to clubs	(181.5)	(160)	(341.5)	(289.5)	(191)	(480.5)	(471)	(351)	(822)	(464)	(425)	(889)	(451.5)	(339)	(790.5)	(915.5)	(764)	(1679.5)

75

Table R4.18 Activity, by type of club

THOSE ATTACHED – FIRST CLUB MENTIONED ONLY

Q. 17 (b)1. & 17 (b) (i)

TYPE OF CLUB / SOCIETY / ORGANIZATION

Activity	Sports	Social	Sports & social	Debating/current affairs	Political	Cultural	Academic	Hobbies	Film	Religious	Uniformed & Red Cross	Youth clubs	Church youth clubs	Chess/Bridge	Common Room/Library	Students Union/Association	Other
	%	%	%	%	%	%	%	%	%	%	%	%	%	%	%	%	%
Active outdoor team games	39	4	27	–	–	–	–	–	–	4	13	24	20	–	2	–	9
Other active outdoor sports & games (not requiring a team)	19	2	23	–	4	–	–	–	–	3	12	9	7	–	2	–	6
Other open-air pursuits, e.g. fishing, walking, climbing	10	1	1	3	12	–	–	7	–	6	44	4	6	–	–	–	12
All active indoor sports & games	30	1	56	–	12	–	3	–	–	6	23	4	6	–	20	8	31
Sports/outdoor games unspecified	9	–	3	–	–	–	–	4	–	21	2	76	75	–	2	–	1
Spectator sports	3	2	10	–	4	–	–	4	–	–	1	2	1	–	2	–	2
Outings	3	6	10	–	24	–	11	4	–	11	7	4	9	–	–	4	6
Creative arts	1	1	–	8	–	7	3	–	–	–	1	1	1	–	2	–	1
Active music and drama	1	3	1	–	–	62	6	–	–	21	14	1	8	–	3	12	5
Listening to music/records	1	17	10	–	–	29	5	–	–	9	1	34	36	–	18	8	7
Listening to pop records/music	–	5	1	–	–	1	–	–	–	1	1	6	6	–	2	–	2
Dancing/discotheques	8	64	44	5	20	3	3	–	–	8	2	42	35	–	9	34	13
Going to theatre/opera/concert/ballet/museum/art gallery/folk, jazz, blues clubs	–	1	1	3	–	3	3	–	–	8	2	1	3	–	9	4	2
Variety shows/fair/zoo	1	3	–	–	4	4	2	4	–	2	–	1	–	–	2	2	1
Seeing/having films; go to cinema/pictures	2	3	1	–	4	2	–	4	96	13	1	2	6	–	–	–	8
Playing cards/chess/draughts/puzzles/crosswords/quizzes/monopoly	2	7	4	3	8	2	32	19	4	–	2	11	13	100	12	–	4
Have refreshments	3	9	6	3	4	1	6	4	7	6	1	11	10	–	28	19	2
Drink/go to pub	14	43	28	–	24	2	2	4	–	3	2	1	4	–	11	11	7
Social work and fund raising for others	–	1	1	3	–	10	2	4	–	15	6	2	8	–	–	2	14

76

continued

Table R4.18 (continued)

TYPE OF CLUB / SOCIETY / ORGANIZATION

Activity	Sports %	Social %	Sports & social %	Debating / current affairs %	Political %	Cultural %	Academic %	Hobbies %	Film %	Religious %	Uniformed & Red Cross %	Youth Clubs %	Church Youth Clubs %	Chess, Bridge %	Common Room / Library %	Students Union / Association %	Other %
Helping out in own organization / for own group	6	2	5	5	8	11	5	14	6	10	34	8	5	4	–	2	12
Talk / chat / meet friends	11	33	27	3	12	9	2	10	4	24	3	35	33	4	73	26	10
Discussions	6	3	5	95	28	5	31	28	12	53	6	2	21	4	7	24	10
Organize / plan / arrange / discuss future events	6	3	12	11	8	4	5	7	4	13	10	3	4	–	–	32	10
Have speakers / lectures	1	2	–	16	32	2	58	5	2	27	6	2	7	–	2	8	14
First aid	–	–	–	–	–	–	–	–	–	–	14	–	–	–	–	–	3
Morse code / map reading / orienteering / knots / tracking / bridge building	–	–	–	–	–	–	–	–	–	–	13	–	–	–	–	–	–
Military matters	–	–	–	–	–	–	–	–	–	–	24	–	–	–	–	–	1
Working for tests / badges	–	–	–	–	–	–	–	–	–	–	10	–	–	–	–	–	1
Games of chance, e.g. bingo, one-arm bandits, raffles	–	–	–	–	–	–	–	–	–	–	1	–	–	–	–	–	1
Other activities	1	9	1	–	8	–	–	7	–	2	30	3	2	19	2	5	6
Social evenings / parties / coffee evenings	7	11	14	8	36	7	32	54	2	30	2	8	14	–	31	25	21
Educational Outings, e.g. visits to factories, farms, fire stations	6	7	10	–	24	2	7	–	–	10	–	3	4	–	4	8	1
Watch T.V. / listen to the radio	–	4	4	–	4	–	21	7	–	–	1	–	1	–	17	–	–
Play games (no further details)	1	–	–	–	4	–	–	–	–	3	–	7	2	–	–	–	5
Dominoes	1	2	3	–	4	–	2	–	–	–	1	2	1	–	2	–	3
Creative crafts	–	–	–	–	–	7	–	–	–	3	6	4	–	–	–	–	2
Total percentages	188	277	308	166	292	170	238	186	133	309	303	312	345	135	251	234	233
Weighted base: All young people attached to clubs	(661)	(329)	(78)	(37)	(25)	(225.5)	(61.5)	(28.5)	(51)	(67.5)	(126)	(444)	(135.5)	(23.5)	(44)	(48.5)	(108)

77

Table R.4.19 Activity, by age of leaving school, age and sex

THOSE ATTACHED – FIRST CLUB MENTIONED ONLY

Q.17 (b)1. & 17 (b) (i)

Activity	Age of leaving school																	
	15									Over 15								
	14-16 years			17-20 years			Total			14-16 years			17-20 years			Total		
	Boys	Girls	Total	Boys	Girls	Total	Boys	Girls	Total	Boys	Girls	Total	Boys	Girls	Total	Boys	Girls	Total
	%	%	%	%	%	%	%	%	%	%	%	%	%	%	%	%	%	%
Active outdoor team games	34	16	26	25	9	19	29	13	22	24	7	16	25	8	17	24	7	16
Other active outdoor sports & games (not requiring a team)	9	9	9	5	7	6	7	8	7	11	12	11	7	9	8	9	11	10
Other open-air pursuits, e.g. fishing, walking, climbing	11	3	7	6	4	5	8	4	6	12	6	9	6	5	5	9	5	7
All active indoor sports & games	55	51	53	50	33	43	52	41	47	31	32	32	28	23	25	30	28	29
Sports/outdoor games unspecified	-	1	1	1	-	-	-	1	-	1	2	1	1	1	1	1	-	-
Spectator sports	3	4	4	6	5	5	5	4	5	3	2	3	3	5	3	3	4	3
Outings	2	4	3	4	7	6	3	5	4	2	4	4	6	5	6	3	4	4
Creative arts	-	2	1	1	1	1	-	1	1	2	2	2	2	1	1	2	1	1
Active music and drama	7	8	7	2	8	5	4	8	6	6	15	10	7	19	12	6	17	11
Listening to music/records	16	23	19	15	18	16	15	20	18	9	16	12	14	15	15	12	16	13
Listening to pop records/music	3	4	3	1	5	3	2	5	3	1	3	2	2	2	2	2	2	2
Dancing/discotheques	15	49	31	27	46	34	22	47	33	8	28	18	16	27	21	12	27	19
Going to theatre/opera/concert/ballet/museum/art gallery/folk, jazz, blues clubs	-	1	1	1	1	1	1	1	1	1	2	1	2	1	1	1	2	1
Variety shows/fair/zoo	-	-	-	2	3	2	1	2	1	1	-	1	1	1	1	1	1	1
Seeing/having films; go to cinema/pictures	3	2	3	2	2	2	2	2	2	8	6	6	8	8	7	7	7	7
Playing cards/chess/draughts/puzzles/crosswords/quizzes/monopoly	7	3	5	11	5	9	10	4	7	11	4	8	4	3	4	7	4	6
Have refreshments	3	11	7	4	7	5	4	9	6	5	7	6	6	10	8	5	8	7
Drink/go to pub	2	2	2	30	32	31	19	18	19	3	2	2	20	16	18	11	8	10
Social work and fund raising for others	1	2	1	1	2	2	1	2	1	2	5	3	2	5	3	2	5	3
Helping out in own organization/for own group	4	11	7	6	8	7	6	10	7	6	6	6	10	10	10	8	8	8

continued

78

Table R.4.19 Activity, by age of leaving school, age and sex (continued)

THOSE ATTACHED – FIRST CLUB MENTIONED ONLY

Q.17 (b)1. & 17 (b) (i)

Activity	15									Over 15								
	14-16 years			17-20 years			Total			14-16 years			17-20 years			Total		
	Boys %	Girls %	Total %	Boys %	Girls %	Total %	Boys %	Girls %	Total %	Boys %	Girls %	Total %	Boys %	Girls %	Total %	Boys %	Girls %	Total %
Talk/chat/meet friends	16	22	19	23	24	23	20	23	22	15	21	18	23	21	22	19	21	20
Discussions	7	6	7	6	7	6	7	6	7	10	13	12	10	13	11	10	13	11
Organize/plan/arrange/discuss future events	1	2	2	6	4	5	4	3	4	5	7	6	8	8	8	6	7	7
Have speakers/lectures	1	4	3	1	3	2	1	4	2	5	7	6	7	9	8	6	8	7
First aid	2	2	2	-	1	-	1	1	1	1	1	1	1	-	-	1	1	1
Morse code/map reading/orienteering/knots/tracking/bridge building	2	-	1	1	1	1	1	-	-	2	1	1	1	-	1	1	1	1
Military matters	2	2	2	1	1	1	1	1	1	3	-	2	1	-	1	2	-	1
Working for tests/badges	1	-	-	1	-	-	1	-	-	2	1	1	-	-	-	1	-	1
Games of chance, e.g. bingo, one-arm bandits, raffles	1	3	2	6	10	7	4	7	5	2	1	2	1	2	2	2	1	2
Other activities	14	10	12	10	16	12	12	13	12	14	12	13	12	14	13	13	13	13
Social evenings/parties/coffee evenings	1	1	1	6	6	6	4	4	4	3	4	3	5	10	7	4	7	5
Educational outings, e.g. visits to factories, farms, fire station	1	1	1	-	-	-	-	-	-	2	2	2	1	1	1	1	1	1
Watch T.V./listen to the radio	4	4	4	3	3	3	4	4	4	2	3	2	1	3	2	1	3	2
Play games (no further details)	-	-	-	-	1	1	-	1	-	2	1	1	1	-	-	1	1	1
Dominoes	2	1	2	5	1	3	4	1	2	-	1	1	-	1	1	-	1	1
Creative crafts	3	4	3	1	1	1	1	2	2	4	2	3	-	1	1	2	2	2
Total percentages	233	269	251	269	281	271	256	276	262	221	236	225	237	258	246	226	244	234
Weighted base: All young people attached to clubs	181.5	160	341.5	289.5	191	480.5	471	351	822	464	425	889	451.5	339	790.5	915.5	764	1679.5

79

Qs. 17 (b)1. & 17 (b) (i)

Table R.4.20 Activity, by age of leaving school, age and type of club

THOSE ATTACHED – FIRST CLUB MENTIONED ONLY

Activity (condensed)	Age of leaving school																							
	15												Over 15											
	14-16 years				17-20 years				Total				14-16 years				17-20 years				Total			
	Sp.	Soc.	Int.	Y.C.	Sp.	Soc.	Int.	Y.C.	Sp.	Soc.	Int.	Y.C.	Sp.	Soc.	Int.	Y.C.	Sp.	Soc.	Int.	Y.C.	Sp.	Soc.	Int.	Y.C.
	%	%	%	%	%	%	%	%	%	%	%	%	%	%	%	%	%	%	%	%	%	%	%	%
Active sport	89	47	24	88	82	52	29	82	85	51	27	86	96	50	43	87	90	56	33	74	93	55	38	83
Spectator sports	8	10	5	5	15	6	-	5	13	6	2	5	9	5	3	2	12	5	3	4	10	5	3	3
Active cultural	1	16	29	8	4	6	21	12	3	7	24	10	8	7	45	12	8	8	52	13	8	8	48	12
Entertainment	17	37	24	49	17	33	50	48	17	34	38	48	25	39	48	45	26	38	61	50	25	38	54	47
Creative crafts	2	-	10	3	-	-	-	2	1	-	4	3	2	-	8	6	-	-	2	3	1	-	6	5
Social	30	82	24	66	59	91	54	60	48	89	40	63	37	87	27	69	59	91	48	74	48	90	36	71
Educational/Instructive	15	8	29	11	15	6	21	9	15	6	24	10	20	20	52	18	20	21	48	22	20	21	50	19
T.V./Radio	4	8	-	10	1	8	-	6	2	8	-	8	2	2	-	8	3	5	4	4	2	4	2	7
Outings	3	8	-	2	5	6	8	8	4	6	4	4	6	3	8	5	7	14	6	11	7	11	7	7
Club organisation	15	13	19	8	15	7	17	16	15	8	18	10	15	12	20	14	26	22	28	23	21	19	24	17
Other	9	21	33	20	24	36	38	17	18	33	36	19	18	22	36	19	21	24	33	21	19	24	34	20
Total percentages	193	250	197	270	237	251	238	265	221	248	217	266	238	247	290	285	272	284	318	299	254	275	302	291
Weighted base: All those attached to club	75.5	38	21	166.5	129.5	165	24	100	205	203	45	266.5	229	58.5	266.5	227	227	145.5	180.5	108	456	204	407	335

KEY   Sp. = Sports club   Soc. = Social/Sports and Social club   Int. = Interest-centred clubs   Y.C. = Youth Clubs

80

Table R4.21 Age Range, by age of leaving school and age

THOSE ATTACHED – FIRST CLUB MENTIONED ONLY

Q.17 (b) (v)

Age Range of club	Age of leaving school													
	15							Over 15						
	14	15	16	17	18	19	20	14	15	16	17	18	19	20
	%	%	%	%	%	%	%	%	%	%	%	%	%	%
Between:														
14-16	44	12	1	1	2	1	-	42	20	6	-	1	-	1
14-18	14	11	12	8	1	-	1	24	32	17	13	3	-	-
14-20	14	20	16	16	3	9	1	10	12	9	13	7	3	1
14-more than 20	16	18	20	11	9	11	8	10	8	11	11	10	9	5
15-20	-	14	9	7	2	1	1	-	11	15	14	5	1	-
15-more than 20	-	6	12	15	9	10	15	-	3	6	7	6	7	6
16-20	-	3	5	1	3	-	-	-	1	14	13	4	3	-
16-more than 20	-	2	8	12	18	11	20	-	-	9	9	14	13	10
17, 18-20	-	-	-	1	3	-	2	-	-	-	4	2	2	1
17, 18-25	-	-	-	4	4	6	-	-	-	-	2	10	21	31
17, 18-30	-	-	-	4	8	4	6	-	-	-	1	7	8	10
17, 18-more than 30	-	1	1	10	22	22	27	-	-	-	4	18	15	15
All ages	4	1	3	1	5	5	3	1	1	2	1	4	4	4
10-13 inclusive-any age	8	10	9	8	8	9	3	12	9	8	4	5	4	5
All others	-	1	5	1	3	11	14	1	2	2	3	4	9	12
Total percentages	100	100	100	100	100	100	100	100	100	100	100	100	100	100
Weighted base:														
All attached to clubs	(115)	(124.5)	(102)	(130)	(112)	(113.5)	(125)	(310.5)	(300.5)	(279)	(229)	(197)	(201.5)	(163)

81

Table R.4.22 Age Range, by age and type of club

THOSE ATTACHED – FIRST CLUB MENTIONED ONLY

Qs 17(b)1 & 17(b)(v)

Age Range	14				15				16				17				18				19				20			
	Sp.	Soc.	Int.	Y.C.	Sp.	Soc.	Int.	Y.C.	Sp.	Soc.	Int.	Y.C.	Sp.	Soc.	Int.	Y.C.	Sp.	Soc.	Int.	Y.C.	Sp.	Soc.	Int.	Y.C.	Sp.	Soc.	Int.	Y.C.
	%	%	%	%	%	%	%	%	%	%	%	%	%	%	%	%	%	%	%	%	%	%	%	%	%	%	%	%
Between:																												
14-16	57	46	55	17	33	11	21	8	7	2	8	2	-	-	-	1	1	-	-	-	-	-	-	2	-	-	-	-
14-18	14	12	31	26	15	15	51	26	10	5	18	22	8	5	23	13	1	-	4	9	-	2	-	2	-	-	-	5
14-20	4	8	4	24	9	30	2	22	-	6	3	27	2	3	13	33	-	1	7	20	-	2	2	24	-	-	-	15
14-more than 20	7	19	4	23	6	7	6	17	11	9	7	22	6	9	8	16	11	4	4	36	6	4	-	37	8	1	1	37
15-20	-	-	-	1	10	11	9	12	13	5	27	11	8	3	14	21	2	4	5	9	1	1	-	2	10	-	-	5
15-more than 20	-	-	-	-	3	4	4	5	8	16	4	6	15	12	5	9	9	9	3	9	8	10	2	10	10	16	7	10
16-20	-	-	-	-	-	4	1	2	13	9	17	2	8	6	14	5	5	2	-	7	-	-	-	4	12	20	11	10
16-more than 20	-	-	-	-	-	-	-	1	12	30	8	1	11	23	6	-	19	12	20	7	8	23	12	6				
17, 18-20	-	-	-	-	-	-	-	-	-	-	-	-	4	3	3	-	2	2	4	-	1	-	4	4	1	2	2	5
17, 18-25	-	-	-	-	-	4	-	-	-	-	-	-	2	6	2	-	7	9	18	-	19	10	31	2	16	7	40	5
17, 18-30	-	-	-	-	-	-	-	-	-	-	-	-	6	2	3	-	7	9	14	-	4	2	29	-	9	8	11	-
17, 18-more than 30	-	-	-	-	1	-	-	-	-	-	-	-	6	20	3	-	22	30	17	-	23	32	12	-	18	32	18	-
All ages	5	4	-	-	5	-	-	-	5	5	1	-	2	2	2	-	5	8	-	-	5	10	2	-	3	5	-	5
10-13 inclusive – any age	14	12	5	8	15	15	2	8	16	9	6	6	13	3	3	2	5	8	2	2	10	6	9	4	8	2	-	-
All others	-	-	1	2	2	-	3	1	5	2	1	2	7	2	-	-	3	2	2	3	15	-	-	2	15	9	11	5
Total percentages	100	100	100	100	100	100	100	100	100	100	100	100	100	100	100	100	100	100	100	100	100	100	100	100	100	100	100	100
Weighted base: All attached to clubs	(122.5)	(26)	(96.5)	(112.5)	(106.5)	(27)	(78.5)	(154)	(75.5)	(43.5)	(72.5)	(127)	(83)	(62)	(62)	(104)	(87.5)	(86)	(56)	(34.5)	(94.5)	(82)	(41)	(49)	(91.5)	(80.5)	(45.5)	(20.5)

KEY   Sp. = Sports clubs   Soc. = Social/Sports and Social clubs   Int. = Interest-centred clubs   Y.C. = Youth Clubs

82

Table R.4.23 Reasons for joining, by age of leaving school, age and sex

THOSE ATTACHED – FIRST CLUB MENTIONED ONLY

Q.17(b)(ii)

Reasons for joining	Age of leaving school																	
	15									Over 15								
	14-16 years			17-20 years			Total			14-16 years			17-20 years			Total		
	Boys	Girls	Total	Boys	Girls	Total	Boys	Girls	Total	Boys	Girls	Total	Boys	Girls	Total	Boys	Girls	Total
	%	%	%	%	%	%	%	%	%	%	%	%	%	%	%	%	%	%
Influence of other people e.g. friends, fiance(e), husband/wife, parents, relatives	62	62	62	53	64	57	56	63	59	52	56	54	46	44	45	49	51	50
Interested in the activity, wanted to take part in it	22	20	21	25	15	21	24	18	21	41	33	37	33	33	33	37	33	35
For something to do/somewhere to go, it's near	22	24	23	19	22	20	20	23	21	12	14	13	14	12	13	13	13	13
Social reasons e.g. to meet new people, meet existing friends	1	8	5	5	7	6	4	7	5	3	6	5	7	11	9	5	8	7
Other reasons	15	18	17	26	19	23	22	19	21	23	22	23	22	27	25	23	24	24
Total percentages	122	132	128	128	127	127	126	130	127	131	131	132	122	127	125	127	129	129
Weighted base: All those attached to clubs	(181.5)	(160)	(341.5)	(289.5)	(191)	(480.5)	(471)	(351)	(822)	(464)	(425)	(889)	(451.5)	(339)	(790.5)	(915.5)	(764)	(1679.5)

83

Table R4.24 Whether first went to club with others, by age of leaving school, age and sex

THOSE ATTACHED – FIRST CLUB MENTIONED ONLY

Q.17(b)(iii)

Age of leaving school

Whether first went to club with others	15									Over 15								
	14-16 years			17-20 years			Total			14-16 years			17-20 years			Total		
	Boys	Girls	Total	Boys	Girls	Total	Boys	Girls	Total	Boys	Girls	Total	Boys	Girls	Total	Boys	Girls	Total
	%	%	%	%	%	%	%	%	%	%	%	%	%	%	%	%	%	%
Went alone	13	2	8	14	8	12	14	5	10	16	9	12	21	10	17	19	10	14
With 1 or 2 friends	48	56	52	51	50	50	49	53	51	44	49	46	41	41	41	42	46	44
In a group	28	33	30	22	25	23	24	29	26	30	33	32	28	32	30	29	33	31
With a relative	10	7	8	10	13	12	10	11	10	7	5	6	5	9	7	6	6	6
With some-one else	1	1	1	2	3	2	1	2	2	2	4	3	2	5	3	2	4	3
Not known	1	1	1	1	1	1	1	1	1	1	1	1	2	2	2	1	1	1
Total percentages	100	100	100	100	100	100	100	100	100	100	100	100	100	100	100	100	100	100
Weighted base: All those attached to clubs	(181.5)	(160)	(341.5)	(289.5)	(191)	(480.5)	(471)	(351)	(822)	(464)	(425)	(889)	(451.5)	(339)	(790.5)	(915.5)	(764)	(1679.5)

Table R.4.25 Reasons for joining, by age of leaving school and type of club

THOSE ATTACHED – FIRST CLUB MENTIONED ONLY

Q.17 (b) (ii)

Reasons for joining	Age of leaving school																							
	15												Over 15											
	14-16 years				17-20 years				Total				14-16 years				17-20 years				Total			
	Sp.	Soc.	Int.	Y.C.	Sp.	Soc.	Int.	Y.C.	Sp.	Soc.	Int.	Y.C.	Sp.	Soc.	Int.	Y.C.	Sp.	Soc.	Int.	Y.C.	Sp.	Soc.	Int.	Y.C.
	%	%	%	%	%	%	%	%	%	%	%	%	%	%	%	%	%	%	%	%	%	%	%	%
Influence of other people e.g. friends, fiance(e), husband/wife, parents/relatives	58	58	48	68	50	68	50	55	53	66	49	63	46	61	42	72	46	56	42	54	46	57	42	66
Interested in the activity, wanted to take part in it	44	26	57	6	42	10	50	4	43	13	53	5	56	15	56	10	49	12	55	5	52	13	56	8
For something to do/somewhere to go, it's near	7	26	5	35	8	22	17	36	8	23	11	36	9	15	7	27	7	24	6	26	8	21	7	27
Social reasons e.g. to meet new people, meet existing friends	-	5	-	6	5	6	-	10	3	6	-	7	2	12	2	8	7	14	6	11	4	14	4	9
Other reasons	11	29	19	14	20	28	21	18	17	28	20	16	15	23	25	20	20	22	24	28	18	22	24	22
Total percentages	120	144	129	129	125	134	138	123	124	136	133	127	128	126	132	137	129	128	133	124	128	127	133	132
Weighted base: All those attached to clubs	(75.5)	(38)	(21)	(166.5)	(129.5)	(165)	(24)	(100)	(205)	(203)	(45)	(266.5)	(229)	(58.5)	(226.5)	(227)	(227)	(145.5)	(180.5)	(108)	(456)	(204)	(407)	(335)

KEY   Sp = Sports clubs   Soc. = Social/Sports and Social clubs   Int = Interest-centred clubs   YC = Youth Clubs

Table R.4.26 Reasons for leaving, by age of leaving school, age and sex

THOSE WHO HAVE EVER LEFT A CLUB

Q.19(a)(ii)

Reasons for leaving	Age of leaving school																	
	15									Over 15								
	14-16 years			17-20 years			Total			14-16 years			17-20 years			Total		
	Boys	Girls	Total	Boys	Girls	Total	Boys	Girls	Total	Boys	Girls	Total	Boys	Girls	Total	Boys	Girls	Total
	%	%	%	%	%	%	%	%	%	%	%	%	%	%	%	%	%	%
ATTACHED BUT HAS LEFT A CLUB IN THE PAST																		
Club unavailable e.g. reached upper age limit, club closed, moved away from area	20	39	30	26	25	26	24	31	27	30	29	29	36	36	36	33	32	33
Lack of time e.g. courting, times clashed with work, homework/study for exams	18	10	14	19	20	20	18	16	17	21	20	21	20	25	22	20	23	21
*Club uncongenial e.g. badly organised, few facilities, people unfriendly, too rough, too strict, too expensive, dislike of uniform	54	45	49	46	39	44	49	42	46	45	47	46	39	35	37	42	41	41
Prevented by other circumstances e.g. parents objected, health/physical reasons	1	2	1	-	3	1	1	2	1	2	2	2	2	1	2	2	2	2
Other reasons	19	13	16	14	21	17	16	17	17	13	14	14	13	12	13	13	13	13
*Lack of friends, no friends to go with	20	25	22	13	23	17	15	24	19	17	16	16	13	17	15	15	16	16
Total percentages	132	134	132	118	131	125	123	132	127	128	128	128	123	126	125	125	127	126
Weighted base: All attached who had left a club	(110.5)	(113)	(223.5)	(211.5)	(134.5)	(346)	(322)	(247.5)	(569.5)	(320)	(317.5)	(637.5)	(364)	(284)	(648)	(684)	(601.5)	(1285.5)

*These items overlap; unfriendliness of other club members is included in both

86

Table **R.4.26** (continued)

Q.19(a)(ii)

Reasons for leaving	Age of leaving school																	
	15									Over 15								
	14-16 years			17-20 years			Total			14-16 years			17-20 years			Total		
	Boys	Girls	Total	Boys	Girls	Total	Boys	Girls	Total	Boys	Girls	Total	Boys	Girls	Total	Boys	Girls	Total
	%	%	%	%	%	%	%	%	%	%	%	%	%	%	%	%	%	%
PAST ATTACHMENT WITH NO PRESENT ATTACHMENT																		
Club unavailable e.g. reached upper age limit, club closed, moved away from area	26	26	26	25	27	26	25	27	26	29	28	28	32	26	28	31	26	28
Lack of time e.g. courting, times clashed with work, homework/study for exams	14	12	13	27	27	27	22	23	22	12	13	13	24	20	22	20	17	18
Club uncongenial e.g. badly organised, few facilities, people unfriendly, too rough, too strict, too expensive, dislike of uniform	48	47	48	37	35	36	41	39	40	44	53	50	43	51	48	44	52	49
Prevented by other circumstances e.g. parents objected, health/physical reasons	1	3	2	1	2	2	1	2	2	-	2	1	2	-	1	1	1	1
Other reasons	17	23	20	16	18	17	16	19	18	17	11	13	14	13	13	15	12	13
Lack of friends, no friends to go with	13	25	20	16	18	17	15	20	18	12	20	17	20	22	21	17	21	20
Total percentages	119	136	129	122	127	125	120	130	126	114	127	122	135	132	133	128	129	129
Weighted base: All attached to a club in the past	(93)	(110)	(203)	(157.5)	(264)	(421.5)	(250.5)	(374)	(624.5)	(60)	(119.5)	(179.5)	(111)	(160.5)	(271.5)	(171)	(280)	(451)

Table R.4.27 Reasons for leaving, by age of leaving school and type of club left

THOSE WHO HAVE EVER LEFT A CLUB

Q.19 (a)(ii)

Reasons for leaving	Age of leaving school																				
	15							Over 15							Total						
	Sp.	Soc.	Int.	Rel.	Unif.	Y.C.	Other	Sp.	Soc.	Int.	Rel.	Unif.	Y.C.	Other	Sp.	Soc.	Int.	Rel.	Unif.	Y.C.	Other
	%	%	%	%	%	%	%	%	%	%	%	%	%	%	%	%	%	%	%	%	%
Club unavailable e.g. reached upper age limit, club closed, moved away from area	26	32	37	33	20	25	51	33	29	36	34	28	29	49	31	31	36	34	26	27	50
Lack of time e.g. courting, times clashed with work, homework/study for exams	22	14	16	20	24	20	20	29	22	22	18	24	16	15	27	17	21	18	24	18	17
*Club uncongenial e.g. badly organized, few facilities, people unfriendly, too rough, too strict, too expensive, dislike of uniform	31	40	26	40	44	47	16	30	37	32	40	45	53	32	30	38	31	40	45	50	26
Prevented by other circumstances e.g. parents objected, health/physical reasons	6	4	-	-	2	1	-	7	2	-	-	-	1	1	7	3	-	-	1	1	1
Other reasons	23	19	25	13	19	16	20	14	22	14	13	13	12	11	17	20	16	13	15	14	14
*Lack of friends, no friends to go with	14	18	12	10	15	21	15	16	26	10	6	13	22	11	15	21	10	8	14	21	13
Total percentages	122	127	116	116	124	130	122	129	138	114	111	123	133	119	127	130	114	113	125	131	121
Weighted base: All who had left a club	(101.5)	(96)	(43.5)	(30)	(153.5)	(722)	(46)	(210.5)	(80.5)	(257.5)	(62)	(366)	(679.5)	(71.5)	(312)	(176.5)	(301)	(92)	(519.5)	(1401.5)	(117.5)

KEY   Sp. = Sports clubs   Soc. = Social/sports & social clubs   Int. = Interest-centred clubs   Rel. = Religious   Unif. = Uniformed & Red Cross   Y.C. = Youth Clubs

*These items overlap; unfriendliness of other club members is included in both

88

Table R.4.28 **Reasons parents wouldn't like their child(ren) to visit certain local places available for young people, by type of place**

Reasons wouldn't like children to visit them	Places would not like child(ren) to visit*				
	Pub(s)	Youth Club(s)	Dance hall, Disco-theques	Indoor sports club	Coffee bar, cafe(s)
They mix with the wrong type of people	25	52	42	58	63
The place has fights, violence, trouble	11	35	41	19	11
They have drugs there	3	9	11	10	29
Not suitable for his/her age group	25	4	12	4	5
Disapprove/fear of drinking	63	–	6	2	–
Disapprove of official activity of the place	–	3	6	4	10
The cost	5	–	1	8	10
Other reasons	5	19	12	6	22
Weighted base: Parents not wanting their child (ren) to visit certain local places	(189)	(182.5)	(141)	(48)	(41.5)

*Only places mentioned by more than 40 parents are given

89

CHAPTER 5

IDEAL CLUBS — WHAT YOUNG PEOPLE WANT FROM VOLUNTARY SOCIAL ORGANISATIONS

5.1 Ideal Activities – What young people would like to be able to do in clubs

Asking people what they *would* like calls on them to undertake a considerable feat of imagination, and not surprisingly, therefore, the relative popularity of the young people's ideal activities generally replicated the pattern for actual club activities.

For boys and girls, the attached and the unattached, sports (mainly indoor) and social activities were the most popular, followed by entertainment (usually listening to music). The traditional interest-centred activities (instructive and active cultural) were favoured rather less than they were pursued in existing clubs, but two new categories of interest centred activities emerged which are labelled 'domestic' and 'motorised'. The first covers such things as cookery lessons, dressmaking, beauty culture, infant care and practical interior design and was of course most often mentioned by girls. The second includes, for example, car maintenance, motorbike scrambles, go-kart racing and driving lessons and was mainly selected by boys. The impression gained by examining examples of these

Table R5.11

Table 5.1 Actual compared with ideal activities, by sex and attachment – percentage of those asked mentioning each main type of activity

| | Actual activities | | | Ideal Activities | | | | | | | | |
| | | | | Attached | | | Unattached | | | Total | | |
	M	F	T	M	F	T	M	F	T	M	F	T
Active sport+	75	59	68	83	77	80	78	73	75	82	75	78
Social	51	64	57	63	79	70	58	79	71	62	79	70
Entertainment	35	40	37	42	54	48	41	52	48	42	53	48
Instructive	27	28	27	14	24	19	10	19	15	13	22	17
Club organization	18	22	20	*	*	*	*	*	*	*	*	*
Active cultural	13	23	17	13	22	17	11	14	13	13	19	16
Domestic	*	*	*	1	13	6	1	14	9	1	13	7
Motorised sport	*	*	*	9	1	5	10	1	4	9	1	5

*Activity occurred insufficiently frequently to form separate category
+Mainly indoor sports

types of ideal activity is; that the girls almost invariably wanted to learn or be shown how to cook, sew or put on make up; but the boys rather rarely wanted (or said they wanted) instruction or demonstration.

About 10% of the young people said they would not want to go to a club or centre of any kind and were therefore not asked to say how they would like it to be.

A further complication in interpreting results arises from the form of the question. We asked people what they would like to do in a club or centre they would really enjoy going to and it seems highly probable that this suggests the undifferentiated type of club of the youth or social variety rather than a group of enthusiasts and amateurs of one kind or another, to which many young people actually belonged. This likelihood is reinforced by a comparison of ideal activities with actual activities in the four main types of club. Table 5.2 shows that the pattern of ideal activities most closely resembles the pattern of activities in existing youth clubs.

Table 5.2 **Ideal activities compared with actual activities in the four main types of club — percentage of those asked mentioning each type of activity**

| | Ideal activities | Actual activities in:- | | | |
		Youth clubs	Social clubs	Interest clubs	Sports clubs
Active sport	78	84	53	37	90
Social	70	68	90	37	48
Entertainment	48	47	36	52	23
Instructive	17	15	13	48	18
Organisation	*	14	13	23	19
Active cultural	16	11	8	46	6
Domestic	7	*	*	*	*
Motorised sport	5	*	*	*	*

*Activity occurred insufficiently frequently to form separate category

There is a difference, however, in that slightly less emphasis is placed on sport, and more on interest centred activities, whether of a traditional or novel (domestic and motorised) kind, in ideal than in actual youth clubs.

Figure 5.1 shows that the later school leavers opted more frequently for the traditional interest centred activities than did the early leavers, although (presumably because they were thinking in terms of undifferentiated clubs), they mentioned them less often than they did as actual activities. The early leavers, on the other hand, chose active cultural pursuits slightly more frequently than they pursued them in actual clubs, and were the

FIG. 5.1.

Actual and ideal club activities, by sex, school leaving age and attachment

Percentages

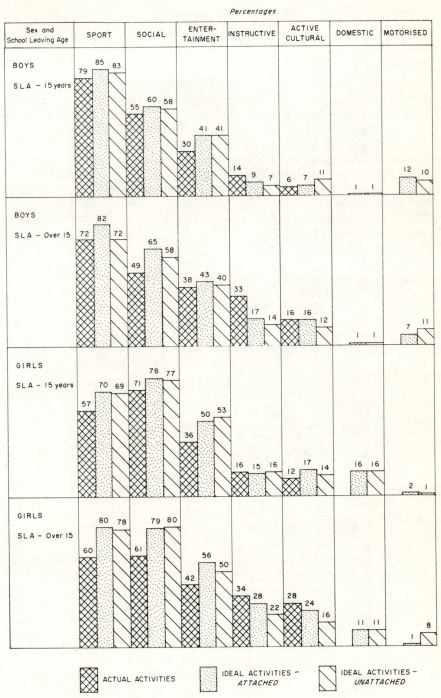

Sex and School Leaving Age	SPORT	SOCIAL	ENTER-TAINMENT	INSTRUCTIVE	ACTIVE CULTURAL	DOMESTIC	MOTORISED
BOYS SLA – 15 years	79 85 83	55 60 58	30 41 41	14 9 7	6 7 11	1 1	12 10
BOYS SLA – Over 15	72 82 72	49 65 58	38 43 40	33 17 14	16 16 12	1 1	7 11
GIRLS SLA – 15 years	57 70 69	71 78 77	36 50 53	16 15 16	12 17 14	16 16	2 1
GIRLS SLA – Over 15	60 80 78	61 79 80	42 56 50	34 28 22	28 24 16	11 11	1 8

ACTUAL ACTIVITIES   IDEAL ACTIVITIES – *ATTACHED*   IDEAL ACTIVITIES – *UNATTACHED*

FIG. 5.2.

Actual and ideal club activities, by school leaving age, age and attachment — Boys

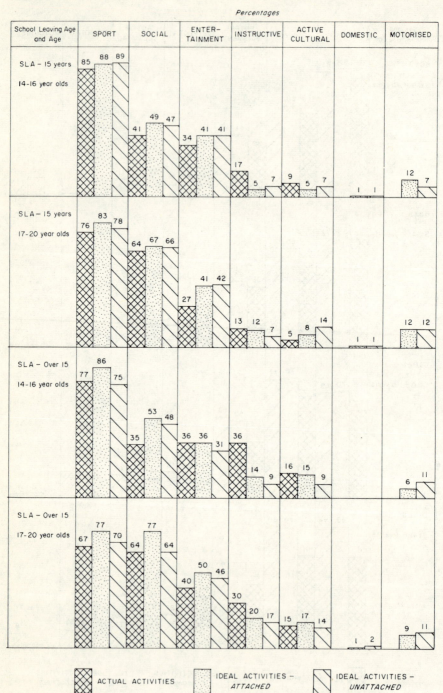

Percentages

School Leaving Age and Age	SPORT	SOCIAL	ENTER-TAINMENT	INSTRUCTIVE	ACTIVE CULTURAL	DOMESTIC	MOTORISED
SLA – 15 years 14-16 year olds	85 88 89	41 49 47	34 41 41	17 5 7	9 5 7	1 1	12 7
SLA – 15 years 17-20 year olds	76 83 78	64 67 66	27 41 42	13 12 7	5 8 14	1 1	12 12
SLA – Over 15 14-16 year olds	77 86 75	35 53 48	36 36 31	36 14 9	16 15 9		6 11
SLA – Over 15 17-20 year olds	67 77 70	64 77 64	40 50 46	30 20 17	15 17 14	1 2	9 11

ACTUAL ACTIVITIES   IDEAL ACTIVITIES – *ATTACHED*   IDEAL ACTIVITIES – *UNATTACHED*

FIG. 5.3.

Actual and idea club activities, by school leaving age, age and attachment — Girls

Percentages

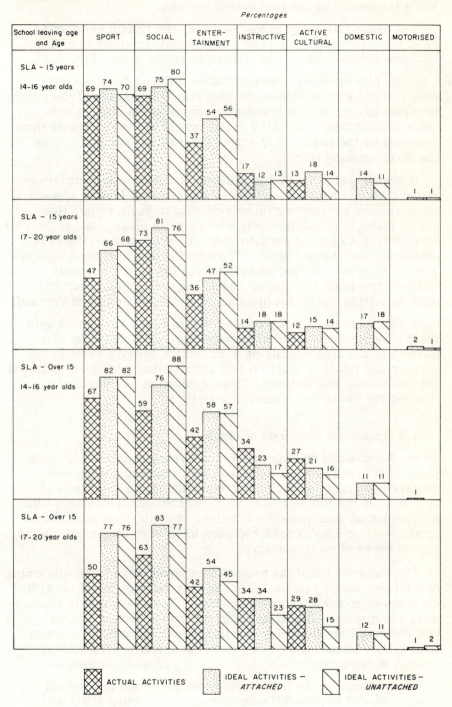

School leaving age and Age	SPORT	SOCIAL	ENTERTAINMENT	INSTRUCTIVE	ACTIVE CULTURAL	DOMESTIC	MOTORISED
SLA – 15 years 14-16 year olds	69 74 70	69 75 80	37 54 56	17 12 13	13 18 14	14 11	1 1
SLA – 15 years 17-20 year olds	47 66 68	73 81 76	36 47 52	14 18 18	12 15 14	17 18	2 1
SLA – Over 15 14-16 year olds	67 82 82	59 76 88	42 58 57	34 23 17	27 21 16	11 11	1
SLA – Over 15 17-20 year olds	50 77 76	63 83 77	42 54 45	34 34 23	29 28 15	12 11	1 2

▨ ACTUAL ACTIVITIES ░ IDEAL ACTIVITIES – *ATTACHED* ▧ IDEAL ACTIVITIES – *UNATTACHED*

95

most enthusiastic about the novel interest-centred activities. This last difference between school leaving groups is very small, but worth noting because most ideal activities were mentioned more frequently by the late school leavers.

The older girl early school leavers, the typical unattached, most often favoured more interest centred activities than the attached amongst them experienced in actual clubs (Fig. 5.3).

Table R5.12   Generally speaking, the unattached differed from the attached only in ways attributable to the different composition of the groups in terms of age, school leaving age and sex. In other words, the activities which appealed to the unattached were largely those favoured by the older early school leavers and particularly by the girls amongst them.

It seems therefore that in thinking of a desirable undifferentiated club, young people whatever their school leaving age opt for activities resembling those available in youth rather than social clubs, but, particularly as they grow older, tend to demand more interest centred pursuits than are currently available in places named 'Youth Clubs'. Considering both that the question was unprompted and that comparatively few of the attached followed interests in existing clubs, the proportions choosing such activities can be taken as an indication of minimum demand.

Table R5.13   A check revealed that parents were in broad agreement with their children about ideal club activities. That is to say that parents of children specifying a particular activity were on the whole more likely to mention that activity than parents of children not mentioning that activity. This agreement was particularly marked for the interest centred activities.

5.2 Important functions of clubs

From discussions and interviews with young people at the pilot stage of this enquiry, it appeared that certain functions were required of clubs, including the provision of desired kinds of activity. In the main enquiry we presented our informants with a short list of such possible functions of clubs, and asked them to say whether they considered each to be very important, fairly important or of no importance.

Table R5.14   The majority rated the provision of novel experiences (learning new things, making new friends and learning how to get on with all sorts of people) as very important. And, looked at in another way, the majority also attached great importance to interest centred activities (learning new things and carrying on existing interests). Least highly rated were opportunities for finding friends of the opposite sex, and escaping from older people.

It was shown in the last chapter that early and late school leavers tended to give different reasons for joining clubs and used them differently, but by contrast there was considerable

Table 5.3 Percentage of young people attaching varying degrees of importance to some possible functions of clubs

A club should be a place where you can:*	Very important			Fairly important			Not important		
	M	F	T	M	F	T	M	F	T
Learn new things/interests	64	71	67	30	26	28	5	3	4
Make new friends	60	70	65	36	28	32	4	2	3
Learn how to get on with all sorts of people	52	68	60	37	27	32	10	5	7
Carry on existing interests	61	57	59	33	38	35	6	5	5
Meet people who think like you	42	40	41	40	42	41	18	17	17
Meet old friends	41	36	38	48	53	50	11	11	11
Find opposite sex friends	36	27	31	42	46	44	21	27	27
Get help with problems	39	44	42	34	34	34	26	21	24
Escape from older people	31	29	30	32	35	33	36	36	36

*The exact wording of statements is given in Table R5.14

agreement between them about the relative importance of different club functions (Fig. 5.4). It seems therefore that the early leavers were hardly any less enthusiastic about provision for following interests than the later leavers, although in reply to the unprompted question about ideal activities they mentioned fewer specific interest centred activities.

Two possible functions of clubs which provided exceptions to the similarity between early and late school leavers were the provision of facilities for help with problems and escaping from older people (Fig. 5.4). Fifty per cent of the early school leavers thought it very important that a club should be a place where they could get help or advice about their problems, compared with 36% of the later leavers. The younger girl early leavers more often than any other group rated this function highly. Although we did not ask what kind of problems people had in mind, the answers of the few who earlier spontaneously mentioned this as something they would like to be available in a club, suggests that the advice sought would range at least from sex education and birth control advice to help with employment and school problems. The fact that the early leavers and the younger groups more often attached great importance to this function does not necessarily mean that they were the most beset by problems, but at least that they were the most inclined to regard clubs as appropriate places to provide help.

There were few considerable and consistent differences between the attached and the unattached which were not due to the different composition of the two groups. But the unattached early school leavers were slightly more eager for facilities to learn new things and find new interests, and all the unattached were more anxious than the attached to be able to carry on existing

Table R5.15

97

FIG. 5.4.

Percentage of young people rating different functions as very important, by sex, age and school leaving age

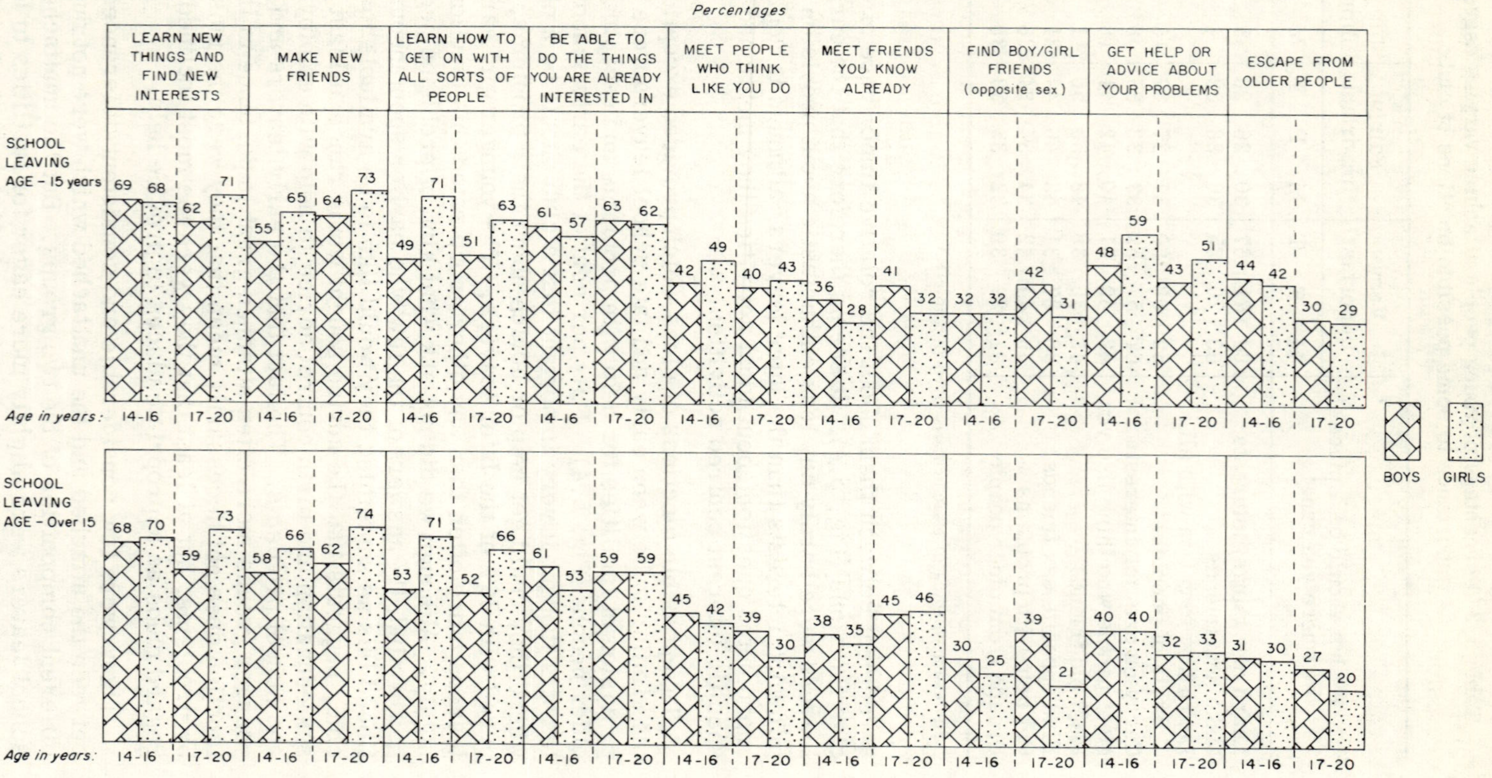

Percentages

GIRLS

BOYS

SCHOOL LEAVING AGE – 15 years

Function	14-16	17-20
LEARN NEW THINGS AND FIND NEW INTERESTS (Boys)	69	62
LEARN NEW THINGS AND FIND NEW INTERESTS (Girls)	68	71
MAKE NEW FRIENDS (Boys)	55	64
MAKE NEW FRIENDS (Girls)	65	73
LEARN HOW TO GET ON WITH ALL SORTS OF PEOPLE (Boys)	49	51
LEARN HOW TO GET ON WITH ALL SORTS OF PEOPLE (Girls)	71	63
BE ABLE TO DO THE THINGS YOU ARE ALREADY INTERESTED IN (Boys)	57	63
BE ABLE TO DO THE THINGS YOU ARE ALREADY INTERESTED IN (Girls)	61	62
MEET PEOPLE WHO THINK LIKE YOU DO (Boys)	42	43
MEET PEOPLE WHO THINK LIKE YOU DO (Girls)	49 / 40	43
MEET FRIENDS YOU KNOW ALREADY (Boys)	36	32
MEET FRIENDS YOU KNOW ALREADY (Girls)	28 / 41	32
FIND BOY/GIRL FRIENDS (opposite sex) (Boys)	32	42
FIND BOY/GIRL FRIENDS (opposite sex) (Girls)	32	31
GET HELP OR ADVICE ABOUT YOUR PROBLEMS (Boys)	48	43
GET HELP OR ADVICE ABOUT YOUR PROBLEMS (Girls)	59	51
ESCAPE FROM OLDER PEOPLE (Boys)	44	30
ESCAPE FROM OLDER PEOPLE (Girls)	42	29

SCHOOL LEAVING AGE – Over 15

Function	14-16	17-20
LEARN NEW THINGS AND FIND NEW INTERESTS (Boys)	68	59
LEARN NEW THINGS AND FIND NEW INTERESTS (Girls)	70	73
MAKE NEW FRIENDS (Boys)	58	62
MAKE NEW FRIENDS (Girls)	66	74
LEARN HOW TO GET ON WITH ALL SORTS OF PEOPLE (Boys)	53	52
LEARN HOW TO GET ON WITH ALL SORTS OF PEOPLE (Girls)	71	66
BE ABLE TO DO THE THINGS YOU ARE ALREADY INTERESTED IN (Boys)	53	59
BE ABLE TO DO THE THINGS YOU ARE ALREADY INTERESTED IN (Girls)	61	59
MEET PEOPLE WHO THINK LIKE YOU DO (Boys)	45	39
MEET PEOPLE WHO THINK LIKE YOU DO (Girls)	42	30
MEET FRIENDS YOU KNOW ALREADY (Boys)	38	45
MEET FRIENDS YOU KNOW ALREADY (Girls)	35 / 45	46
FIND BOY/GIRL FRIENDS (opposite sex) (Boys)	30	39
FIND BOY/GIRL FRIENDS (opposite sex) (Girls)	25	21
GET HELP OR ADVICE ABOUT YOUR PROBLEMS (Boys)	40	32
GET HELP OR ADVICE ABOUT YOUR PROBLEMS (Girls)	40	33
ESCAPE FROM OLDER PEOPLE (Boys)	31	27
ESCAPE FROM OLDER PEOPLE (Girls)	30	20

Age in years:

interests. The greatest difference, however, related to the provision of advice and help with problems, to which more of the unattached attributed great importance. The difference was most marked for the younger late school leavers amongst whom un-attachment was rare, and this suggests that their unattachment may have been related to their problems.

5.3 How often should clubs be open

The question which asked, 'How often would you like (the club or centre) to be open?' undoubtedly reinforced the implication Table R5.16 that we were concerned with undifferentiated rather than interest centred types of club, for which it would probably have been more appropriate to refer to the frequency of meetings.

The most popular opening frequencies were 7 nights a week or all the time, closely followed by 3 and 2 nights a week. Only 5% selected one night a week. This does not mean that the people who made these choices wanted to use a club so frequently, but only that they wanted it to be available on this number of occasions, since the question included the qualification '..even if you didn't go every time it was open'. In fact the indications from pilot work and the question on commercial provision (discussed in section 5.5), suggest that at least some young people disliked the feeling of obligation to attend a club every time it was open. Rather, the answers may be taken to imply either that the young person would like to be able to use a club up to the chosen number of occasions, or that he would like the choice of attending on any of the chosen number of occasions.

Maximum availability was most favoured by boys, the older age groups and the late school leavers, and conversely, a club open 2, 3 or 4 nights a week was most preferred by the 14-16 year olds whatever their school leaving age or sex. It may be that the younger group found it more difficult to imagine a club which was open without their feeling they were expected to attend, or they may genuinely have preferred a more restricted choice. The section on views of Youth Clubs in the preceding chapter supports the first explanation.

Table 5.4 Number of occasions on which ideal club should be open – percentages of young people making each choice, by sex, age and school leaving age

School leaving age	Age	7 nights/ all the time			6 nights			5 nights			4 nights			3 nights			2 nights			1 night		
		M	F	T	M	F	T	M	F	T	M	F	T	M	F	T	M	F	T	M	F	T
15	14-16	17	14	16	8	8	8	6	12	9	14	13	13	25	26	25	24	21	22	3	5	4
	17-20	32	21	27	7	5	6	12	9	11	12	18	15	20	26	23	12	17	15	2	2	2
	T	26	19	22	8	6	7	10	10	10	12	16	14	22	26	24	17	18	18	2	3	3
16+	14-16	19	15	16	8	7	7	8	9	8	8	14	11	25	23	24	22	22	22	6	8	7
	17-20	41	31	37	7	5	6	9	7	8	9	12	10	12	21	16	13	13	13	3	7	5
	T	30	22	26	8	6	7	8	8	8	8	13	11	18	22	20	18	18	18	5	8	6
	Total	29	21	25	8	6	7	9	9	9	10	14	12	20	24	22	17	18	18	4	6	5

5.4 Ideal Age Range

It was shown in the last chapter that the age range of an existing club is related to its type and that it is therefore important to consider the two aspects together. As indicated, it is almost certain that in the case of ideal clubs, the questions asked had suggested undifferentiated clubs to the young people and their preferences should ultimately be related to clubs of this kind. But in the first place it is useful to compare ideal with actual ranges for all clubs to which the young people were attached.

Table R5.17
The 14 and 15 year olds appeared to prefer higher upper age limits than those they quoted for the clubs they actually attended. 14 to 17 or 18, was the most popular single range for the two years together, although just over 30% of the 15 year olds wanted a lower limit of 15 years. This illustrates the considerable incompatibility of the choices of the younger and older members of the whole 14 to 20 year group. Thus, although most of the 14 and 15 year olds wanted an upper limit of from 17 to 20, very few of the 17 to 20 year olds favoured these ranges.

The selections of the 16 and 17 year olds were rather widely scattered, although many of them were evidently happy to mix with younger children. The 18 to 20 year olds on the other hand most commonly chose a range of from 17 or 18 to between 21 and 25. This contrasts with their clustering in existing clubs with age ranges of from 17 or 18 up to 30 and above.

Table 5.5 Actual compared with Ideal Age Ranges, by age – percentage attending or preferring clubs with each range

Age Range	14		15		16		17		18		19		20	
	Actual	Ideal	Actual	Ideal	Actual	Ideal	Actual	Ideal	Actual	Ideal	Actual	Ideal	Actual	Ideal
14-16	42	28	17	5	5	1	1	-	1	-	-	-	-	-
-18	21	41	26	26	16	9	11	2	2	-	-	-	-	-
-20	11	15	14	21	11	13	14	7	5	3	5	2	1	1
-over 20	12	8	11	9	13	11	11	8	10	9	10	9	6	8
15-20			12	26	14	26	12	14	4	4	1	2	-	1
-over 20			4	5	7	12	10	11	7	10	8	9	10	8
16-20					11	12	9	18	3	7	2	2	-	1
-over 20					8	10	10	18	16	21	12	17	14	14
17, 18-20					2		3	6	3	5	1	2	1	1
-25					1		3	7	8	24	16	28	18	28
-30					2		2	1	8	9	7	10	8	16
-over 30					6		6	2	19	2	18	7	20	8

Comparison between ideal age ranges and those given for the four main types of club shows that up to and including the age of 17 years there is no close resemblance between preferred and actual ranges. But it is clear that on the whole the broad ranges offered by youth clubs and social clubs were not the most popular, although it was evidently this sort of club which was being considered. From 18 years upwards the distribution of preferences is more like that given for existing interest

Table 5.6 Ideal compared with Actual Age Ranges in three main types of club, by age – percentage attending or preferring clubs with each age range

Age Range	14				15				16				17				18				19				20			
	I	AI	AYC	AS	I	AI	AYC	AS	I	AI	AYC	AS	I	AI	AYC	AS	I	AI	AYC	AS	I	AI	AYC	AS	I	AI	AYC	AS
14–16	28	55	17	(46)	5	21	8	(11)	1	8	2	(2)	–	–	1	–	–	–	–	–	–	–	(2)	–	–	–	–	–
–18	41	31	26	(12)	26	51	26	(15)	9	18	22	(5)	2	23	13	5	–	4	(9)	1	–	–	(2)	–	–	–	(5)	–
–20	15	4	24	(8)	21	2	22	(30)	13	3	27	(6)	7	13	33	3	3	7	(20)	1	2	2	(24)	2	1	1	(15)	1
– over 20	8	4	22	(19)	9	6	17	(7)	11	7	22	(9)	8	8	16	9	9	4	(36)	4	9	–	(37)	4	8	1	(37)	1
15–20					26	9	12	(11)	26	27	11	(5)	14	14	21	3	4	5	(9)	4	2	–	(2)	1	1	–	(5)	–
– over 20					5	4	5	(4)	12	4	6	(16)	11	5	9	12	10	3	(9)	9	9	2	(10)	10	8	7	(10)	16
16–20									12	17	2	(9)	18	15	5	6	7	–	(7)	2	2	–	(4)	–	1	–	–	–
– over 20									10	8	1	(30)	18	6	–	23	21	20	(7)	12	17	12	(6)	23	14	11	(10)	20
17, 18–20													6	3	–	3	5	4	–	2	2	–	(4)	–	1	2	(5)	–
–25													7	2	–	6	24	18	–	9	28	31	(2)	10	28	40	(5)	7
–30													1	3	–	2	9	14	–	9	10	29	–	2	16	11	–	8
– over 30													2	3	–	20	2	17	–	30	7	12	–	32	8	18	–	32

(1) I = Ideal Age Range; AI = actual age range in interest centred clubs; AYC = actual age range in Youth Clubs; AS = actual age range in social clubs
(2) Figures in brackets are based on less than 50 cases
(3) Sports clubs omitted for lack of space. From 14 to 16 they resemble interest – centred clubs and from 18 to 20 they resemble social clubs in Age Range.

101

centred clubs than for any other type. Specifically people opted for more restricted ranges than those offered by undifferentiated clubs and in particular the recognised Youth Service age range of 14 to 20 and the typical social club range of from 17 or 18 to over 30 were rarely chosen. The rejection of the latter range may of course be incompatible with the preferences of older people, just as the rejection of lower limits of below 17 or 18 years is in conflict with the choices of younger children. But the rather wide dispersal of choices suggests that no single club age range will suit every one it covers.

Differences between early and late school leavers, the attached and unattached were negligible and there was no indication that the early leavers and the unattached favoured less restricted age ranges than the other groups.

5.5 Commercial versus non-commercial provision

It seemed possible that commercially provided leisure facilities might correspond more closely to what was wanted, at least by the unattached, than existing non-commercial organisations. Accordingly we asked the young people which kind of provision they would expect to enjoy more and why. Because the question immediately followed those about characteristics of an ideal club, most probably answered in terms of an undifferentiated club, it seems likely that comparisons were made with this type rather than with the club the young person actually went to if this was of a different kind. Specifically the comparison was almost certainly made between clubs of the youth type on the one hand and commercial provision such as 'coffee bars, night clubs, dance halls and so on', as exemplified in the question on commercial provision.

Table
R5.18   Thirty-three per cent of the young people said they would expect to enjoy a commercially run place more, 43% less and 20% thought they would enjoy both to the same extent.

Preferences varied with school leaving age, age and sex, although in no group did a majority opt unequivocally for commercial provision. The later leavers and the younger children were least enthusiastic about commercial places, but there were sex differences within each group. Thus, amongst 14-16 year olds the girls were most inclined to prefer commercial places, but within the older group there was little difference between the sexes.

Table
R5.19   The differences between the attached and unattached were in part a reflection of their different characteristics, but within each sub group the unattached were most likely to favour commercial provision. Forty-seven per cent of the older early school leavers who were unattached thought they would enjoy commercial facilities most, compared with 40% of the attached in the same group.

Table 5.7 Preference for commercial rather than non-commercial provision, by sex, age and school leaving age – percentages saying they would expect to enjoy commercially run places more, less or the same

School leaving age	Age	Males			Females			Total		
		More	Less	Same	More	Less	Same	More	Less	Same
15	14-16	27	53	14	37	45	15	32	49	14
	17-20	44	31	20	42	34	21	43	33	21
	T	38	40	18	40	38	19	39	39	18
16 or over	14-16	22	61	15	26	50	21	24	55	18
	17-20	35	40	22	33	36	27	34	38	24
	T	29	50	18	29	43	24	29	47	21

Table 5.8 Preference for commercial rather than non-commercial provision by age, school leaving age and attachment – percentages saying they would expect to enjoy commercially run places more, less or the same

School leaving age	Age	Attached			Unattached		
		More	Less	Same	More	Less	Same
15	14-16	29	53	15	36	45	14
	17-20	40	37	21	47	29	21
	T	35	43	18	43	35	18
16 or over	14-16	22	58	17	30	47	20
	17-20	32	42	23	39	29	29
	T	27	50	20	35	37	25
	Total	30	48	19	40	35	21

Either because of the crudity of the question, or because the young people had never considered it before, the reasons they gave for their preferences were not illuminating. The majority of those preferring commercial places gave answers which in effect restated their premises. Over 50% said they provided better facilities, entertainment or equipment, for example a 16 year old school boy said; 'It's more professional, you can get your money's worth. If you go to a Youth Club it's very amateur – the groups are amateur. If you go to a commercially run place you get good groups and you can enjoy yourself'. And nearly 30% said such places must necessarily be

Table R5.20

103

better because they were commercial; 'If people know they can get money for doing something, they always do a better job' or; '...... it stands to reason, the person running it will try to give the best value to keep the customers happy'. More interestingly, 17% thought commercial places more sociable and 10% said they attracted a greater variety of people. 16% thought they would feel freer, less restricted by rules and obligations; 'You'd get more freedom. In Youth Clubs you've always got somebody there watching you' said one, and another commented; 'You don't have anyone to push you around'. Only 6% mentioned the advantage of being able to drink, (Table 5.9).

Table 5.9 **Some reasons for preferring commercial provision – percentage of those preferring commercial provision giving each reason by age and school leaving age**

Some reasons for preferring commercial provision	School leaving age = 15			School leaving age = 16 or over		
	14-16	17-20	Total	14-16	17-20	Total
Better facilities etc.	42	49	47	54	60	58
Run for profit	14	26	22	31	40	36
Meet more/new people	22	14	17	23	14	18
Meet greater variety of people	11	9	9	13	9	10
More freedom	11	19	16	13	17	15
Have a better time	9	8	8	14	12	13
Not so rough	6	3	4	4	6	5
No responsibility	1	3	2	2	3	3

Because of the dubious validity of the results it is hazardous to emphasize differences between subgroups, but it appears that the younger group, particularly the early leavers were most likely to mention the greater friendliness and variety of people, and that the older people, especially the early leavers were most attracted by the greater freedom of commercial places.

Table R5.21 By contrast the reasons for liking commercial places less were rather more often specific, although 34% said they were less good and 16% disliked their being commercial. Said one apprentice electrician; 'At a well run Youth Club, you know they've got your interest at heart, at a commercial organisation all they're interested in is your money and getting it out of you', and a young bank clerk explained; 'They're out to make a profit – whereas if the members are involved, they're working to keep it going for their own good'. 36% considered commercial places less sociable and 19% that they offered less freedom. Lack of freedom covered not only feelings of being over-organised but also of lack of choice of activity, and similar to this was the idea that in commercial places there was no opportunity for

members to arrange and organise what happened themselves.
For example, a girl of 20 who had left school at 15 commented;
'In a non-commercial place there are not so many restrictions –
if it's run by members of the club there are not so many rules –
we have the same points of view and it's run by ourselves and we
make up the rules we want, because the club would be run by us'
and a 20 year old technician said; '...... in your own club.. you
can do what you like and help in the running of the place and the
decor – whereas in a commercially run place you couldn't'. As
might be expected it was the older later school leavers who most
often mentioned this disadvantage of commercial organisations.

It is antithetical to the reported advantage which commercial
organisations had of relieving the member of responsibility for
what went on, but which was mentioned by only 3% of those preferring commercial provision, (Table 5.10).

Table 5.10 Some reasons for not preferring commercial provision –
percentage of those not preferring commercial provision
giving each reason, by age and school leaving age

Some reasons for *not* preferring commercial provision	School leaving age = 15			School leaving age = 16 or over		
	14-16	17-20	Total	14-16	17-20	Total
Not so easy to meet people	29	34	32	38	40	39
Not such good facilities	36	29	32	35	36	35
Less freedom	15	19	17	18	22	20
Only out for profit	11	16	13	17	20	18
Too expensive	14	11	12	15	14	15
Do not cater for own age group	17	7	12	12	7	10
No opportunity for responsibility	4	8	6	8	18	12
Too rough	8	8	8	10	4	8

It appears that some young people felt that commercial
organisations provided something they wanted which non-
commercial clubs did not but others believed the same facilities
were more readily available in non-commercial clubs. To some
extent this was, no doubt, due to the different experiences of
different individuals of each kind of provision, for example
some found more friendliness in commercial places and others
in non-commercial clubs. However an examination of some of
the answers falling into similarly labelled categories of reasons
for being for and against commercial provision suggests that in
each case the young people were referring to something rather
different. Thus those who preferred commercial places because
they offered better facilities and so on, were often speaking of
the greater luxury and professionally smooth organisation of the
place, but those who preferred non-commercial places for the

same reason were normally talking about the greater variety of facilities offered. Similarly, the feeling of greater freedom in commercial places was the negative freedom of absence of obligation and surveillance but the freedom in non-commercial places was felt to be a freedom to choose and influence what was available. Nevertheless some young people felt they could behave more naturally in commercial and others in non-commercial environments.

To sum up, apart from real disagreements about what each type of place had to offer, the impression is that commercial places were preferred for their greater lavishness and unrestrictive and undemanding provision, but that they were rejected for the lack of influence the individual had on what he could do there or on the kind of place it was.

5.6 Summary

Because of the imaginative demands made by the questions about ideal clubs the results presented in this chapter should be regarded as suggestive rather than predictive of what would appeal to young people if it were available. Bearing this in mind, it seems that among undifferentiated clubs young people favour places providing similar activities to Youth rather than social clubs, but that they want more interest centred activities and narrower age ranges than either type of club currently offers, in general. The evidence is not conclusive, but it seems probable that the early school leavers and the unattached did not differ from others in their general requirements of clubs, but that they tended to prefer different kinds of interest centred activities. On the other hand as the greater supporters of commercial provision they appeared to favour more freedom from surveillance and responsibility than they believed was possible in non-commercial clubs.

It is worth pointing out, however, that in a study of this kind, it is not possible to determine what efforts have already been made to engage the children prone to unattachment in interest centred activities. It may well be that in many cases such attempts have been made in Youth Clubs, (the groups most commonly patronised by the younger early leavers), and that, in spite of what these young people say they want, when presented with opportunities, for example, to sing, discuss, or learn dress-making or car maintenance they often do not respond. If this is so, as has been suggested to us, two kinds of explanation are possible: either the young people were mistaken in thinking they wanted more of such activities, or the way in which the opportunities have been presented have for some reason been unattractive to them. If efforts are to be made to prolong attachment, the second explanation offers a more constructive implication; namely that experiments with different methods of harnessing demand to provision are required. Here almost the only clue offered by the present data is the evidence for the role played by friends in first visiting a club. It seems possible that if young people join clubs as members of a group they will also be inclined to take up activities in the same way. In which case the agreement of friendship groups that they would like to try something new would often be more useful than the agreement of separate individuals; a suggestion supported by evidence quoted by Katz and Lazarsfeld (1960, pp 73-81). There was also a hint that some of the attempts to promote interest centred activities have been too rigid. For example one girl shop assistant who had left a Youth Centre said; 'It was a bore, you had to study – you have to do that at school, I wasn't bothered to study..... well there were classes in maths, English and typing – just like studying – I didn't want that!'. Similarly, a boy who was a wireman explained that he had left a Youth Club because; 'the idea of doing those sort of things dropped – I just don't like doing that sort of thing any more – up there they've got classes for different things like archery and pottery..... If you aren't going to the classes, they don't like you being there and doing nothing.

It would seem useful then, to accept the young peoples preferences at their face value and to try out different ways of involving them in the activities they say they want. But it is important to remember that different age, sex and educational groups have rather different preferences. Moreover, on the whole, the older people were not happy about being in the same groups as the younger children, although, equally, they preferred not to be in all-age groups.

Table R5.11 Ideal club activities, by age of leaving school, age and sex

Q.20(a)

Ideal club activities	Age of leaving school																	
	15									Over 15								
	14-16 years			17-20 years			Total			14-16 years			17-20 years			Total		
	Boys	Girls	Total	Boys	Girls	Total	Boys	Girls	Total	Boys	Girls	Total	Boys	Girls	Total	Boys	Girls	Total
	%	%	%	%	%	%	%	%	%	%	%	%	%	%	%	%	%	%
Active sports	88	72	80	81	67	74	84	69	76	84	82	83	76	76	76	80	79	79
Social	48	78	64	67	78	72	59	78	69	52	78	66	74	81	77	63	79	71
Entertainment	41	55	48	41	50	46	41	52	47	36	58	47	49	51	50	43	54	48
Instructive	6	12	9	10	18	14	9	16	12	13	22	18	19	31	25	16	26	21
Active cultural	6	16	11	11	14	13	9	15	12	14	20	17	16	24	20	15	22	18
Domestic	1	13	7	1	18	10	1	16	9	-	11	6	1	12	6	1	11	6
Motorised sport	10	1	5	12	2	7	11	1	6	7	1	4	9	1	6	8	1	5
Craft	8	5	6	5	4	5	6	4	5	7	4	6	5	5	5	6	5	5
Other activities	51	54	52	44	50	47	47	52	49	54	65	60	51	53	52	53	59	56
Total percentages	259	306	282	272	301	288	267	303	285	267	341	307	300	334	317	285	336	309
Weighted base: Young people not averse to belonging to a club	(273.5)	(293.5)	(567)	(401)	(451)	(852)	(674.5)	(744.5)	(1419)	(513.5)	(553.5)	(1067)	(529)	(468.5)	(997.5)	(1042.5)	(1022)	(2064.5)

108

Table R5.12 Ideal club activities, by age of leaving school, age, sex and attachment

THOSE WHO WERE NOT AVERSE TO BELONGING TO A CLUB ONLY

Q.20(a)

Ideal club activities	Age of leaving school																	
	15									Over 15								
	14-16 years			17-20 years			Total			14-16 years			17-20 years			Total		
	Boys	Girls	Total	Boys	Girls	Total	Boys	Girls	Total	Boys	Girls	Total	Boys	Girls	Total	Boys	Girls	Total
	%	%	%	%	%	%	%	%	%	%	%	%	%	%	%	%	%	%
PRESENT ATTACHMENT																		
Active sport	88	74	81	83	66	77	85	70	79	86	82	84	77	77	77	82	80	81
Social	49	75	61	67	81	73	60	78	68	53	76	64	77	83	80	65	79	71
Entertainment	41	54	47	41	47	43	41	50	45	36	58	47	50	54	52	43	56	49
Instructive	5	12	8	12	18	14	9	15	12	14	23	18	20	34	26	17	28	22
Active cultural	5	18	11	8	15	11	7	17	11	15	21	18	17	28	22	16	24	20
Domestic	1	14	7	1	17	8	1	16	8	-	11	5	9	12	6	1	11	6
Motorised sport	12	1	7	12	2	8	12	2	8	6	11	4	9	6	5	7	11	4
Crafts	7	5	6	4	6	5	5	5	5	7	5	6	4	6	5	6	5	5
Other activities	48	58	53	48	46	48	48	52	50	59	66	62	54	54	54	56	61	58
Total percentages	256	311	281	376	298	287	268	305	286	276	343	308	309	349	327	293	345	316
Weighted base: All those attached to a club	(168)	(151.5)	(319.5)	(259)	(175)	(434)	(427)	(326.5)	(753.5)	(439.5)	(412.5)	(852)	(414)	(311)	(725)	(853.5)	(723.5)	(1577)
NO PRESENT ATTACHMENT																		
Active sport	89	70	77	78	68	71	83	69	74	75	82	80	70	76	73	72	78	76
Social	47	80	66	66	76	72	58	77	70	48	88	72	64	77	72	58	80	72
Entertainment	41	56	50	42	52	49	41	53	49	31	57	48	46	45	45	40	50	47
Instructive	7	13	10	7	18	14	7	16	13	9	17	14	17	23	22	14	22	19
Active cultural	1	14	11	14	14	14	11	14	13	9	16	14	14	15	14	12	16	14
Domestic	1	11	7	1	18	12	1	16	10	-	11	7	2	11	7	1	11	7
Motorised sport	7	1	3	12	1	5	10	1	4	11	-	4	11	2	6	11	8	5
Crafts	9	5	7	7	3	5	8	4	6	11	3	5	5	5	5	7	4	5
Other activities	57	49	52	36	52	47	46	51	49	30	60	50	41	50	46	36	55	48
Total percentages	265	299	283	263	302	289	265	301	288	222	334	294	270	304	290	251	324	293
Weighted base: Those with no present attachment	(105.5)	(142)	(247.5)	(141)	(276)	(417)	(246.5)	(418)	(664.5)	(74)	(141)	(215)	(115)	(157.5)	(272.5)	(189)	(298.5)	(487.5)

109

Table R5.13 Parent's ideal club activities, by young person's ideal club activities

Parent Q.6(a) Parent's ideal club activities	Q.20(a) Young person's ideal club activities									
	Sport	Social	Entertainment	Cultural	Instructive	Domestic	Crafts	Outings	T.V.	Other
	%	%	%	%	%	%	%	%	%	%
Sport	77	74	75	77	71	65	75	74	72	77
Social	55	57	58	56	54	54	56	55	55	58
Entertainment	32	33	36	34	34	32	30	29	37	34
Cultural	28	28	30	43	35	30	35	31	26	31
Instructive	23	24	26	26	29	21	24	27	25	27
Domestic	18	19	20	21	20	41	20	21	19	20
Crafts	15	14	15	18	15	15	28	16	14	16
Outings	3	3	3	4	3	3	3	6	4	3
T.V.	2	2	3	2	2	3	2	4	5	3
Other activities	43	44	48	47	46	42	44	47	43	48
Total percentages	296	298	314	328	309	306	317	310	300	317
Weighted base: Young people not averse to belonging to a club	(2768)	(2451)	(1665)	(554.5)	(608)	(249.5)	(178.5)	(200.5)	(220)	(1702)

Table R5.14 Important club functions, by age of leaving school, age and sex

Club functions	Importance	Age of leaving school																	
		15									Over 15								
		14-16 years			17-20 years			Total			14-16 years			17-20 years			Total		
		Boys	Girls	Total	Boys	Girls	Total	Boys	Girls	Total	Boys	Girls	Total	Boys	Girls	Total	Boys	Girls	Total
		%	%	%	%	%	%	%	%	%	%	%	%	%	%	%	%	%	%
1. To make new friends	Very	55	65	61	64	73	68	60	70	65	58	66	63	62	74	68	60	70	65
	Fairly	40	32	36	34	26	30	37	28	34	38	32	34	34	24	29	36	28	32
	Not	4	2	3	2	1	2	3	2	2	4	2	3	4	1	3	4	2	3
2. Meet friends you know already	Very	36	28	32	41	32	36	39	30	35	38	35	36	45	46	46	42	40	41
	Fairly	50	50	50	46	56	51	47	54	51	50	56	53	46	47	46	48	52	50
	Not	13	22	18	13	12	12	13	16	14	11	9	10	9	7	8	10	8	9
3. Find boy/girl friends (opp. sex)	Very	32	32	32	42	31	36	38	32	35	30	25	27	39	21	30	34	23	29
	Fairly	46	45	46	37	34	35	41	38	40	48	54	51	38	48	43	43	51	47
	Not	20	22	21	21	34	28	20	29	25	22	21	22	22	30	26	22	25	24
4. Learn new things and find new interests	Very	69	68	69	62	71	67	65	70	68	68	70	69	59	73	66	64	71	67
	Fairly	25	27	26	33	26	29	30	26	28	27	27	27	34	24	29	30	26	28
	Not	5	4	5	4	3	4	5	4	4	5	3	4	7	3	5	6	3	4
5. Be able to do things you are already interested in	Very	61	57	59	63	62	62	62	59	61	61	53	57	59	59	58	60	56	58
	Fairly	32	35	34	30	35	33	31	35	33	34	42	38	34	37	36	34	40	37
	Not	6	8	7	7	4	5	6	5	6	5	4	5	6	4	5	6	4	5
6. Escape from older people	Very	44	42	43	30	29	29	36	34	35	31	30	29	27	20	24	29	25	27
	Fairly	30	33	31	30	32	31	30	32	31	41	39	40	27	33	30	34	36	35
	Not	25	25	25	40	38	39	34	33	33	28	30	29	46	46	46	37	37	37
7. Meet people who think like you do	Very	42	49	45	40	43	41	41	45	43	45	42	44	39	30	35	42	37	40
	Fairly	41	40	41	41	43	42	41	42	42	39	40	39	40	45	42	39	42	41
	Not	16	11	13	18	14	16	17	13	15	15	18	17	21	24	22	18	21	19
8. Get help or advice about your problems	Very	48	59	53	43	51	47	45	54	50	40	40	40	32	33	32	36	37	36
	Fairly	29	29	29	31	27	29	30	28	29	39	38	39	34	39	36	36	39	38
	Not	22	12	17	26	21	24	25	18	21	21	22	21	34	27	31	27	24	26
9. Learn how to get on with all sorts of people	Very	49	71	60	51	63	58	50	66	59	53	71	62	52	66	59	53	68	60
	Fairly	43	26	34	37	29	32	39	28	33	39	26	32	34	28	31	36	27	32
	Not	8	3	5	12	8	10	10	6	8	7	3	5	13	5	9	10	4	7
Weighted base: Young people not averse to belonging to a club		(273.5)	(293.5)	(567)	(401)	(451)	(852)	(674.5)	(744.5)	(1419)	(513.5)	(553.5)	(1067)	(529)	(468.5)	(997.5)	(1042.5)	(1022)	(2064.5)

Note.—'Don't know' and 'no answer' are omitted from the table so the numbers may not always add to 100%

Q. 21

Table R5.15 Important club functions, by age of leaving school, age, sex and attachment

Club functions	Importance	Age of leaving school																	
		15									Over 15								
		14-16 years			17-20 years			Total			14-16 years			17-20 years			Total		
		Boys	Girls	Total	Boys	Girls	Total	Boys	Girls	Total	Boys	Girls	Total	Boys	Girls	Total	Boys	Girls	Total
		%	%	%	%	%	%	%	%	%	%	%	%	%	%	%	%	%	%
1. To make new friends	ATTACHED Very	54	65	60	66	75	70	61	71	65	59	64	62	63	76	69	61	69	65
	Fairly	41	33	37	32	23	29	36	28	32	37	33	35	33	22	28	35	29	32
	Not	4	2	3	2	1	2	3	2	2	4	2	3	4	1	3	4	2	3
	NOT ATTACHED Very	57	66	62	58	71	67	58	69	65	52	72	65	59	71	66	56	72	66
	Fairly	38	31	34	39	28	31	38	29	32	41	27	32	36	28	31	38	27	31
	Not	5	3	4	3	1	2	4	2	3	7	1	3	5	1	3	6	1	3
2. Meet friends you know already	ATTACHED Very	36	29	33	42	30	37	40	30	36	39	34	36	45	46	45	42	39	40
	Fairly	49	50	49	45	57	50	47	54	50	50	57	53	46	49	47	48	54	50
	Not	13	21	17	12	13	13	13	17	14	11	9	10	9	5	8	10	7	9
	NOT ATTACHED Very	36	26	30	39	34	36	38	31	34	36	37	36	45	47	46	42	42	42
	Fairly	51	51	51	47	55	52	49	54	52	53	53	53	45	44	44	48	48	48
	Not	12	23	18	14	11	12	14	15	15	11	10	10	10	10	10	10	10	10
3. Find boy/girl friends (opp. sex)	ATTACHED Very	30	33	32	42	27	36	38	30	34	30	24	27	38	20	30	34	22	28
	Fairly	49	51	50	37	37	37	42	44	42	50	54	52	40	50	44	45	52	49
	Not	17	16	16	21	34	26	19	25	22	20	22	21	21	30	25	20	25	22
	NOT ATTACHED Very	34	32	33	43	33	36	39	33	35	30	27	28	40	24	31	36	26	30
	Fairly	41	39	40	36	32	34	38	35	36	36	53	47	33	43	39	34	48	43
	Not	25	28	27	20	34	29	22	32	28	33	20	25	27	31	30	30	26	27
4. Learn new things and find new interests	ATTACHED Very	68	66	67	60	70	64	63	68	65	68	69	68	61	74	67	64	71	68
	Fairly	27	27	27	36	28	33	32	27	30	27	28	27	32	23	28	29	26	28
	Not	4	7	5	4	2	4	4	4	4	5	3	4	8	2	5	6	2	4
	NOT ATTACHED Very	71	71	71	68	72	70	69	71	70	68	72	70	54	70	64	60	71	67
	Fairly	23	27	25	27	25	26	25	26	26	26	24	25	40	26	32	35	25	29
	Not	7	2	4	5	3	4	6	3	4	7	4	5	4	4	4	5	4	4

continued

112

Table R5.15 (continued)

Q. 21

Club functions	Importance	Age of leaving school																	
		15									Over 15								
		14-16 years			17-20 years			Total			14-16 years			17-20 years			Total		
		Boys	Girls	Total	Boys	Girls	Total	Boys	Girls	Total	Boys	Girls	Total	Boys	Girls	Total	Boys	Girls	Total
		%	%	%	%	%	%	%	%	%	%	%	%	%	%	%	%	%
5. Be able to do the things you are already interested in	ATTACHED																		
	Very	60	55	58	62	61	61	61	58	60	60	53	57	57	58	57	59	55	57
	Fairly	33	38	36	29	34	31	31	36	33	35	43	39	35	38	36	35	41	38
	Not	5	7	6	9	5	7	8	6	7	5	4	5	7	3	6	6	4	5
	NOT ATTACHED																		
	Very	63	59	61	65	61	62	64	60	62	65	55	58	64	61	62	64	58	60
	Fairly	30	32	31	32	35	34	31	34	33	28	41	36	32	34	33	31	37	35
	Not	7	9	8	3	3	3	4	5	5	7	4	5	4	6	5	5	5	5
6. Escape from older people	ATTACHED																		
	Very	45	43	44	28	28	28	34	35	35	31	30	30	24	21	23	28	26	27
	Fairly	32	33	32	29	31	30	30	32	31	40	40	40	28	32	30	34	37	35
	Not	23	23	23	42	40	41	35	32	34	29	30	29	47	46	47	38	37	37
	NOT ATTACHED																		
	Very	44	42	42	33	30	31	38	34	35	28	30	29	36	20	27	33	25	28
	Fairly	27	32	30	31	32	32	29	32	31	49	38	42	24	33	29	34	36	35
	Not	28	26	27	35	38	37	32	34	33	23	31	28	40	47	44	33	39	37
7. Meet people who think like you do	ATTACHED																		
	Very	39	52	45	39	38	39	39	45	42	45	41	43	38	29	34	42	36	39
	Fairly	44	37	41	41	47	44	42	42	42	40	39	39	41	47	43	40	42	41
	Not	16	11	14	19	15	17	18	13	16	15	20	17	20	24	22	18	22	19
	NOT ATTACHED																		
	Very	46	45	46	42	46	44	44	45	45	49	45	46	43	33	37	45	39	41
	Fairly	36	44	41	42	41	41	39	42	41	34	42	39	35	42	39	35	42	39
	Not	17	10	13	17	13	14	17	12	14	16	13	14	22	25	24	19	19	19
8. Get help or advice about your problems	ATTACHED																		
	Very	45	60	52	44	47	45	44	53	48	38	37	38	31	33	32	35	35	35
	Fairly	30	30	30	30	29	30	30	29	30	40	40	40	34	39	36	37	40	38
	Not	23	10	17	26	23	25	25	17	22	21	22	22	34	28	32	27	25	26
	NOT ATTACHED																		
	Very	52	57	55	41	54	50	46	55	52	50	48	49	34	34	34	40	41	40
	Fairly	26	29	28	32	26	28	30	27	28	30	32	31	35	40	38	33	36	35
	Not	21	14	17	27	20	22	25	18	20	20	20	20	31	26	28	27	23	24

continued

113

Table R5,15 (continued)

Q. 21

Club functions	Importance	Age of leaving school																	
		15									Over 15								
		14-16 years			17-20 years			Total			14-16 years			17-20 years			Total		
		Boys	Girls	Total	Boys	Girls	Total	Boys	Girls	Total	Boys	Girls	Total	Boys	Girls	Total	Boys	Girls	Total
		%	%	%	%	%	%	%	%	%	%	%	%	%	%	%	%	%	%
9. Learn how to get on with all sorts of people	ATTACHED Very	48	70	58	52	63	57	51	66	57	53	70	62	52	69	60	53	70	61
	Fairly	42	26	35	37	29	34	39	28	34	39	26	33	34	26	31	36	26	32
	Not	9	3	6	10	8	9	10	6	8	7	3	5	13	4	9	10	4	7
	NOT ATTACHED Very	51	72	63	49	64	59	50	67	60	51	71	64	51	59	56	51	65	60
	Fairly	43	25	32	36	29	31	39	27	32	38	26	30	34	32	33	36	29	32
	Not	6	3	4	16	7	10	11	6	8	9	3	5	14	8	11	12	6	8
Weighted base: Young people not averse to belonging to a club	ATTACHED	(168)	(151.5)	(319.5)	(259)	(175)	(434)	(427)	(326.5)	(753.5)	(439.5)	(412.5)	(852)	(414)	(311)	(725)	(853.5)	(723.5)	(1577)
	NOT ATTACHED	(105.5)	(142)	(247.5)	(141)	(276)	(417)	(246.5)	(418)	(664.5)	(74)	(141)	(215)	(115)	(157.5)	(272.5)	(189)	(298.5)	(487.5)

114

Table R5.16 How often clubs should be open, by age of leaving school, age and sex

Q.20(f)

How often clubs should be open	Age of leaving school																	
	15									Over 15								
	14-16 years			17-20 years			Total			14-16 years			17-20 years			Total		
	Boys	Girls	Total	Boys	Girls	Total	Boys	Girls	Total	Boys	Girls	Total	Boys	Girls	Total	Boys	Girls	Total
	%	%	%	%	%	%	%	%	%	%	%	%	%	%	%	%	%	%
Every night (7 nights a week)	16	14	15	30	20	25	24	18	21	17	12	14	35	25	31	26	18	22
6 nights a week	8	8	8	7	5	6	8	6	7	8	7	7	7	5	6	8	6	7
5 nights a week	6	12	9	12	9	11	10	10	10	8	9	8	9	7	8	8	8	8
4 nights a week	14	13	13	12	18	15	12	16	14	8	14	11	9	12	10	8	13	11
3 nights a week	25	26	25	20	26	23	22	26	24	25	23	24	12	21	16	18	22	20
2 nights a week	24	21	22	12	17	15	17	18	18	22	22	22	13	13	13	18	18	18
1 night a week	3	5	4	2	2	2	2	3	3	6	8	7	3	7	5	5	8	6
Weekends only	1	1	1	1	1	1	1	1	1	1	1	1	1	1	1	1	1	1
All the time (incl. daytime)	1	-	1	2	1	2	2	1	1	2	3	2	6	6	6	4	4	4
Other	1	1	1	2	1	2	2	1	1	4	2	3	4	2	3	4	2	3
Total percentages	100	100	100	100	100	100	100	100	100	100	100	100	100	100	100	100	100	100
Weighted base: Young people not averse to belonging to a club	(273.5)	(293.5)	(567)	(401)	(451)	(852)	(674.5)	(744.5)	(1419)	(513.5)	(553.5)	(1067)	(529)	(468.5)	(997.5)	(1042.5)	(1022)	(2064.5)

115

Table R5.17 Ideal Age Range, by age

Q.20(c)	Age						
Ideal Age Range	14	15	16	17	18	19	20
	%	%	%	%	%	%	%
14-16	28	5	1	-	-	-	-
14-18	41	26	9	2	-	-	-
14-20	15	21	13	7	3	2	1
14-over 20	8	9	11	8	9	9	8
15-20	1	26	26	14	4	2	1
15-over 20	-	5	12	11	10	9	8
16-20	-	3	12	18	7	2	1
16-over 20	-	1	10	18	21	17	14
17, 18-20	-	-	2	6	5	2	1
17, 18-25	-	-	1	7	24	28	28
17, 18-30	-	-	-	1	9	10	16
17, 18-over 30	-	-	-	2	2	7	8
All ages	1	1	1	2	2	3	3
10-13-any age	6	3	3	2	2	1	2
Other	-	-	-	-	1	6	10
Total percentages	100	100	100	100	100	100	100
Weighted base: Young people not averse to belonging to a club	(538.5)	(563)	(532.5)	(506.5)	(456.5)	(445)	(441.5)

Table R5.18 Commercial versus non-commercial provision, by age of leaving school, age and sex

Q.22

Commercial versus non-commercial provision	Age of leaving school																	
	15									Over 15								
	14-16 years			17-20 years			Total			14-16 years			17-20 years			Total		
	Boys	Girls	Total	Boys	Girls	Total	Boys	Girls	Total	Boys	Girls	Total	Boys	Girls	Total	Boys	Girls	Total
	%	%	%	%	%	%	%	%	%	%	%	%	%	%	%	%	%	%
Would enjoy commercially run place:																		
More	27	37	32	44	42	43	38	40	39	22	26	24	35	33	34	29	29	29
Less	53	45	49	31	34	33	40	38	39	61	50	55	40	36	38	50	43	47
Both the same	14	15	14	20	21	21	18	19	18	15	21	18	22	27	24	18	24	21
Don't know, can't answer	5	2	3	3	2	2	4	2	3	1	3	2	1	2	2	1	2	2
Depends on the mood you are in, the people there and the atmosphere etc.	1	1	1	-	-	-	-	1	1	-	1	-	2	1	1	1	1	1
Other answers	-	-	-	-	-	-	-	-	-	-	-	-	-	-	-	-	-	-
Total percentages	100	100	100	100	100	100	100	100	100	100	100	100	100	100	100	100	100	100
Weighted base: All young people	(307)	(316.5)	(623.5)	(471)	(522)	(993)	(778)	(838.5)	(1616.5)	(549)	(576)	(1125)	(584.5)	(523)	(1107.5)	(1133.5)	(1099)	(2232.5)

117

Table R5.19 Commercial versus non-commercial provision, by age of leaving school, age, sex and attachment

Q.22

Commercial versus non-commercial provision	Age of leaving school																	
	15									Over 15								
	14-16 years			17-20 years			Total			14-16 years			17-20 years			Total		
	Boys	Girls	Total	Boys	Girls	Total	Boys	Girls	Total	Boys	Girls	Total	Boys	Girls	Total	Boys	Girls	Total
	%	%	%	%	%	%	%	%	%	%	%	%	%	%	%	%	%	%
ATTACHED																		
Would enjoy commercially run place:																		
More	26	31	29	43	35	40	36	33	35	21	24	22	35	28	32	28	26	27
Less	55	49	53	35	39	37	43	44	43	64	51	58	40	43	42	52	48	50
Both the same	14	17	15	19	23	21	17	20	18	14	21	17	20	26	23	17	23	20
Don't know, can't answer	3	1	2	2	3	2	2	2	2	1	3	2	1	2	1	1	2	2
Depends	-	2	1	-	-	-	-	1	1	-	1	1	2	1	2	1	1	1
Other answers	1	-	-	-	-	-	-	-	-	-	-	-	-	-	-	1	-	-
Total percentages	100	100	100	100	100	100	100	100	100	100	100	100	100	100	100	100	100	100
Weighted base: those attached to clubs	(181.5)	(160)	(341.5)	(289.5)	(191)	(480.5)	(471)	(351)	(822)	(464)	(426)	(890)	(451.5)	(339)	(790.5)	(915.5)	(765)	(1680.5)
NOT ATTACHED																		
Would enjoy commercially run place:																		
More	28	43	36	47	46	47	40	45	43	29	30	30	35	42	39	33	36	35
Less	50	40	45	25	31	29	36	34	35	49	46	47	36	24	29	41	34	37
Both the same	14	13	14	22	20	21	18	18	18	19	20	20	26	31	29	23	26	25
Don't know, can't answer	6	4	5	4	2	2	5	2	3	2	3	3	2	3	2	2	3	2
Depends	2	-	1	1	-	-	1	-	-	-	1	-	-	-	-	-	1	-
Other answers	-	-	-	1	-	1	1	-	-	-	-	-	-	-	-	-	-	-
Total percentages	100	100	100	100	100	100	100	100	100	100	100	100	100	100	100	100	100	100
Weighted base: those not attached to clubs	(125.5)	(156.5)	(282)	(180.5)	(330)	(510.5)	(306)	(486.5)	(792.5)	(85)	(150)	(235)	(133)	(184)	(317)	(218)	(334)	(552)

118

Table R5.20 Reasons for preferring commercial provision, by age of leaving school, age and sex

Q.22(a)

Reasons for preferring commercial provision	Age of leaving school																	
	15									Over 15								
	14-16 years			17-20 years			Total			14-16 years			17-20 years			Total		
	Boys	Girls	Total	Boys	Girls	Total	Boys	Girls	Total	Boys	Girls	Total	Boys	Girls	Total	Boys	Girls	Total
	%	%	%	%	%	%	%	%	%	%	%	%	%	%	%	%	%	%
They cater better for entertainment, better facilities/equipment	54	33	42	52	47	49	53	42	47	56	53	54	66	53	60	63	53	58
Better because run for profit, is competitive	18	12	14	33	19	26	28	17	22	34	29	31	49	29	40	44	29	36
Meet more/new people	17	26	22	11	18	14	13	21	17	19	26	23	13	15	14	15	20	18
Feel freer	13	9	11	20	19	19	18	15	16	16	10	13	14	19	17	15	15	15
Have a better time, more enjoyable, more of a change	4	13	9	8	7	8	7	9	8	13	15	14	13	11	12	13	13	13
Meet greater variety of people	9	13	11	7	10	9	8	11	9	9	16	13	7	11	9	8	13	10
Your friends/your sort of people would be there	5	10	8	11	8	9	9	10	9	7	5	6	7	6	7	7	6	7
They cater for older people only	1	7	5	5	15	10	4	12	8	2	2	2	2	9	6	2	6	4
Licenced bar available	1	2	2	8	8	8	6	6	6	4	2	3	12	1	7	9	2	5
Know better how to cope with rough elements, not so rowdy	4	8	6	3	3	3	3	4	4	4	4	4	5	6	6	5	5	5
Meet people of different ages	1	2	2	2	3	3	2	2	2	-	5	3	2	4	3	1	5	3
No responsibility	-	2	1	2	3	3	2	2	2	4	1	2	1	6	3	2	4	3
You and the others only go there if you like that activity	2	1	2	3	1	2	3	1	2	2	3	3	2	4	2	2	3	3
Other answers	5	5	5	2	3	3	3	4	4	6	3	4	2	2	2	4	3	3
Don't know	9	9	9	6	5	6	6	7	7	4	8	6	2	5	3	3	6	4
Total percentages	143	152	149	173	169	172	165	163	163	180	182	181	197	181	191	193	183	187
Weighted base: Those who prefer commercial provision	(83.5)	(117)	(200.5)	(209.5)	(220.5)	(430)	(293)	(337.5)	(630.5)	(121)	(147.5)	(268.5)	(206.5)	(171.5)	(378)	(327.5)	(319)	(646.5)

119

Table R5.21 Reasons for liking commercial places less, by age of leaving school, age and sex

Q.22(a)

Reasons for liking commercial places less	Age of leaving school																	
	15									Over 15								
	14-16 years			17-20 years			Total			14-16 years			17-20 years			Total		
	Boys	Girls	Total	Boys	Girls	Total	Boys	Girls	Total	Boys	Girls	Total	Boys	Girls	Total	Boys	Girls	Total
	%	%	%	%	%	%	%	%	%	%	%	%	%	%	%	%	%	%
Not so easy to mix or meet people	27	32	29	38	32	34	32	32	32	29	48	38	36	45	40	32	47	39
Don't provide such good facilities/don't cater for the interests of the young people	35	36	36	28	29	29	32	32	32	37	33	35	36	36	36	37	34	35
Not so free/relaxed	16	14	15	20	19	19	18	17	17	22	14	18	20	23	22	22	17	20
Too commercialized/only out for profit	10	12	11	17	15	16	13	14	13	20	14	17	24	14	20	22	14	18
Too expensive	18	9	14	16	7	11	17	8	12	16	15	15	16	11	14	16	14	15
Don't cater for own age group	16	18	17	7	7	7	12	12	12	12	13	12	6	8	7	10	11	10
No opportunity for responsibility	4	5	4	9	8	8	6	7	6	9	6	8	18	17	18	13	10	12
Too rough/too much violence	9	7	8	10	6	8	9	7	8	9	12	10	3	6	4	6	9	8
Atmosphere too hot, crowded, stuffy, smokey, noisy	5	4	4	3	4	4	4	4	4	3	2	2	4	7	6	3	4	4
Don't like the types who go there	3	1	2	5	2	3	4	2	3	3	3	3	4	1	3	4	2	3
Non-commercially run place is more worthwhile/you put more into it/get something worthwhile out of it	1	1	1	3	1	2	2	1	2	1	–	1	4	2	3	2	1	2
Other reasons	1	2	2	3	3	3	2	3	2	2	2	2	2	4	3	2	3	2
Don't know, vague reasons given	8	11	10	5	13	10	7	12	10	6	8	7	4	3	3	5	6	6
Total percentages	153	152	153	164	146	154	158	150	153	169	170	168	177	177	176	174	172	174
Weighted base: those who would enjoy a commercially run place less	(163.5)	(142)	(305.5)	(148)	(176.5)	(324.5)	(311.5)	(318.5)	(630)	(336.5)	(285)	(621.5)	(231.5)	(190)	(421.5)	(568)	(475)	(1043)

CHAPTER 6

VOLUNTARY COMMUNITY SERVICE AND
RESIDENTIAL COURSES

These are two forms of extra club activities which may be provided through the Youth Service and are therefore important in
considering the whole range of Youth Service and allied provision. Both facilities may be organised through existing clubs,
or through schools, colleges, or other organisations or they
may be independent of any of these. In this chapter we are concerned with the kind of young people involved and whether they
differ from those who are attached to clubs; the sort of activities
in which they participate and the way they came to do so.

A. VOLUNTARY COMMUNITY SERVICE

The term was intended to cover any unpaid service for others
or for the community in general, the examples included in the
question were, looking after handicapped children, visiting old
people and helping in a work camp.

6.1 The Characteristics of the Young People involved

35% of the young people said they had undertaken voluntary
community service at some time, but only 11% said they were
active at the time of interview.

(a) Age and Sex

Age was unrelated to total experience of community service,
but the younger groups were rather more often involved in
voluntary service at the time of interview than the older people.

Table 6.1 Percentage of young people who had ever done or were
currently doing voluntary community service, by age and
sex

Age	Had ever done voluntary community service			Doing voluntary community service at time of interview		
	M	F	T	M	F	T
14-16	27	42	34	10	16	13
17-20	29	41	35	8	10	9
Total	27	41	35	9	13	11

The fall out occurred after 16 years, similar to the fall out in attachment at about the same age, and seems to be related to leaving school as will be shown shortly.

Girls were considerably more likely to report experience of voluntary service than boys, and rather more likely to be doing it at the time of interview, whichever age group they belonged to. Thus at the extremes 16% of the younger girls were currently involved, but only 8% of the older boys.

(b) School leaving age and occupational status

These two variables are closely related in the present context, and it is therefore useful to consider them together.

Those who stayed on longer at school and those in full time education were about twice as likely to be engaged in voluntary community service at the time of interview as other groups, and rather more likely ever to have done such work, (Fig. 6.1)

FIG. 6.1.

Percentage of young people who had ever done or were currently doing voluntary community service (a) by school leaving age and (b) by occupational status

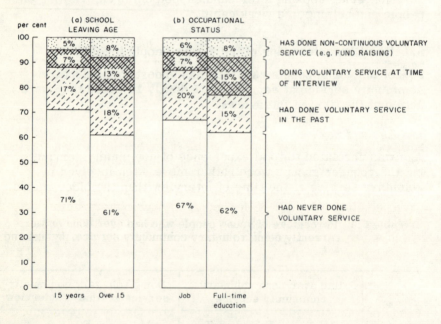

Table R6.15 These differences, however, were both due to the close association between education and voluntary work. Thus amongst those 14 to 16 years olds still in full time education early leavers were just as frequently engaged in voluntary work as the later leavers, and amongst the 17-20 year olds who were

122

working, the early leavers were only a little less likely to be doing voluntary work (6% compared with 9%). In other words, and unlike attachment to clubs, involvement in voluntary service seems to depend more on whether a young person is still at school or college, on the one hand or in a job, on the other, than on school leaving age.

Table 6.2 Percentage of young people doing voluntary community service at time of interview, by age, sex, school leaving age, and occupational status

School leaving age	Age	In full time education			In full time employment		
		M	F	T	M	F	T
15	14-16	10	21	16	3	7	5
	17-20	7*	-*	4*	6	5	6
	T	10	20	15	5	6	6
16 and over	14-16	13	18	15	3	15	9
	17-20	9	23	15	8	10	9
	T	12	19	15	8	11	9
	Total	11	19	15	6	7	7

*Percentages are unreliable because of small bases

(c) Area and regional variations

Although the number of people living in truly rural areas was too small to yield any firm conclusions, it appears that the young people there were rather less likely to be doing or to have done voluntary work than those living elsewhere. This may have been because of lack of opportunity through negligible demand for this type of work or because the organisations which arrange much of voluntary community service are centred in more urban areas.

Table R6.16

(d) Relationship to Attachment

Young people who were attached were most likely to be engaged in voluntary service at the time of interview and they were also most likely ever to have done such service. Those who had never been attached were least likely ever to have been involved (Fig. 6.2). Looked at the other way round, 84% of those currently doing voluntary work were attached, but only about 64% of those not doing such work.

Table R6.17

123

FIG. 6.2.

Percentage of young people who had ever done or were currently doing voluntary community service, by attachment

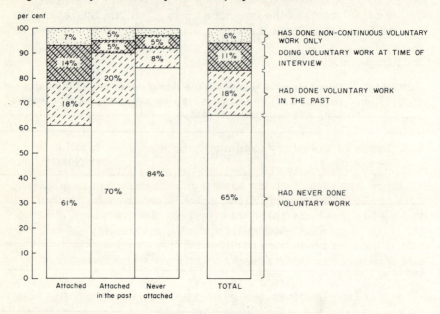

Attachment, like involvement in voluntary work, is related to occupational status, so that the relationship between attachment and voluntary work could be fortuitous, for example both might be affected by occupational status, but neither by the other. But this was not the case; on the contrary, within each occupational status category the attached were more than twice as often involved in voluntary work as the unattached.

Table 6.3 Percentage of young people currently doing voluntary community service by occupational status and attachment

Occupational status	Attached	Unattached	Total
In full time paid job	9	4	7
In full time education	17	8	15
Other	11	4	7

The relationship of voluntary work with attachment to what the young people regarded at Youth clubs was even more marked, and those attached to what they called Youth clubs were rather more often involved in voluntary work than any other group.

In summary, the young people engaged in voluntary community service were most likely to be girls, still at school and attached, and in particular attached to what they called Youth Clubs.

124

Table 6.4 Percentage of young people currently doing voluntary community service by occupational status and youth club attachment

Occupational status	Attached to Youth Club	Total Attached	Not Attached
In full time paid job	11	9	4
In full time education	19	17	7
Other	10	11	4
Total	15	14	5

6.2 Types of Voluntary Community Service

Voluntary community service took two main forms. First of all there was that of giving practical help to people in some sort of need, old people, sick people, handicapped children and so on. Secondly there was the kind of work which is rather different from what is usually meant by community *service;* that of raising funds for charities by, for example, selling flags and sponsored walks. These are unlikely to involve direct contact with those in need.

The majority of those who had done voluntary work had been involved in the first type of work, and 60% of them had helped old people in some way. 25% said they had helped with fund raising, which may be an underestimate both because the question wording did not suggest that this type of activity was included, and also because, being sporadic, it is more easily forgotten.

It was shown earlier that girls were more likely than boys to have done voluntary work, and it can be seen from Table 6.5

Table 6.5 Percentage of young people ever involved in voluntary community service who had done various kinds of work

Type of Service	M	F	T
Helping old people	53	64	60
Fund raising	33	19	25
Helping children (other than handicapped children)	4	15	10
Helping handicapped children	4	11	8
Helping ill people (other than children or old people)	5	8	7
Helping handicapped people (other than children or old people)	5	7	6
Doing odd jobs	5	2	3
Maintenance of property (for Youth Clubs, Churches etc.)	4	1	2
Helping children in hospital	1	2	1
Meals on wheels	1	2	1
Other	13	9	10

that amongst those who were involved they were more likely
to have rendered a service to people. Although boys had also
more often helped individual people than done anything else, they
were much more likely than girls to have helped raise funds and,
albeit tiny proportions were involved, to have done odd jobs and
helped maintain property. The more dramatic kinds of work,
like environmental improvements and assistance in disasters
occurred too rarely to form separate categories.

Table
R6.18
The type of voluntary work being undertaken did not vary
considerably or systematically with occupational status or school
leaving age, although school children were rather more often
involved with normal healthy children.

There was some evidence of a shift over time in emphasis
from helping old people to work with handicapped people and
with children, who were neither handicapped nor sick.

**Table 6.6 Type of voluntary community service undertaken, by
whether currently engaged in any such work – selected
types of work only**

Experience of voluntary service	Work with					
	Old people	children not handicapped or sick	handi- capped children	Ill people	handi- capped people	sick children
Current	65	14	10	9	10	1
Past	70	11	9	7	5	2

6.3 How the young people found out about voluntary community service

Some voluntary community service is arranged by schools,
clubs, churches and voluntary service organisations, whilst
some springs from individual initiative. It was not possible
to find out exactly who had arranged the work which the young
people interviewed had done, but instead we asked them how
they first found out about the opportunity for voluntary service.
The availability of such channels of communication of course
must depend on the young person's contact with appropriate
groups and individuals in the community.

The most important source of information about voluntary
service was the school. It was shown earlier that those who
were still at school were the most likely to be currently
engaged in voluntary service and it may be because access to
such work is most readily available through schools. Youth
clubs (i. e. those named as such by the informants) also
played a considerable role, but this was clearly dependent

on attachment to such groups, and as this was maximal during and immediately after schooling, it was not a source widely available to those at work.

Table 6.7 Source of information about voluntary community service (a) by attachment (b) by occupational status – percentage of young people who had ever done such work

Source of information	(a) Attachment			(b) Occupational status		Total
	Attached	Past attachment	Never attached	In a job	In FT.Ed.	
School	40	45	(52)	37	45	41
Youth organisation	27	18	(2)	26	22	24
Friends, relatives	19	19	(15)	19	19	19
Church	10	8	(5)	8	10	9
Personal initiative	8	11	(15)	9	8	9
Other organisations	6	6	(7)	7	5	6
Other people	6	4	(2)	5	5	5
College	2	4	(2)	3	3	3
Mass media	2	2	-	1	2	2
Other	6	3	(2)	5	5	5

Percentages in brackets are based on less than 50 cases

6.4 Reasons for stopping voluntary community service

Two main themes emerged for abandoning voluntary service, firstly the loss of opportunity, and secondly a loss of desire for one reason or another.

The first covers the young person's detachment from the organisation which arranged the work, and lack of work to do. The second includes loss of interest, lack of friends or relatives to do it with, and lack of time, which implies that priority is given to other activities.

18% of the young people had done voluntary service in the past but had given it up by the time of interview. Reasons reflecting a loss of opportunity because of detachment from an organisation were most frequently given by the unattached and those at work, whilst loss of desire was most often cited by the attached and those at school.

Because of the many other questions covered by this enquiry it was not possible to consider more than a few aspects of voluntary community service. The data shows that very few young people were involved but that those in full time education and the attached were most likely to be so. This seems to be explicable in terms of the dominant role of schools and youth organisations in organising or facilitating voluntary work.

If voluntary work is considered a worthwhile activity for young people there seems to be enormous scope for expansion, particularly amongst those who have left school, since so few

Table 6.8 **Reasons for abandoning voluntary community service – percentage of young people who had given up such work, giving various reasons (a) by attachment (b) by occupational status**

Reasons for giving up	(a) Attachment		(b) Occupational Status		(c) Total
	Attached	Not Attached	In a job	At school	
Left school	22	29	32	–	24
Lack of time	24	24	25	21	24
Left organisation that ran it	14	17	15	13	16
Job ended	11	13	10	18	12
Moved	8	9	6	6	8
Lost interest	8	5	6	13	7
Organisation closed down	4	4	3	6	4
Friends/relatives stopped going	3	1	2	3	3
Not enough work	2	2	–	5	2
Only available in certain forms	2	2	1	6	2
Other	11	6	8	19	10

are currently involved. Very few people had taken up voluntary work on their own initiative or because of information they had received from the mass media, so that it must be assumed that the organisations to which young people belonged were at this time the most effective means of channelling them into such work. This suggests the possibility of exploiting other means of informing and attracting the young than through schools and youth groups. However, we do not know how many people would be interested if the means of engagement were available to them, nor whether the rather small proportion involved, even amongst the attached in full time education, means that few were interested or that many schools and youth groups were not offering them the opportunity to be so.

Most of the people who had done voluntary work had helped old people, rather few reported work with children and even less mentioned the more adventurous types of work. But it is not possible to say from this enquiry whether the current deployment of their energies made the best use of what the young people had to offer, either from their own or the recipients' point of view.

B. RESIDENTIAL COURSES

Residential course was intended to mean any course which entailed the young person's staying away from home, except for purely vocational courses. Examples were given to the informants of courses in mountaineering, music, how to get on with other people and Outward Bound Schools.

6.5 The characteristics of young people who had been on courses

(a) Sex and school leaving age

27% of all the young people said they had been on a residential course at some time, but whilst 32% of the boys had had this experience, only 22% of girls reported it. This difference may be due to the boys' greater interest in sport, which, as will be shown later, was the most common activity provided by such courses.

Table R6.19

The later school leavers were almost twice as likely to have been on a course as the early leavers, and this may have been due to their extended connection with schools, which were the major organisers of courses (section 6.7)

Table 6.9 Percentage of young people who had been on a residential course by sex and school leaving age

School leaving age	M	F	T
15	23	14	18
16 and over	38	29	33
Total	32	22	27

However, if only those aged 14-16 and still at school are considered the same difference, persists, so that it is school leaving age and not being at school which accounts for the difference.

Table 6.10 Percentage of young people who had been on a residential course by sex and school leaving age — those aged 14-16 and at school only

School leaving Age	M	F	T
15	20	15	17
16 and over	38	26	32
Total	35	24	29

School leaving age was related not only to whether young people attended a course at all but also, to a lesser extent, to the number of courses attended by those who had. 26% of the late school leavers who had been on a course, had been on more than one, but only 19% of the early leavers.

Table R6.20

Since attending a course is likely to cost money, parental income may be important and the fact that only about 10% of the parents of early school leavers had earned over £ 25 net in the week before the interview compared with 30% of the parents of later leavers lends some support to this possibility.

(b) Relationship to Attachment

Young people who were attached at the time of interview were more likely to have been on a residential course than any other group, whilst those who had never been attached were least likely to have done so.

Table 6.11 Percentage of young people who had been on a residential course by attachment

	Never Attached	Past Attachment	Present Attachment	Total
Has attended Residential Course	10	19	32	27
Has not attended Residential Course	90	81	68	73

In fact the currently attached were almost twice as likely to have attended a course as those who were not attached.

Table R6.21 Attachment itself is, of course, related to school leaving age but within each group of school leavers the attached were more likely than the unattached to have been on a residential course and more of those who were attached to what they called a Youth Club had attended a course than any other group.

Table 6.12 Percentage of young people who had been on a residential course by school leaving age, attachment and attachment to what they called a Youth Club

School Leaving Age	All Attached	Attached to Youth Club	Not Attached	Total
15	23	30	14	18
16 and over	37	37	32	33
Total	32	35	16	27

6.6 Types of Residential Course

More than half of the young people who had been on a residential course had been on one concerned with outdoor sport like sailing, hiking or camping. And nearly 30% had experienced the similar activity of orienteering.

Such adventurous courses including Outward Bound Schools were reported most frequently by boys and the early school leavers, whilst educational and cultural courses were more often mentioned by girls. Educational courses in particular, such as field studies and courses on academic subjects, were most often quoted by late school leavers.

Table 6.13 Types of activity followed on courses attended, by sex and school leaving age − percentage of those who had attended a course mentioning each type of course − 1st course mentioned only

| Type of Activity | School leaving Age | | | | | | Total | | |
| | 15 years | | | 16 and over | | | | | |
	M	F	T	M	F	T	M	F	T
Outdoor sport	68	59	65	60	45	54	62	49	57
Orienteering	32	32	32	29	25	27	30	27	29
Visiting towns/sightseeing	15	15	15	17	17	17	17	17	17
Field studies	7	8	7	13	21	17	12	17	14
Job orientation	8	11	12	8	7	8	8	8	8
Drama/pottery, music etc.	5	8	6	4	9	6	4	9	6
Educational trips abroad	3	8	5	4	8	6	4	8	6
Discussions	3	7	5	4	6	5	4	7	5
Outward Bound School	7	4	6	5	3	4	6	3	4
Academic courses	-	4	2	3	7	5	2	7	4
Religious	2	5	3	2	5	4	2	5	4
Socialisation	1	1	1	1	2	2	1	2	2
Other	17	10	14	16	14	15	16	13	15

6.7 Bodies organising courses

The young people were asked who had organised the courses which they had attended, and their replies are likely to refer to the bodies through which they were enabled to go on the

Table 6.14 Bodies organising courses by school leaving age of those who had attended − 1st course mentioned only

| Organising Body | School leaving Age | | Total |
	15	16 or over	
School	53	50	51
Uniformed organisation	15	17	17
Other club	15	8	10
Church	3	3	3
Education Committee	2	3	3
College	-	3	2
Work	2	2	2
Other	8	13	12

131

courses, rather than the bodies which actually provided the facilities, if these differed. Schools played the predominant role from this point of view, 51% of the courses had been organised through schools, 17% through uniformed organisations and 10% by other clubs of one kind or another.

Although schools always played the dominant role in organising courses, the early leavers cited schools and clubs more frequently than later leavers who in turn rather more often mentioned uniformed organisations and colleges, but the differences were small.

6.8 Summary

Residential courses were even more closely related to full time education than voluntary work but in this case when early leavers were still at school they were less likely than their late leaving contemporaries to have been on a course. Similarly, the attached were more likely than the unattached to have attended a course because courses were frequently organised through the clubs they belonged to.

In this case too, we were unable to explore the unmet demand for residential courses, or the young people's satisfaction or otherwise with the existing type of provision.

Both residential courses and voluntary community service were catering mainly for those who already enjoyed the advantages of attachment and were only to a very limited extent providing an alternative, partly because the means of becoming involved in either was through the organisations to which the attached already belonged, whether club, school or college. It seems that any expansion amongst the unattached must be made through the organisations to which they in turn belong, which, if no other, would be where they work.

Table R.6.15 Voluntary Service, by age of leaving school, age, occupational status and sex

Q.25

	Age of leaving school											
	15						Over 15					
	14-16 years		17-20 years		Total		14-16 years		17-20 years		Total	
Voluntary Service	Job	Ed.	Job	Ed.	Job	Ed.	Job	Ed.	Job	Ed.	Job	Ed.
	%	%	%	%	%	%	%	%	%	%	%	%
BOYS												
Never done voluntary work	78	77	79	73	79	77	77	69	67	61	68	67
†Has done some in the past	19	13	14	20	16	14	20	18	24	30	24	22
Still doing voluntary work	3	10	6	7	5	10	3	13	8	9	8	12
Total percentages	100	100	100	100	100	100	100	100	100	100	100	100
Weighted base: All boys in a job or full-time education	(165.5)	(129.5)	(441)	(15)*	(606.5)	(144.5)	(30.5)	(510.5)	(339.5)	(219)	(370)	(729.5)
GIRLS												
Never done voluntary work	53	56	68	71	64	56	33	62	54	40	52	56
†Has done some in the past	41	23	26	29	30	23	52	20	40	37	42	24
Still doing voluntary work	7	21	5	-	6	20	15	18	10	23	11	19
Total percentages	100	100	100	100	100	100	100	100	100	100	100	100
Weighted base: All girls in a job or full-time education	(161.5)	(135.5)	(422)	(7)*	(583.5)	(142.5)	(33)	(532)	(293.5)	(181.5)	(326.5)	(713.5)
TOTAL												
Never done voluntary work	65	66	74	73	72	67	54	65	61	52	60	62
†Has done some in the past	30	18	20	23	23	18	36	19	30	33	30	23
Still doing voluntary work	5	16	6	4	6	15	9	15	9	15	9	15
Total percentages	100	100	100	100	100	100	100	100	100	100	100	100
Weighted base: All young people in a job or full-time education	(327)	(265)	(863)	(22)*	(1190)	(287)	(63.5)	(1042.5)	(633)	(400.5)	(696.5)	(1443)

*percentages are unreliable because of small bases
†includes non-continuous voluntary work such as selling flags

Table R.6.16 Voluntary Service, by type of area

Q.25 Voluntary Service	Type of area				Total
	Conurbation	Urban	Semi-Rural	Rural	
	%	%	%	%	%
Never done voluntary work	62	67	66	74	65
Has done some in the past	27	23	23	19	24
Is still doing voluntary work	11	11	11	7	11
Total percentages	100	100	100	100	100
Weighted base: All young people	(1329)	(1762)	(691)	(67)	(3849)

Table R.6.17 Voluntary Service, by occupational status and attachment

Q.25 Voluntary Service	Job		Education		Neither	
	Attached	Unattached	Attached	Unattached	Attached	Unattached
	%	%	%	%	%	%
Never done voluntary work	63	72	59	75	62	70
Has done some in the past	27	24	24	18	28	25
Is still doing voluntary work	9	4	17	8	11	4
Total percentages	100	100	100	100	100	100
Weighted base: All young people	(1026)	(860.5)	(1382.5)	(347.5)	(94)	(138.5)

134

Table R6.18 Type of voluntary work, by age of leaving school, age and sex

Type of Voluntary Work	Age of leaving school																	
	15									Over 15								
	14-16 years			17-20 years			Total			14-16 years			17-20 years			Total		
	Boys	Girls	Total	Boys	Girls	Total	Boys	Girls	Total	Boys	Girls	Total	Boys	Girls	Total	Boys	Girls	Total
	%	%	%	%	%	%	%	%	%	%	%	%	%	%	%	%	%	%
Helping old people	58	68	65	51	69	62	54	68	63	49	58	54	56	63	60	53	61	57
Helping handicapped children	4	11	8	7	11	10	6	11	9	4	10	7	3	12	8	4	11	8
Helping other children	-	14	9	3	8	6	2	11	8	5	18	13	4	17	11	5	17	12
Helping ill people	3	5	4	4	7	6	4	6	5	1	8	5	9	10	10	6	9	7
Helping handicapped people	3	5	4	4	6	5	4	5	5	5	7	6	6	8	7	5	8	7
Fund raising	24	15	18	34	15	22	30	15	21	39	22	29	30	22	26	34	22	27
Meals on wheels	-	2	1	1	2	2	1	2	1	1	1	1	-	2	1	1	1	1
Odd jobs, errands	4	1	2	8	1	4	6	1	3	6	3	4	3	2	2	4	3	3
Helping sick children	1	1	1	1	1	1	1	1	1	1	2	2	-	2	1	1	2	1
Maintenance of property (for Church, Youth Club, etc)	6	1	3	5	1	2	5	1	3	2	-	1	4	2	3	3	1	2
Other work	6	4	5	11	6	8	9	5	7	11	6	8	18	15	16	14	11	12
Total percentages	109	127	120	129	127	128	122	126	126	124	135	130	133	155	145	130	146	137
Weighted base: All young people who have done voluntary work	(69.5)	(142.5)	(212)	(98.5)	(160.5)	(259)	(168)	(303)	(471)	(165.5)	(231)	(396.5)	(206)	(266)	(472)	(371.5)	(497)	(868.5)

135

Q.26

Table R.6.19 Whether had ever been on a residential course, by age of leaving school, age and sex

Whether been on a residential course	Age of leaving school																	
	15									Over 15								
	14-16 years			17-20 years			Total			14-16 years			17-20 years			Total		
	Boys	Girls	Total	Boys	Girls	Total	Boys	Girls	Total	Boys	Girls	Total	Boys	Girls	Total	Boys	Girls	Total
	%	%	%	%	%	%	%	%	%	%	%	%	%	%	%	%	%	%
Yes	26	16	21	21	12	16	23	14	18	39	26	32	38	32	35	38	29	33
No	74	84	79	79	88	84	77	86	82	61	74	68	62	68	65	62	71	66
Total percentages	100	100	100	100	100	100	100	100	100	100	100	100	100	100	100	100	100	100
Weighted base: All young people	(306.5)	(316)	(622.5)	(471)	(522)	(993)	(777.5)	(838)	(1615.5)	(549.5)	(576.5)	(1126)	(584.5)	(523)	(1107.5)	(1134)	(1099.5)	(2233.5)

136

Table R6.20 Number of residential courses attended, by age of leaving school and age

Q.26	Age of leaving school					
Number of residential courses attended	15			Over 15		
	14-16 years	17-20 years	Total	14-16 years	17-20 years	Total
	%	%	%	%	%	%
One	87	77	81	81	68	74
Two	9	19	15	16	24	20
Three	2	4	3	3	6	5
Four	2	1	1	1	1	1
Five	1	-	-	-	1	-
Total percentages	100	100	100	100	100	100
Weighted base: All young people who attended a residential course	(128.5)	(164)	(292.5)	(360.5)	(386)	(746.5)

Table R.6.21 Whether had ever been on a residential course, by age of leaving school and attachment

Q.26	Age of leaving school				Total	
Whether been on a residential course	15		Over 15			
	Attached	Unattached	Attached	Unattached	Attached	Unattached
	%	%	%	%	%	%
Yes	24	13	37	24	32	17
No	76	87	63	76	68	83
Total percentages	100	100	100	100	100	100
Weighted base: All young people	(822)	(793.5)	(1679.5)	(554)	(2501.5)	(1347.5)

CHAPTER 7

LEISURE ACTIVITIES OF THE YOUNG PEOPLE

Our main concern in this chapter is to find out whether the
leisure patterns of the attached differ from those of the unattached. It is already clear that the attached differ in important
demographic and social respects from the unattached, and it is
to be expected that the different age, sex and educational groups
will spend their spare time in different ways, but the question
examined here is whether, within each group, the leisure lives
of the unattached were any less rich and varied than those of the
attached.

The most valid way of examining leisure patterns is by means
of Time Budgets, which require informants to account for each
short interval of their free time in detail over a given period.
At the pilot stage of the present enquiry informants were asked
to say how they had spent each half hour of one evening, and
one weekend day, but because this was time consuming, and the
alternative (and better) method of diary keeping was impractic-
ably expensive we were unable to use either for the main enquiry.
Instead, the young people were asked what they did in their spare
time when they were with friends, their families and on their
own and the results pooled for each individual. However, the
pilot Time Budget results will be used to support or qualify the
data from the main enquiry, where appropriate. The main conclusion from the Pilot which is worth mentioning here, is that
the simple question about leisure activities yields a much more
exciting picture of spare time than is actually the case, since
in fact, the single most time consuming activity is watching
television, followed by travelling, eating and personal care.

7.1 Leisure Activities in general

The most frequently mentioned pastimes were social, such as   Table
dancing, talking, drinking and visiting or entertaining friends   R7.10
and relations (86%). In section 7.2 this category will be examined
more closely. 70% reported watching television and 69% mentioned entertainment like cinema going and listening to music.
67% said they took part in active sport, and 54% said they spent
some time reading.

The most frequently mentioned sports were outdoor pursuits
like cycling, fishing or walking, this was followed, in order,
by outdoor non-team games, indoor sports (like Ten-pin bowling,
table tennis and ice skating), and outdoor team games.

139

No other activity was mentioned by as many as half the young people, but outings and short walks (as distinct from country hikes), creative domestic activities, like dressmaking and gardening and other domestic pursuits were each cited by over a third of the sample, whilst crafts, active culture and study were each reported by about one fifth.

(a) Sex, age and school leaving age differences

The boys mentioned sport and crafts, like woodwork and car maintenance much more frequently than girls, who in turn more often said they spent some of their time on social and domestic pastimes, entertainment and reading.

Table 7.1 Percentage of young people mentioning various leisure activities, by sex

Activity	Male	Female	Total
Social	81	91	86
Television, radio	70	70	70
Entertainment	64	75	69
Active sport	77	57	67
Reading	46	62	54
Outings, walks	47	50	49
Domestic creative	24	56	40
Other domestic	19	52	36
Active cultural	20	23	22
Creative crafts	35	6	20
Study	22	17	19
Sedentary games	20	17	18
Spectator sports	14	9	12
Laze about	9	8	8
Other	34	41	38

NOTE: Boxes indicate differences of 10% or more between the sexes

Active sport was reported most frequently by the 14-16 year olds, whilst social pursuits and entertainment were evidently most prevalent amongst 17-20 year olds.

The late school leavers mentioned most types of activity more frequently than the early leavers, so that the average number of kinds of activity mentioned by the late leavers was 6.4 compared with 5.6 for the early leavers.

It is a commonplace of social survey research that the better educated tend to reply to open ended questions in more dimensions than the less educated, and the problem is to know whether this reflects different behaviour or only different degrees of

140

fluency. In the present case it was possible to use the pilot Time Budget results as a check, and this showed the same kind of difference: on average the late leavers had each spent their time on 6.6 different kinds of activities compared with 5.9 for the early leavers. Thus the late school leavers appear to have led a more varied leisure life than those who left school at the minimum age.

Amongst the many activities reported more frequently by the late school leavers, certain types were considerably more prevalent in this group. These were; active sport, reading, active cultural pursuits and study. Television watching alone, was mentioned slightly more frequently by early rather than late school leavers. All these differences were confirmed by the Time Budget evidence. That is to say the activities mentioned more frequently by each group also occupied a greater proportion of that group's time. In particular, the early leavers spent more of their spare time watching television and the late leavers spent much more time on homework and study.

Table 7.2 **Percentage of young people mentioning various leisure activities by school leaving age**

Activity	SLA 15	SLA 16 or over	Total
Social	86	87	86
Television, radio	72	68	70
Entertainment	66	72	69
Active sport	61	72	67
Reading	43	62	54
Outings, walks	44	52	49
Domestic creative	41	40	40
Other domestic	34	37	36
Active cultural	13	28	22
Creative crafts	20	20	20
Study	9	27	19
Sedentary games	19	18	18
Spectator sports	11	13	12
Laze about	8	8	8
Other	32	41	38

NOTE: Boxes indicate differences of 10% or more between
        school leaving groups

(b) Occupational status

Whatever the school leaving age reported by the young people, whether they were in full time education or not made a difference to how they spent their spare time. Those in full time education were considerably more likely to mention active sport, study, Table R7.11

141

reading and active culture than those in a job. This is presumably both because the facilities for pursuing such occupations are more readily available during people's school days, and because encouragement to do so is more systematic. The young people at work, on the other hand, more often reported social activities and entertainment. But on the whole the young people in full time education mentioned the majority of types of activity more frequently than those at work. In other words they were more active.

Table 7.3 Percentage of young people mentioning various leisure activities by sex and occupational status

Type of activity	In full time education			In full time employment		
	M	F	T	M	F	T
Social	74	90	82	88	93	90
Television, radio	69	68	69	70	74	72
Entertainment	60	74	67	67	78	72
Active sport	83	67	75	72	51	62
Reading	54	71	63	39	55	47
Outings, walks	50	57	53	45	46	45
Domestic creative	22	54	38	26	56	41
Other domestic	25	51	38	15	53	33
Active cultural	25	35	30	16	14	15
Creative crafts	33	5	19	38	7	23
Study	31	30	31	14	7	11
Sedentary games	22	17	19	17	17	17
Spectator sports	15	9	12	14	11	12
Laze about	7	6	7	10	8	9
Other	40	46	43	29	38	33

(c) Differences associated with attachment

Table R7.12 The attached on average mentioned 6.4 activities each, compared with 5.7 for the unattached. This was not due to the different composition of the two groups, but held for every sub group. The only noteworthy exceptions to this, (noteworthy because of the direction rather than the size of the differences), were television watching and domestic activities, which were reported slightly more often by most groups of the unattached.

The activities which were considerably more common amongst the attached were; active sport, active culture, and study, followed by reading.

On the whole there were more considerable differences between the attached and unattached late school leavers, than between the same groups of early leavers, for whom only social activities and active sport were much more prevalent amongst the attached. It seems very likely that this is in part due to the different types of club patronised by the two educational groups. Early leavers,

142

Table 7.4 Percentages of young people mentioning various leisure activities, by sex, school leaving age and attachment

Activities	Attached							Unattached						
	SLA 15			SLA 16 or over			T	SLA 15			SLA 16 or over			T
	M	F	T	M	F	T		M	F	T	M	F	T	
Social	87	93	90	83	94	88	89	73	88	82	73	87	82	82
Television, radio	72	72	72	68	66	67	69	71	75	73	70	72	71	72
Entertainment	64	70	66	67	79	73	71	56	72	66	62	72	68	67
Active sport	78	58	69	81	69	75	73	68	42	52	74	53	61	56
Reading	35	54	43	57	73	64	57	30	51	43	47	63	57	49
Outings, walks	45	44	44	51	57	53	50	41	46	44	46	50	49	46
Domestic, creative	27	52	38	23	58	38	38	26	56	44	22	58	44	44
Other domestic	14	54	31	23	50	35	34	16	52	38	18	56	41	39
Active cultural	14	14	14	26	34	31	25	11	13	12	21	17	19	15
Creative arts	37	7	24	33	7	21	22	34	4	16	38	5	18	17
Study	13	8	11	31	27	29	23	10	4	6	22	20	21	12
Sedentary games	19	19	19	20	18	19	19	21	18	19	18	15	16	18
Spectator sport	17	10	14	15	12	14	14	10	7	8	13	9	10	9
Laze about	9	6	7	8	8	8	8	9	8	9	10	8	9	9
Other	26	43	33	39	39	43	40	29	33	32	35	39	37	34

it will be recalled, tend to go overwhelmingly to Youth, social and sports clubs, in which the main activity which is difficult to follow outside an organised group is sport; whereas considerable proportions of late leavers also attend interest-centred clubs which offer facilities for active culture, not easily pursued outside a formal group.

The differences in the prevalence of reading and study between the attached and unattached are more difficult to explain and in the absence of any other evidence, it can only be attributed to the tendency for the attached to be interested, for one reason or another, in a wider range of activities.

7.2 More about Social Activities

The attached mentioned social activities rather more often than the unattached, but the difference was not great (89% compared with 82%). The smallness of the difference is rather surprising, because it might be expected that club membership would affect this aspect of leisure to a greater extent than any other. The category comprised various activities which were considered to be primarily sociable in purpose, and as the following table shows, their popularity varied amongst the different groups.

Obviously this is a very crude measure of social interaction and the figures for club visiting alone cast doubt on its validity since in fact two thirds of the young people should have mentioned it. But other evidence was available from the answers to two questions about the frequency of contacts with friends

Table 7.5 Percentages of young people mentioning each type of social activity by age, sex and school leaving age

Activity	Male				Female			
	SLA 15		SLA 16 or over		SLA 15		SLA 16 or over	
	14-16	17-20	14-16	17-20	14-16	17-20	14-16	17-20
Dancing	21	49	8	46	45	48	45	55
Visiting, entertaining friends	23	32	30	41	47	47	51	56
Talking	22	29	31	40	39	52	46	52
Drinking	6	62	5	62	9	52	5	45
Eating out	11	9	6	14	9	15	13	25
Visiting non-commercial clubs	20	17	27	19	26	10	32	14
Visiting other clubs	2	6	2	6	5	6	4	5
Chatting up boys/girls	4	3	2	1	2	1	-	-
Base	307	471	549	584.5	316.5	522	576	523

during the week preceding interview. In the first the young person was asked on how many days he had seen his friends to talk to during the previous week, and the second concerned the number of days on which he had 'got together with friends to do things like going out or visiting one another's homes'.

Table R7.13 The answers to the first question showed that the attached were considerably more likely to have seen their friends to talk to every day during the previous week, whilst the unattached were more likely than the attached to have seen them for up to five days only.

Table 7.6 Frequency of seeing friends to talk to during week preceding interview, by sex, age, school leaving age and attachment

School leaving age	Age	Number of days friends seen to talk to during previous week											
		0-5 days						6 or 7 days					
		Males		Female		Total		Male		Female		Total	
		A	U	A	U	A	U	A	U	A	U	A	U
15	14-16	27	47	29	45	29	43	70	56	71	58	70	57
	17-20	37	59	53	54	44	57	63	41	47	45	57	43
	T	34	52	43	50	38	52	66	48	58	48	63	48
16 or over	14-16	28	45	34	43	33	43	73	56	66	57	69	56
	17-20	38	53	38	61	38	57	62	46	62	40	62	42
	T	33	50	36	52	34	52	67	50	64	47	66	48
Total		33	52	38	52	35	52	67	48	62	48	65	48

Note: A = attached U = unattached

144

The differences between the attached and unattached in patterns Table R7.14 of doing things with friends was of another kind. Here the distinction lay between those who had got together with friends at all during the preceding week and those who had not. The attached were much more likely to have done things with their friends than the unattached. In fact the differences shown in Tables 7.6 and 7.7 are considerably greater than is suggested by the reports of social activities (Table 7.4), and it may be concluded that in addition to being less physically and apparently intellectually active, the unattached also led less intensely sociable lives.

Table 7.7 **Frequency of getting together with friends to do things like going out or visiting each other's homes, by sex, age, school leaving age and attachment**

School leaving age	Age	Number of days got together with friends during previous week											
		O						1-7					
		Male		Female		Total		Male		Female		Total	
		A	U	A	U	A	U	A	U	A	U	A	U
15	14-16	14	30	12	32	13	31	86	70	88	68	88	68
	17-20	12	23	26	32	17	29	88	77	75	69	83	71
	T	12	26	20	32	16	30	88	74	80	69	85	72
16 or over	14-16	17	41	20	37	18	38	83	59	81	62	82	61
	17-20	12	19	18	31	14	26	87	80	82	68	86	73
	T	14	28	19	34	16	31	80	72	81	66	84	68
	Total	14	27	19	33	16	30	86	73	81	67	84	70

It is incidentally worth noting, from the same tables, that whilst the boys mentioned fewer social pastimes than girls, they actually had more contacts with friends than girls did. This is born out by the Time Budget evidence, which showed the boys spent a rather greater proportion of their spare time in the company of friends than girls did. It is a common finding of social research that girls and women claim more social activities than males, but the data from this enquiry suggests that whilst girls value them more, they in fact meet their friends less often.

7.3 Part-time Education

It was suggested above on the basis of their reported involvement in active cultural pastimes, study and reading, that the unattached are less intellectually active than the attached, within each educational group. Further evidence of this is provided by information on the extent of part-time education amongst the attached and unattached. The former were considerably more likely to be experiencing some kind of part-time education than the unattached. Of course not all such education took place in the young people's spare time, some of it was covered by Day Release courses, but it serves to illustrate once again the fact that the unattached were not compensating for what they missed in clubs by being more active in other ways, including intellectually.

Table 7.8 Percentage of those not in full-time education who were receiving part-time education at the time of interview, by age, sex, school leaving age and attachment

School leaving age	Age	Male		Female		Total	
		Att'd	Unatt'd	Att'd	Unatt'd	Att'd	Unatt'd
15	14-16	37	19	17	12	29	15
	17-20	36	18	13	10	28	13
	T	37	18	14	10	28	14
16 or over	14-16	*	*	*	*	*	*
	17-20	55	44	29	23	45	32
	T	57	42	33	26	47	33
	Total	45	26	22	15	36	20

*Bases too small to provide reliable percentages

7.4 Leisure Activities young people would like to do if they could

Table R7.15

57% of the young people said there was something they would like to be able to do in their spare time which they currently could not do; 59% of the attached and 53% of the unattached.

By far the most desired of unavailable activities was sport, mentioned by 58%, but unlike the relative popularity of sports actually pursued, indoor sports like skating, judo or ten-pin bowling were most favoured, followed by open air pursuits, outdoor non-team games, and motorised sport, in that order. Team games were mentioned by only 3% of those who wanted to be able to do things they could not.

The next most desired of unavailable facilities, were opportunities for social activities such as dancing and meeting people, (20%). No other desired pastime was mentioned by as many as 10% of the young people, but opportunities for entertainment, active culture, learning to drive, travel and more Youth Clubs were each mentioned by over 5% of the sample.

Sports were particularly desired by boys, as social activities were by girls, especially the younger ones. Youth clubs were most often specified by the 14 to 16 year olds, driving lessons by the older boys, and active culture by the older late school

146

Table 7.9 Percentages of young people who would like more opportunities to carry on selected leisure activities, by sex, age, school leaving age and attachment – (those who would like more opportunities only)

Desired Activities	Attached								Unattached							
	SLA 15				SLA 16 or over				SLA 15				SLA 16 or over			
	Males		Females		Males		Females		Males		Females		Males		Females	
	14-16	17-20	14-16	17-20	14-16	17-20	14-16	17-20	14-16	17-20	14-16	17-20	14-16	17-20	14-16	17-20
Sports	67	62	61	57	64	57	59	56	57	62	54	47	52	63	50	63
Social	11	10	26	22	11	15	29	22	18	22	35	24	12	10	34	19
Entertainment	10	3	10	1	9	8	11	13	7	3	20	6	7	4	10	4
Youth Clubs	9	3	12	8	10	3	14	2	14	3	18	4	7	-	17	2
Active culture	3	7	1	7	4	9	9	11	2	3	2	13	2	6	6	7
Learn to drive	7	9	-	7	5	10	3	4	9	9	1	6	12	16	4	9
Travel	3	6	5	4	3	10	3	7	2	11	2	4	-	10	3	3
Attend classes	3	4	3	11	-	1	2	4	-	3	1	9	-	3	1	9
Domestic	-	1	2	3	-	-	3	2	-	-	6	11	2	-	5	6
Weighted Base	(95.5)	(148)	(92.5)	(88)	(177)	(289.5)	(276)	(202.5)	(56.5)	(89)	(86.5)	(157)	(42)	(70)	(93.5)	(115.5)

147

leavers. Facilities for following creative domestic activities, like dressmaking and beauty culture were mentioned by only 3% of the sample but by 8% of the older girl early leavers.

The attached did not differ from the unattached in the average number of additional activities they mentioned, (although of course they were rather more likely in the first place to say there were extra things they would like to be able to do which at present they could not) and there were few considerable and consistent differences between them. But on the whole the attached were more enthusiastic about more sport and the unattached about more opportunities for mixing. Of some interest, because it supports evidence about desired activities in clubs, is the fact that the unattached girl early leavers most often mentioned a wish for more opportunities to do or learn things like dressmaking and other domestic crafts.

7.5 Conclusions

The evidence presented suggests that the unattached led rather less active and varied leisure lives than the attached. In fact they were less physically, socially and intellectually energetic than the attached. The differences between the two groups in the case of sporting activities and social contacts were similar for both early and late school leavers. But the differences for intellectual and cultural pursuits were greatest for late school leavers. This suggests once again that attachment was most rewarding for the later school leavers, the experience enriched their lives more than those of the early leavers and this is presumably due to the different types of club each group tended to patronise.

In general, the attached showed rather more interest than the unattached in having more provided, so that it is not clear that the unattached were consciously dissatisfied with their less active lives, although of course, being evidently more lethargic they may have found it more difficult to think of ways in which their leisure lives could be improved.

Q.8

Table R7.10 Leisure Activities by age of leaving school, age and sex

	Age of leaving school																	
	15									Over 15								
	14-16 years			17-20 years			Total			14-16 years			17-20 years			Total		
Activity	Boys	Girls	Total	Boys	Girls	Total	Boys	Girls	Total	Boys	Girls	Total	Boys	Girls	Total	Boys	Girls	Total
	%	%	%	%	%	%	%	%	%	%	%	%	%	%	%	%	%	%
Active sport	83	51	67	67	47	57	74	48	61	87	67	77	72	61	67	80	64	72
Spectator sport	14	7	11	14	8	11	14	8	11	15	9	12	15	13	14	15	11	13
Domestic	16	35	25	14	52	34	15	53	34	28	52	40	17	51	33	22	52	37
Domestic creative	28	46	37	25	59	43	26	54	41	24	52	38	21	64	41	22	58	40
Active cultural	16	17	16	12	12	12	13	14	13	22	35	29	27	27	27	25	31	28
Other cultural/entertainment	54	73	64	64	70	68	60	71	66	56	73	65	76	81	78	66	77	72
Creative crafts	32	4	18	38	7	22	36	6	20	34	4	19	34	9	22	34	6	20
Social	67	86	77	91	92	92	82	90	86	68	90	80	94	94	94	81	92	87
Study	11	11	11	12	3	7	12	6	9	30	31	31	28	18	23	29	25	27
Reading	33	56	45	33	50	42	33	52	43	54	73	64	57	66	61	55	70	62
T.V./Radio	74	77	76	70	72	71	71	74	72	71	68	69	66	67	67	69	68	68
Outings/walks	41	48	44	45	43	44	43	45	44	51	56	54	49	53	51	50	55	52
Sedentary games	23	20	21	18	18	18	20	18	19	22	17	19	17	16	17	19	17	18
Other	33	41	37	24	35	30	27	37	32	42	46	44	35	43	39	38	45	41
Sit around/laze about etc.	5	6	6	11	8	10	9	7	8	4	6	5	13	10	12	9	8	8
Total percentages	607	653	641	619	656	642	615	661	638	671	742	709	691	741	715	681	745	711
Weighted Base: All young people	(307)	(316.5)	(623.5)	(471)	(522)	(993)	(778)	(838.5)	(1616.5)	(549)	(576)	(1125)	(584.5)	(523)	(1107.5)	(1133.5)	(1099)	(2232.5)

149

Q.8

Table R7.11 Leisure Activities by age of leaving school, age, sex and occupational status

Activity	Occupational Status	Age of leaving school																	
		15									Over 15								
		14-16 years			17-20 years			Total			14-16 years			17-20 years			Total		
		Boys	Girls	Total	Boys	Girls	Total	Boys	Girls	Total	Boys	Girls	Total	Boys	Girls	Total	Boys	Girls	Total
		%	%	%	%	%	%	%	%	%	%	%	%	%	%	%	%	%	%
Active sport	Full-time employment	81	46	64	67	51	59	71	50	61	77	48	62	75	54	65	75	53	65
	Full-time education	87	58	72	87	29	68	87	56	72	88	68	78	69	71	70	82	69	76
Spectator sport	Full-time employment	16	9	13	14	9	12	15	9	12	15	15	15	12	14	13	12	14	13
	Full-time education	12	6	9	10	-	7	12	6	9	15	8	12	20	14	17	16	10	13
Domestic	Full-time employment	15	50	32	14	53	33	14	52	33	13	48	32	16	54	33	15	53	33
	Full-time education	17	58	38	27	14	23	18	56	37	30	52	41	18	47	31	26	51	38
Domestic creative	Full-time employment	26	40	33	27	58	42	26	53	39	36	61	49	25	63	43	26	63	43
	Full-time education	33	51	42	-	57	18	29	52	40	23	51	38	14	63	36	21	54	37
Active cultural	Full-time employment	8	12	10	11	12	11	11	12	11	16	18	17	25	19	22	24	19	22
	Full-time education	24	23	23	13	-	9	23	22	22	23	37	30	31	40	35	25	38	31
Other cultural/entertainment	Full-time employment	60	81	71	64	74	69	63	76	70	82	82	82	73	79	76	74	80	77
	Full-time education	43	65	54	63	86	70	45	66	55	54	73	64	81	85	83	62	76	69
Creative crafts	Full-time employment	31	4	18	38	7	23	37	6	22	36	-	17	41	10	27	40	9	26
	Full-time education	34	4	19	47	-	32	36	4	20	35	4	19	25	8	18	32	5	19
Social	Full-time employment	72	90	81	91	92	91	86	91	88	82	97	90	94	94	94	93	95	94
	Full-time education	60	82	71	93	86	91	63	83	73	68	90	79	94	95	94	76	91	83
Study	Full-time employment	7	4	6	10	3	7	9	4	6	20	27	24	22	12	18	22	14	18
	Full-time education	17	20	18	70	14	52	22	20	21	31	32	32	38	31	35	35	32	33
Reading	Full-time employment	36	55	45	32	52	42	33	53	43	38	61	50	50	60	55	49	60	54
	Full-time education	30	57	44	57	86	66	32	59	46	55	74	65	64	74	69	58	74	66
T.V./Radio	Full-time employment	74	78	76	70	75	72	71	76	73	80	70	75	67	70	69	68	70	69
	Full-time education	74	76	76	73	57	68	74	76	75	71	67	69	64	63	63	69	66	67
Outings/Walks	Full-time employment	38	44	41	46	46	46	44	45	44	36	39	38	49	48	48	48	47	47
	Full-time education	45	53	49	30	29	30	43	52	48	52	57	55	50	61	55	51	58	55
Sedentary games	Full-time employment	20	16	18	18	16	17	18	16	17	16	18	17	14	19	16	15	19	16
	Full-time education	25	24	24	27	-	18	25	23	24	23	17	20	19	12	16	21	16	18
Other activities	Full-time employment	26	37	31	25	37	31	25	37	31	39	67	54	35	37	36	36	40	38
	Full-time education	40	46	43	20	-	14	38	44	41	43	45	44	34	51	42	40	46	43

continued

Table R7.11 (continued)

Q.8

Age of leaving school

Activity	Occupational Status	15									Over 15								
		14-16 years			17-20 years			Total			14-16 years			17-20 years			Total		
		Boys	Girls	Total	Boys	Girls	Total	Boys	Girls	Total	Boys	Girls	Total	Boys	Girls	Total	Boys	Girls	Total
		%	%	%	%	%	%	%	%	%	%	%	%	%	%	%	%	%	%
Sit around/ laze about etc.	Full-time employment	5	7	6	12	8	10	10	8	9	10	3	6	12	10	11	12	9	10
	Full-time education	5	3	4	7	–	4	5	3	4	4	6	5	16	8	12	7	7	7
Weighted Bases:	All young people in full-time employment	(165.5)	(161.5)	(327)	(441)	(422)	(863)	(606.5)	(583.5)	(1190)	(30.5)	(33)	(63.5)	(339.5)	(293.5)	(633)	(370)	(326.5)	(696.5)
	All young people in full-time education	(129.5)	(135.5)	(265)	(15)	(7)	(22)	(144.5)	(142.5)	(287)	(510.5)	(532)	(1042.5)	(219)	(181.5)	(400.5)	(729.5)	(713.5)	(1443)

151

Q.8

Table R7.12 Leisure Activities by age of leaving school, age, sex and attachment

Activity	Club Attachment	15 14-16 years Boys %	Girls %	Total %	15 17-20 years Boys %	Girls %	Total %	15 Total Boys %	Girls %	Total %	Over 15 14-16 years Boys %	Girls %	Total %	Over 15 17-20 years Boys %	Girls %	Total %	Over 15 Total Boys %	Girls %	Total %
Active sport	Attached	86	59	73	72	57	66	78	58	69	88	69	79	74	68	72	81	69	75
	Not attached	80	42	59	60	41	48	68	42	52	86	60	70	66	47	55	74	53	61
Spectator sport	Attached	18	8	13	17	12	15	17	10	14	15	10	13	15	14	15	15	12	14
	Not attached	9	7	8	10	6	8	10	7	8	11	6	8	14	11	12	13	9	10
Domestic	Attached	17	56	35	12	52	28	14	54	31	30	51	40	17	48	30	23	50	35
	Not attached	14	51	34	18	52	40	16	52	38	21	54	42	16	57	40	18	56	41
Domestic creative	Attached	26	43	34	27	59	40	27	52	38	24	52	38	21	64	40	23	58	38
	Not attached	32	49	41	22	59	46	26	56	44	22	53	42	21	63	45	22	58	44
Active Cultural	Attached	18	18	18	12	11	12	14	14	14	24	39	31	27	35	30	26	37	31
	Not attached	13	15	14	10	12	11	11	13	12	10	24	19	28	11	18	21	17	19
Other cultural/ entertainment	Attached	59	71	64	67	69	68	64	70	66	57	75	65	78	85	81	67	79	73
	Not attached	48	75	63	61	71	67	56	72	66	51	70	63	69	73	72	62	72	68
Creative crafts	Attached	36	6	22	38	8	26	37	7	24	33	4	19	33	10	23	33	7	21
	Not attached	27	2	13	39	6	18	34	4	16	44	2	17	34	7	18	38	5	18
Social	Attached	78	91	84	93	94	93	87	93	90	71	93	82	96	96	96	83	94	88
	Not attached	51	82	68	89	91	90	73	88	82	53	83	72	86	91	89	73	87	82
Study	Attached	12	14	13	14	3	10	13	8	11	32	31	31	30	23	26	31	27	29
	Not attached	10	8	9	9	3	5	10	4	6	24	33	29	21	10	14	22	20	21
Reading	Attached	34	60	46	36	49	41	35	54	43	55	74	64	59	71	64	57	73	64
	Not attached	31	52	42	30	51	43	30	51	43	46	70	61	48	58	54	47	63	57
T.V./Radio	Attached	76	78	77	69	67	68	72	72	72	72	66	69	65	65	65	68	66	67
	Not attached	71	76	74	71	74	73	71	75	73	67	72	70	71	72	72	70	72	71
Outings/ Walks	Attached	42	49	45	47	40	44	45	44	44	52	57	54	50	57	53	51	57	53
	Not attached	41	46	44	42	45	44	41	46	44	46	54	51	46	47	46	46	50	49
Sedentary games	Attached	23	19	21	17	19	18	19	19	19	22	20	21	17	15	16	20	18	19
	Not attached	23	20	22	19	16	17	21	18	19	21	9	13	16	20	19	18	15	16
Other	Attached	28	47	36	25	40	31	26	42	33	42	48	45	36	46	40	39	47	43
	Not attached	40	36	37	22	32	29	29	33	32	44	39	41	29	38	34	35	39	37
Laze about/ sit around etc.	Attached	6	4	5	10	7	9	9	6	7	4	6	5	13	10	12	8	8	8
	Not attached	4	8	6	13	9	10	9	8	9	4	7	6	14	9	11	10	8	9

Table R7.12 (continued)

Q.8

Activity	Age of leaving school																	
	15									Over 15								
	14-16 years			17-20 years			Total			14-16 years			17-20 years			Total		
Club Attachment	Boys	Girls	Total	Boys	Girls	Total	Boys	Girls	Total	Boys	Girls	Total	Boys	Girls	Total	Boys	Girls	Total
	%	%	%	%	%	%	%	%	%	%	%	%	%	%	%	%	%	%
Weighted Bases:																		
All young people who were attached to clubs	(181.5)	(160)	(341.5)	(289.5)	(191)	(480.5)	(471)	(351)	(822)	(464)	(425)	(889)	(451.5)	(339)	(790.5)	(915.5)	(764)	(1679.5)
All young people who were unattached	(125)	(156)	(281)	(181.5)	(331)	(512.5)	(306.5)	(487)	(793.5)	(85.5)	(151.5)	(237)	(133)	(184)	(317)	(218.5)	(335.5)	(554)

153

Table R7.13 Number of days has seen friends to talk to during past week, by age of leaving school, age, sex and attachment

Q.12(b) No. of days during past week has seen friends	Club Attachment	Age of leaving school																	
		15									Over 15								
		14-16 years			17-20 years			Total			14-16 years			17-20 years			Total		
		Boys	Girls	Total	Boys	Girls	Total	Boys	Girls	Total	Boys	Girls	Total	Boys	Girls	Total	Boys	Girls	Total
		%	%	%	%	%	%	%	%	%	%	%	%	%	%	%	%	%
None	Attached	2	2	2	2	8	5	2	5	4	-	1	1	3	3	3	2	2	2
	Unattached	2	5	4	10	8	9	7	7	7	6	2	4	5	14	10	5	9	7
One	Attached	3	2	3	4	6	5	3	5	4	2	2	2	2	3	3	2	2	2
	Unattached	5	6	5	4	9	8	4	8	7	-	3	2	6	1	3	4	2	3
Two	Attached	5	4	4	7	8	7	6	6	6	3	2	2	6	4	5	4	3	4
	Unattached	6	3	4	13	6	9	10	5	7	5	5	5	8	9	9	7	7	7
Three	Attached	4	4	4	4	8	6	4	6	5	4	6	5	7	7	7	5	6	6
	Unattached	3	8	6	13	8	10	9	8	8	4	5	4	7	7	7	6	6	6
Four	Attached	6	5	5	9	4	7	8	5	6	4	4	4	10	6	8	7	6	6
	Unattached	3	7	5	10	6	7	7	6	7	5	4	4	12	9	10	9	6	8
Five	Attached	11	12	11	11	19	14	11	16	13	15	18	17	10	15	12	13	17	14
	Unattached	24	16	19	9	17	14	15	16	16	25	24	24	15	21	18	19	22	21
Six	Attached	14	10	12	10	10	10	12	10	11	19	20	19	12	13	12	15	17	16
	Unattached	10	14	12	6	13	10	8	13	11	16	15	15	10	10	10	13	12	12
Seven	Attached	56	61	58	53	37	47	54	48	52	54	46	50	50	49	50	52	47	50
	Unattached	46	42	44	35	32	33	40	35	37	40	42	41	36	30	32	37	35	36
Total percentages:	Attached	100	100	100	100	100	100	100	100	100	100	100	100	100	100	100	100	100	100
	Unattached	100	100	100	100	100	100	100	100	100	100	100	100	100	100	100	100	100	100
Weighted Bases:	All young people who were attached to clubs	(181.5)	(160)	(341.5)	(289.5)	(191)	(480.5)	(471)	(351)	(822)	(464)	(425)	(889)	(451.5)	(339)	(790.5)	(915.5)	(764)	(1679.5)
	All young people who were unattached	(125)	(156)	(281)	(181.5)	(331)	(512.5)	(306.5)	(487)	(793.5)	(85.5)	(151.5)	(237)	(133)	(184)	(317)	(218.5)	(335.5)	(554)

Table R7.14 Number of days has got together with friends during past week, by age of leaving school, age, sex and attachment

Q. 12(c) No. of days during past week has got together with friends	Club Attachment	Age of leaving school																	
		15									Over 15								
		14-16 years			17-20 years			Total			14-16 years			17-20 years			Total		
		Boys	Girls	Total	Boys	Girls	Total	Boys	Girls	Total	Boys	Girls	Total	Boys	Girls	Total	Boys	Girls	Total
		%	%	%	%	%	%	%	%	%	%	%	%	%	%	%	%	%	%
None	Attached	14	12	13	12	26	17	12	20	16	17	20	18	12	18	14	14	19	16
	Unattached	30	32	31	23	32	29	26	32	30	41	37	38	19	31	26	28	34	31
One	Attached	9	12	11	14	20	16	12	16	14	18	20	19	12	21	16	15	20	18
	Unattached	9	15	13	14	22	19	14	20	17	12	13	13	24	16	19	19	15	16
Two	Attached	18	12	15	19	16	18	18	14	16	22	18	19	18	17	18	20	18	19
	Unattached	19	20	19	18	14	15	18	16	17	8	18	13	16	17	16	13	18	16
Three	Attached	12	19	15	15	12	13	14	15	14	17	17	17	16	15	16	16	16	16
	Unattached	9	6	7	10	12	11	10	10	10	11	7	8	16	12	14	14	10	12
Four	Attached	10	14	12	12	6	10	12	10	11	7	10	9	12	8	10	10	9	10
	Unattached	5	6	5	8	8	8	7	7	7	7	5	6	8	8	8	8	7	7
Five	Attached	12	11	12	8	8	8	10	9	10	8	7	7	10	7	9	9	7	8
	Unattached	12	6	9	9	4	6	10	5	7	5	7	6	8	8	8	7	7	7
Six	Attached	9	2	6	5	6	6	7	4	6	4	3	4	4	4	4	4	3	4
	Unattached	5	4	4	7	4	5	6	4	5	5	3	4	2	3	3	3	3	3
Seven	Attached	16	18	17	15	7	12	15	12	14	7	6	6	15	10	13	11	8	9
	Unattached	11	11	11	11	5	7	11	7	9	12	9	10	6	4	5	8	6	7
Total percentages:	Attached	100	100	100	100	100	100	100	100	100	100	100	100	100	100	100	100	100	100
	Unattached	100	100	100	100	100	100	100	100	100	100	100	100	100	100	100	100	100	100
Weighted Bases:	All young people who were attached to clubs	(181.5)	(160)	(341.5)	(289.5)	(191)	(480.5)	(471)	(351)	(822)	(464)	(425)	(889)	(451.5)	(339)	(790.5)	(915.5)	(764)	(1679.5)
	All young people who were unattached	(125)	(156)	(281)	(181.5)	(331)	(512.5)	(306.5)	(487)	(793.5)	(85.5)	(151.5)	(237)	(133)	(184)	(317)	(218.5)	(335.5)	(554)

Q.9

Table R7.15 Whether would like to do anything in spare time which finds difficult to do at the moment, by age of leaving school, age and attachment

Whether or not would like to do anything in spare time which finds difficult to do at the moment	Age of leaving school																	
	15									over 15								
	14-16 years			17-20 years			Total			14-16 years			17-20 years			Total		
	Attached	Unattached	Total	Attached	Unattached	Total	Attached	Unattached	Total	Attached	Unattached	Total	Attached	Unattached	Total	Attached	Unattached	Total
	%	%	%	%	%	%	%	%	%	%	%	%	%	%	%	%	%	%
Yes	55	51	53	49	48	48	52	49	50	62	58	61	62	58	61	62	58	61
No	45	49	47	51	52	52	48	51	50	38	42	39	38	42	39	38	42	39
Total percentages	100	100	100	100	100	100	100	100	100	100	100	100	100	100	100	100	100	100
Weighted base: All young people	(341.5)	(281)	(622.5)	(480.5)	(512.5)	(993)	(822)	(793.5)	(1615.5)	(889)	(237)	(1126)	(790.5)	(317)	(1107.5)	(1679.5)	(554)	(2233.5)

OTHER DIFFERENCES BETWEEN
THE ATTACHED AND UNATTACHED
AND MEMBERS OF DIFFERENT TYPES OF CLUB

The fact that the unattached led rather less active and varied leisure lives than the attached does not of itself mean that they found their free time any less satisfactory. They may have been people who preferred less excitement, who had less desire to mix with other young people or who were more family centred. In this chapter we shall examine differences of this kind between the various groups of young people in order to find out firstly which groups appear to have been the most fortunate in the ways we shall describe and secondly to attempt an assessment of the extent to which the existing facilities contributed to their good fortune.

8.1 The Measures Used

Three main aspects of the young people's lives were selected for study; their interest in people and events beyond their immediate experience, which together we have termed 'adventurousness', although this refers to a mental state rather than physical activity; their ability to make friends easily; and their relationships with the older generation, as represented by their family and older people in general. These areas were chosen both because exploratory work suggested that experience within them was related to the satisfaction young people felt with their lives, and because they appeared relevent to what the Youth Service and allied facilities do or might provide.

Details of the way in which the measures for each area were constructed are given in Appendix 4, but briefly the method was as follows: pilot work suggested not only the important areas themselves, but also the questions or statements which might be used to define a young person's position within each area, for example whether he found it easy or difficult to mix with other people. The responses to these questions and statements were then analysed by the statistical technique of factor analysis which identified cohesive groups of items, such that someone responding in a particular way to one of the items was also likely to respond in a similar way to another item in the same group. For example, taking as an illustration the measure of capacity for mixing, someone who said he found it easy to make new friends was also likely to agree that he found it easy to talk to others and to deny that he was rather a shy person, and so on. Each young person was then allotted a score according to the number of items in the group to which he had responded, in a predetermined way. Thus someone who denied that he found it easy to make friends, agreed that he was shy, not a good mixer, did not find it easy to talk to other people, and hated going to new places without friends received the highest score on this measure, whilst someone who responded in the opposite way to all these statements received the lowest score. The resulting scale was then divided into two, so that people with three or more difficulties (in this case) were counted as finding it difficult to mix, and those with 2 or less were regarded as not finding it difficult. In general the division was made at, or adjacent to, the mid way point.

8.2 Boredom

Unlike the measures discussed above which refer to all but one of the other measures used in this chapter, 'boredom' was assessed by the response to a single question, 'do you usually enjoy your spare time, or are you often bored.'

As suggested above, there is no reason to suppose that because the unattached experienced a less energetic leisure their lives were less satisfactory, but the fact is that they more often reported boredom than the attached.

Table 8.1 **Percentage of 14-20 year olds who were often bored in their spare time, by sex, age, school leaving age and attachment**

School leaving Age	Age	Attached			Unattached			Total		
		M	F	T	M	F	T	M	F	T
15	14-16	25	42	33	38	46	42	30	44	37
	17-20	20	37	27	27	35	32	23	36	30
	T	22	39	29	31	39	36	26	39	32
16 or over	14-16	20	21	21	28	37	34	22	26	24
	17-20	19	13	17	18	27	23	19	18	18
	T	20	18	19	22	32	28	20	22	21
Total		20	25	22	28	36	32	22	29	26

Note: For bases see table R8.24 .

As the report on Young School Leavers (Morton-Williams and Finch, 1968) showed, early leavers are more likely to report boredom than later leavers, and boredom is evidently particularly associated with the early teens and being a girl. But within most groups, the unattached more often said they were often bored in their spare time. At the two extremes, 46% of the younger

158

unattached girls leaving school at 15 said they were often bored, but only 13% of the older attached girls giving a school leaving age of 16 or over.

The differences between the attached and unattached vary in degree and in two cases, (the older girl early leavers, and the older boy late leavers) there is a slight reversal of the relationship. Considering the variety of experiences which attachment subsumes, it is perhaps remarkable that such a relationship appears at all. This is illustrated by the relationship between prevalence of boredom and type of club, shown in Table 8.2. The least often bored were those who went to interest centred clubs, and amongst the early leavers, who rarely went to interest centred groups, it was sports clubs which evidently provided the strongest antidote to boredom, or alternatively which attracted those least prone to boredom. But the people who attended places called Youth Clubs were only a little less often bored than the unattached.

Table 8.2 Percentage of young people who were often bored, by age, school leaving age and type of club (first or only club mentioned)

School leaving age	Age	Type of Club				Unattached
		Sports	Social	Interest-centred	Youth	
15	14-16	24	(34)	(33)	37	42
	17-20	19	29	(29)	34	32
	T	21	30	(31)	36	36
16 or over	14-16	22	19	16	25	34
	17-20	18	21	13	18	23
	T	20	20	15	23	28
Total		20	25	16	28	32

NOTE: 1. Percentages in brackets are based on less than 50 cases
2. For bases see table R8.25

8.3 Adventurousness

Is it true that the unattached in some sense preferred a less exciting life than the attached? Under the heading of adventurousness three measures were included, which were composed of the following items

(1) Attitudes towards varied experiences
I'd like to have the opportunity to get to know another country really well.

I'd like to make friends with people who have different
   attitudes and experiences from myself.
I'd like to have all sorts of different friends.
As far as holidays are concerned, I'd like to explore a
   different place each year.

(2) Social Conservatism
I like to spend my spare time with the same group of people.
I don't mind what I do in my spare time as long as I'm with
   friends.
I prefer to stay where I know people rather than go to new
   places.
I prefer to do the things I know about rather than learn com-
   pletely new things.

(3) Interest in wider world
I like to hear what's going on in the world.
Regularly watches documentary/current affairs programmes.
Wider interest in the news (i.e. interested in more than local
   news, crime, scandal or gossip).
Stayed on later or left school to get a better education.

On all three measures the unattached as a group appeared to
be rather more timid or inward-looking than the attached, being
less enthusiastic about varied experiences, preferring the company of known people and having less interest in the wider world.
But in the two latter cases the differences between school leaving
age groups were greater than differences between the attached
and unattached. That is to say the early leavers were less
socially adventurous and considerably less interested in the
wider world than the later leavers, whether attached or not.
(Table 8.3).

Table 8.3 Adventurousness and Attachment

(a) Percentage of young people who were less keen on varied experiences, by
   age, sex, school leaving age and attachment.

School leaving age	Age	Attached			Unattached			Total		
		M	F	T	M	F	T	M	F	T
15	14-16	36	30	33	42	39	40	38	34	36
	17-20	30	27	28	39	33	35	33	30	32
	T	32	28	30	40	35	37	35	32	33
16 or over	14-16	35	24	30	45	32	36	36	26	31
	17-20	29	19	24	41	29	34	31	25	27
	T	32	22	27	43	30	35	34	26	29
Total		32	24	28	41	33	36	34	28	31

(b) Percentage of young people who were more socially conservative by age, sex, school leaving age and attachment.

School leaving age	Age	Attached			Unattached			Total		
		M	F	T	M	F	T	M	F	T
15	14-16	38	35	37	47	38	43	42	37	39
	17-20	21	26	30	39	32	35	34	30	32
	T	34	30	32	43	35	38	37	33	35
16 or over	14-16	28	20	24	46	29	35	32	22	26
	17-20	20	15	18	22	22	22	20	17	19
	T	24	18	21	32	25	28	25	20	23
Total		27	22	25	38	31	34	30	25	28

(c) Percentage of young people who were less interested in the wider world, by age, sex, school leaving age and attachment.

School leaving age	Age	Attached			Unattached			Total		
		M	F	T	M	F	T	M	F	T
15	14-16	39	50	44	42	52	47	40	51	46
	17-20	30	37	33	33	39	36	31	39	34
	T	33	43	37	37	42	40	36	42	39
16 or over	14-16	17	24	21	26	29	28	19	26	22
	17-20	12	15	14	22	19	21	14	17	16
	T	15	20	17	24	26	24	16	21	19
Total		21	27	24	31	35	33	24	30	27

NOTE: For bases see table R8.24

Again the type of club which the attached used made some difference. Those who belonged to undifferentiated clubs, and youth clubs in particular were on the whole rather less keen on varied experiences, tended to prefer the company of known people and to have little interest in the wider world. Conversely, members of sports and especially interest centred clubs were more adventurous. The only noteworthy exception was that sports club members who were late school leavers were less keen than others on varied experiences. (Table 8.4).

In the case of interest in the wider world, youth club members were evidently no more interested than the unattached.

161

It seems therefore that whilst the attached are less inclined to boredom and more to adventurousness, in the sense described, than the unattached, it is those who go to sports or interest-centred clubs who are least bored and most enterprising.

Table 8.4 Adventurousness and type of club attended (first or only club mentioned)

(a) Percentage of young people who were less keen on varied experiences by age, school leaving age and type of club (first or only club mentioned).

| School leaving age | Age | Type of club | | | | Unattached |
		Sports	Social	Interest	Youth	
15	14-16	28	(26)	(38)	38	40
	17-20	23	33	(12)	30	35
	T	25	32	(24)	35	37
16 or over	14-16	33	22	29	32	36
	17-20	30	26	22	20	34
	T	31	25	25	28	35
Total		29	29	25	31	36

(b) Percentage of young people who were more socially conservative by age, school leaving age and type of club (first or only club mentioned).

| School leaving age | Age | Type of club | | | | Unattached |
		Sports	Social	Interest	Youth	
15	14-16	27	(47)	(33)	38	43
	17-20	31	30	(16)	34	35
	T	30	33	(24)	37	38
16 or over	14-16	27	26	20	26	35
	17-20	17	24	12	20	22
	T	22	24	17	24	28
Total		24	29	16	30	34

(c) Percentage of young people less interested in the wider world, by age, school leaving age and type of club (first or only club mentioned).

School leaving age	Age	Type of club				Unattached
		Sports	Social	Interest	Youth	
15	14-16	39	(42)	(28)	50	47
	17-20	27	36	(33)	33	36
	T	32	37	(31)	42	40
16 or over	14-16	20	27	14	28	28
	17-20	13	14	12	17	21
	T	16	18	13	24	24
Total		21	27	15	32	33

NOTE: 1. Percentages in brackets are based on less than 50 cases
2. For bases see table R8.25

8.4 Capacity for mixing

It was shown in the last chapter that the unattached had fewer contacts with friends than the attached. Ideally we should have tried to discover whether they preferred a less sociable life. But because of the limited interview time which could be devoted to each area, we concentrated on the extent to which people found it easy or difficult to make friends. The items used in the measure were:

I find it easy to make new friends.
I'm rather a shy person, in fact.
I'm not what you call a good mixer.
I find it easy to talk to other people when I first meet them.
I hate going to new places like a club unless I have friends with me.

44% of the young people were scored as having difficulties on three out of the 5 items included, and the girl early leavers most often reported difficulties. The greatest difference however was between the attached and the unattached. 40% of those who went to clubs found mixing difficult, but 51% of those who did not.

Amongst the attached, social ease varied with the type of club, but in this case it was those attached to interest-centred clubs who were most often unsure of themselves. The early leavers who belonged to sports clubs least often had difficulties in mixing, but the late leavers who went to the undifferentiated (youth and social) clubs were least bothered by problems of making friends.

163

Table 8.5 Percentage of young people who found it more difficult to mix, by age, school leaving age, sex and attachment

School leaving age	Age	Attached			Unattached			Total		
		M	F	T	M	F	T	M	F	T
15	14-16	41	47	44	61	56	58	49	52	50
	17-20	32	43	36	45	51	49	37	48	43
	T	36	45	40	51	53	52	42	49	46
16 or over	14-16	46	42	44	56	52	52	48	45	46
	17-20	35	38	36	49	45	46	38	40	39
	T	41	40	40	52	48	49	43	42	43
Total		39	42	40	52	51	51	42	46	44

NOTE: For bases see table R8.24

Table 8.6 Percentage of young people who found it more difficult to mix by age, school leaving age and type of club (first or only club mentioned)

School leaving age	Age	Type of Club				Unattached
		Sports	Social	Interest	Youth	
15	14-16	41	(45)	(48)	43	58
	17-20	32	42	(29)	34	49
	T	36	43	(38)	40	52
16 or over	14-16	43	43	51	37	52
	17-20	35	30	41	32	46
	T	39	34	46	35	49
Total		38	38	45	37	51

NOTE: 1. Percentages in brackets are based on less than 50 cases
2. For bases see table R8.25

8.5 Family Relationships

Family relationships have many components and of these we were able to select aspects of only two which we believed were relevent to the satisfactoriness of spare time and possibly to attachment and which we could make some attempt to measure in a survey of this type. The first component was family integration and here we were interested in the extent to which the young person could turn to his family for emotional support and interest. The second was that of parental restrictiveness, and in this case it was the parent's attempts to limit or direct the young person's activities which seemed important. Originally we

164

aimed to examine these areas from both the young person's and
his parents' view points, but in the event it was possible to
construct measures of the young person's perception of the
salience of his family and of his parents' restrictiveness. But in
the case of parents the task proved more difficult, and it was
only feasible to examine narrow aspects of each relationship,
specifically, the parent's anxieties about firstly the adequacy of
the young person's social life, and secondly the possibility of his
misbehaving. Clearly parental interest in a child and his control
have many more constituents than these.

(a) Family Integration

It seemed possible that the unattached might be more closely
integrated with their families than the attached and therefore
feel less desire for contacts outside the home.

The measure used was constructed from the following items:

As a family we are always discussing things together.
My parents are always interested to know what I've been doing.
I would always ask my parents' advice before taking a really
    big decision.
Parents understand you more than anyone else does.
Most enjoys spending spare time with family.

It seems possible that in part this is a measure of the person's
dependence on his family.

In fact there was little difference between the attached and
unattached, and the greatest difference was between the older
late school leavers and the rest. Specifically the 17 to 20 year
olds giving a school leaving age above the minimum were least
often closely integrated with their families. This strongly
suggests that one of the main components of a lack of integration
was the young person's independence rather than parental lack

Table 8.7 Percentage of young people who were less closely integrated within
their family by age, sex and school leaving age

School leaving age	Age	Attached			Unattached			Total		
		M	F	T	M	F	T	M	F	T
15	14-16	41	31	36	45	38	41	43	34	38
	17-20	42	42	42	41	34	37	42	37	39
	T	42	37	40	43	35	38	42	36	39
16 or over	14-16	38	35	37	33	37	33	37	35	36
	17-20	53	46	50	57	43	49	54	45	50
	T	46	40	43	48	40	43	46	40	43
Total		44	39	42	45	37	40	44	38	41

NOTE: For bases see table R8.24

of interest. This is firstly because parents of late leavers are usually most actively concerned about their children's lives (e.g. Morton-Williams and Finch, 1968, p.115 and 126), and secondly because it was this older group of later leavers who were most adventurous.

This interpretation helps to explain the small differences between members of different kinds of clubs, for in this case it was members of interest centred clubs who were least often closely integrated or most independent.

But there is here no evidence that the unattached compensated for their lack of contact with organised groups by being more family centred.

Table 8.8 **Percentage of young people who were less closely integrated with their families by type of club (first or only club mentioned)**

School leav-ing age	Age	Type of Club				Unattached
		Sports	Social	Interest	Youth	
15	14-16	27	(42)	(5)	41	41
	17-20	41	44	(42)	40	37
	T	36	44	(25)	41	38
16 or over	14-16	36	40	41	38	33
	17-20	50	47	58	53	49
	T	43	45	48	43	43
Total		41	44	46	42	40

NOTE: 1. Percentages in brackets are based on less than 50 cases
2. For bases see table R8.25

(b) Parental Restrictiveness

The extent to which the parents were felt to limit the young person's activities seemed likely to influence whether or not he used a club, and possibly the type of club he used, although it is also evident that two equally authoritarian parents may differ in their ideas of what their respective children should do.

The items included in the measure were:

My parents quite understand that I can make up my own mind about things.
My parents realise I need more freedom at my age.
I sometimes feel my parents are a bit too strict.
Informant feels he should decide about how to behave.
Number of items parent makes rules about.

166

Overall there was little difference in the extent of parental restrictiveness reported by the attached and the unattached. But whilst restrictive parents of younger early school leavers evidently tended to encourage or induce attachment, restrictive parents of younger late leavers were apparently more inclined to discourage it. But the greatest difference not surprisingly was between the younger children and the 17 to 20 year olds. Two and a half times as many of the younger than the older groups reported restrictions.

Table 8.9 Percentage of young people who felt their parents were more restrictive, by school leaving age, age, sex and attachment

School leaving age	Age	Attached			Unattached			Total		
		M	F	T	M	F	T	M	F	T
15	14-16	54	54	54	43	49	46	50	51	51
	17-20	18	25	21	20	19	19	19	22	20
	T	32	38	35	29	29	29	31	33	32
16 or over	14-16	44	45	45	49	50	50	45	46	46
	17-20	19	18	19	20	16	18	19	17	18
	T	32	33	33	31	31	32	32	33	29
	Total	32	35	33	30	30	30	31	33	32

NOTE: For bases see table R8.24

Since it seems probable that parental pressure would be used to induce membership of various types of club, according to which the parent thought most suitable, it is surprising to find that except amongst the younger early leavers it was the youth club members who most often reported restrictiveness, and the members of social clubs least. Is this really because restrictive parents tend to encourage youth club rather than other attachments, or is a young person's attachment to a youth club likely to activate authoritarianism in his parents? Because it seems unlikely that restrictive parents on the whole would tend to favour youth clubs rather than say a football team or an academic club, it seems possible that membership of youth clubs may have some effect on parental behaviour, and some evidence for this is provided in the next section. However, as the measure used is of parental restrictiveness as perceived by the young person, it is also possible that certain types of attachment sensitize young people to this aspect of parental behaviour, so that, what is acceptable to members of interest centred clubs is irksome to Youth Club members.

Table 8.10   Percentage of young people who felt their parents were more restrictive by school leaving age, age and type of club (first or only club mentioned)

School leaving age	Age	Type of Club				Unattached
		Sports	Social	Interest-centred	Youth	
15	14-16	62	(50)	(62)	54	46
	17-20	14	21	(25)	26	19
	T	31	27	(42)	43	29
16 or over	14-16	42	46	43	47	50
	17-20	19	17	19	26	18
	T	31	26	33	40	32
	Total	31	26	34	42	30

NOTE: 1. Percentages in brackets are based on less than 50 cases
2. For bases see table R8.25

(c) Parental Anxieties
(i) About antisocial activities/loss of control

This was a measure of the worries of the mother about her child doing something socially unacceptable or which might get him into trouble and included the following items:

I worry about him (trying) drinking.
I am sometimes afraid he might get into trouble.
I worry in case he tries taking drugs.
Number of items of behaviour parent has to say anything about.
Would like advice about child.
I am anxious in case he is attacked.

For technical reasons the analysis had to be limited to parents with only one child in the sample.

The parents of the younger children were more often anxious than the parents of the 17 to 20 year olds, perhaps because they felt more reponsible for controlling their children's behaviour. But the parents of the younger early leavers were considerably more often worried than the parents of younger late leavers. However there was no difference between parents of the attached and unattached.

The parents of children who went to undifferentiated clubs, and particularly Youth Clubs, were more prone to anxiety than parents of members of other types of club or of the unattached. This suggests that the restrictiveness experienced particularly by Youth Club members may in part be a result of the anxiety their parents feel about the way they may behave. It does seem

Table 8.11 Parental anxiety about loss of control, by sex, age and school leaving age of child. (Parents with only one child in the sample)

School leaving Age	Age	Attached			Unattached			Total		
		M	F	T	M	F	T	M	F	T
15	14-16	37	45	41	41	41	41	39	44	41
	17-20	29	25	28	26	26	26	28	25	26
	T	32	35	33	32	31	32	32	33	32
16 or over	14-16	28	31	29	22	31	28	27	31	29
	17-20	20	24	22	20	21	20	20	23	21
	T	25	28	26	21	26	24	24	27	26
Total		27	30	28	27	29	28	27	30	28

NOTE: For bases see table R8.26

as likely that Youth Club attachment in some way arouses this anxiety, as that children who stimulate anxiety join Youth Clubs. A possible explanation would be that young people who go to undifferentiated clubs, and Youth Clubs in particular, perhaps already a little wild in their behaviour because they lack any focus for their mental energies, often find there little effective encouragement to concentrate their minds constructively and so are peculiarly open to suggestions from other members that they should behave in ways disturbing to adults. Even if they never actually do so, they may worry their parents by talking as if they might. This, however, is a very tentative explanation.

Table 8.12 Parental anxiety about loss of control, by sex, age, school leaving age and type of club to which child belongs (parents with only one child in the sample and first or only club mentioned)

School leaving age	Age	Type of club				Unattached
		Sports	Social	Interest	Youth	
15	14-16	(30)	(55)	...	44	41
	17-20	20	29	...	(39)	26
	T	23	35	...	42	32
16 or over	14-16	29	(40)	20	36	28
	17-20	24	20	17	31	20
	T	26	27	19	34	24
Total		26	31	20	37	28

NOTE: 1. Figures in brackets are based on less than 50 cases
2. . . . bases too small to use
3. For bases see table R8.27

(ii) About the young person's social life

Another type of anxiety a mother may have about her child is
that his social life is inadequate, and the following items were
used in constructing a measure of such anxiety:

I wish he had more friends.
Thinks child does not meet enough of the kind of people she
likes him to mix with.
I wish there were more for him to do round here.
On the whole child is not the sort of person who makes friends
easily.
Is not happy about the amount of time child spends at home.

Again parents of younger children were more often worried
than parents of older children and the parents of early school
leavers were more prone to anxiety than parents of later leavers.
But the greatest difference was between the parents of the attached
children and parents of the unattached. 25% of parents of the
attached were scored as anxious, but 39% of parents of the
unattached.

Table 8.13 Parental anxiety about young person's social life by age, sex
and school leaving age of young person (those with only one
child in sample)

School leaving Age	Age	Attached			Unattached			Total		
		M	F	T	M	F	T	M	F	T
15	14-16	30	33	31	59	50	53	43	42	42
	17-20	25	30	27	28	39	34	26	36	31
	T	26	31	28	40	43	42	32	38	35
16 and over	14-16	28	31	29	37	51	46	29	36	33
	17-20	15	15	15	20	32	27	16	21	18
	T	22	25	23	27	42	36	23	30	26
	Total	23	26	25	35	42	39	26	33	30

NOTE: For bases see table R8.26

In this case, the type of club to which the attached young
people went made little difference. Compared with parents of
the unattached, the parents of children who went to any kind of
club were much less likely to be worried about the adequacy of
their child's social life.

It is worth looking in more detail at parents' anxieties to see
which problems most concerned them. Mothers most often
expressed anxiety about circumstances or hazards which were
largely beyond the control of their children. The most common
worry, for example, was that the child might be involved in an
accident, this was followed by concern that there was not enough

Table 8.14 Parental anxiety about young person's social life by age, school leaving age and type of club to which young person is attached. (Parents with only one child in sample and first or only club mentioned)

School leaving Age	Age	Type of Club				Unattached
		Sports	Social	Interest	Youth	
15	14-16	(24)	(25)	. . .	29	53
	17-20	20	25	. . .	(30)	34
	T	22	25	. . .	29	42
16 and over	14-16	31	(34)	30	24	46
	17-20	15	23	11	19	27
	T	23	27	23	22	36
	Total	23	26	24	25	39

NOTE: 1. Percentages in brackets are based on less than 50 cases
2. . . . bases too small to use
3. For bases see table R8.27

for the child to do in the area, and thirdly by the fear that the child would be attacked. And worries about socially unacceptable behaviour or social isolation were much less prevalent.

Except for the wish that their child had more friends, all anxieties were more frequent amongst working class than middle class parents. In fact in all other cases anxieties were least prevalent amongst the Registrar General's class I and II parents and most prevalent amongst Class IV and V and the unemployed. In particular, the least skilled parents were considerably more often worried than middle class parents about there not being enough to do in the area, that their child would be attacked, and that he or she would get into trouble. Perhaps this is a realistic assessment of the hazards of the bleaker working class areas.

Comparatively few parents (13%) actually felt they needed advice about their child's problems, although, of course, in absolute numbers, 13% of the parents of all adolescents is no mean figure. That is to say, if an advisory service were to be provided, as these parents evidently needed, the facilities required would be considerable, although some of the problems mentioned were ones for which, theoretically, sources of advice already exist. The most frequently mentioned problems for which advice was desired were difficulties of communication, worries about jobs, relationships with boy or girl friends, concern about the frequency or infrequency of the child's going out, and doubt about how permissive or restrictive the parent should be. The general impression is that the most pervasive parental concern was uncertainty about how they (the parents)

Table 8.15 Percentage of parents who sometimes worried, by Registrar General's Socio-economic Class

Anxiety	Registrar General's Socio-economic Class						Total
	I & II	III non-manual	All non-manual	III manual	IV, V or unemployed	All manual	
Wishes there were more for child to do in area	54	59	56	70	74	71	66
Wishes he had more friends	32	29	30	26	32	28	29
Afraid he might get into trouble	29	31	30	36	40	37	35
Worries in case he is in accident	68	69	68	73	76	74	72
Worries in case he takes drugs	18	21	19	21	22	21	21
Anxious in case he is attacked	47	54	50	54	60	56	54
Worries about him drinking	17	21	19	20	25	22	21
Weighted base: All parents	(499)	(406.5)	(905.5)	(1081)	(581.5)	(1662.5)	(2592)*

*The total includes 24 parents who gave an inadequate description of their work

should behave. But whether this is a phenomenon peculiar to the present time or is characteristic of some parents during their child's transition to adulthood, it is not possible to say. The problems about which advice should already be available are those concerning jobs, education and mental or physical health, which accounted for 29% of all the problems mentioned.

Table 8.16 Problems mentioned by parents who said they would like to be able to obtain advice about their child(ren), by Registrar General's Socio-economic Class. (Percentages of all problems)

Problems for which advice needed	Registrar General's Social Class						Total
	I & II	III non-manual	All non-manual	III manual	IV, V or unemployed	All manual	
Difficulty of communication	9	18	13	22	20	21	18
Jobs	19	16	17	12	12	12	14
Boy/girl friends, sex	7	8	8	12	19	14	12
Going out	7	14	11	9	13	10	11
How permissive to be	11	12	11	12	5	9	10
Discipline	10	10	10	5	10	7	8
Education	18	8	13	6	2	5	7
Type of friends	2	8	5	6	11	8	7
Difficulty in making friends	9	2	6	6	1	4	5
Mental health	6	2	4	4	6	4	4
Drugs	2	8	5	3	6	4	4
Getting into trouble	6	4	5	2	5	3	4
Money	-	12	6	3	1	2	3
Physical health	-	-	-	4	6	4	3
How spends spare time	-	-	-	4	4	4	3
Weighted base: Parents who wanted advice	(53)	(51)	(104)	(137.5)	(83.5)	(221)	(329)*

*The total includes 4 parents who gave an inadequate description of their work

172

8.6 Attitudes towards older people in general

Finally, because this was a subject on which many young people expressed opinions during the exploratory phase, and because it seemed possible that attachment might play some part in either dividing or uniting the generations, we sought the young people's views on 'older people'.

In this case the items used allowed young people to express considerable hostility to older people if they chose, and it is therefore surprising that 40% of the sample agreed with four or more of the 6 following statements:

The older generation go on so much about young people that
   it makes me sick.
Older people irritate me with the things they say.
Older people often blame young people for things that aren't
   really their fault.
Whatever age you are older people treat you like a child
Older people often say one thing and do another.
You usually reject your parents' advice at my age.

The younger children expressed more hostility than 17 to 20 year olds, and the early school leavers were considerably more hostile than those who gave a school leaving age of 16 or over. Possibly this is because it is these groups whom adults feel most obliged to restrict, although as far as parents are concerned this appears to be clearly true only of the younger group (see Table 8.11). Some evidence for this explanation of the difference between early and later school leavers comes again from the Morton-Williams and Finch study (1968), which showed that the early leavers were more likely to have their school behaviour rated as unacceptable by their teachers than later leavers. This suggests that the 'generation gap' as instanced by mutual disapproval or hostility is a phenomenon largely characteristic of relations between the early leavers and older people in authority.

Table 8.17 Percentage of young people who were hostile to older people, by age, school leaving age, sex and attachment

School leaving Age	Age	Attached			Unattached			Total		
		M	F	T	M	F	T	M	F	T
15	14-16	55	57	56	55	46	50	55	53	53
	17-20	45	36	41	43	40	41	44	38	41
	T	49	45	48	48	42	44	49	43	46
16 and over	14-16	41	36	39	46	37	40	42	37	39
	17-20	32	25	29	29	35	32	31	29	30
	T	37	31	34	36	36	36	36	33	35
Total		41	36	38	43	40	41	41	37	40

NOTE: For bases see table R8.24

173

There was no difference in the extent of hostility between the attached and the unattached.

Although the differences are not large youth club members, particularly the older early leavers, were more often hostile towards older people than those who went to other kinds of club, in particular interest centred clubs, and more hostile than the unattached. This could be explained in several ways. For example young people who are antagonistic towards their elders

Table 8.18 Percentage of young people who were hostile to older people, by age, school leaving age, and type of club, (first or only club mentioned)

School leaving age	Age	Sports club	Social club	Interest centred club	Youth club	Unattached
15	14-16	56	(47)	(62)	58	50
	17-20	34	45	(29)	48	41
	T	42	46	(38)	54	44
16 or over	14-16	43	41	32	44	40
	17-20	31	34	26	32	32
	T	37	36	29	40	36
Total		39	41	31	46	41

NOTE: For bases see table R8.25

may opt for youth clubs, because the name suggests the absence of older people, as one girl of 16 said; 'In a Youth Club you would all be of a similar age, it doesn't matter how you dress, how you dance, there'll be no one criticising you all the time'. They may experience more authoritarianism from the youth leaders, than people who go to interest centred clubs are subjected to, though we have no evidence for this. Or there may be less provided in youth clubs to serve as a link with older people, either as a subject of common interest, or to bring the two generations into contact with one another. Also, as suggested earlier, youth clubs may possibly stimulate behaviour which encourages mutual antagonism.

Another possible and quite different explanation is that Youth Clubs foster a healthy objectivity in young people's view of older people. The Youth Club experience, in other words, may comparatively speaking, free young people from the conventions which require them say, to acquiesce in adult hypocrisy or submit to adult authoritarianism. But to test any of these possibilities would necessitate other measures than those we used.

8.7 Happiness

In addition to the other measures discussed, the young people were also asked: 'Taking all things together, how would you say things are nowadays, would you say you are very happy, fairly happy or not very happy?' This is the scale used and explored by Bradburn (1969), working in the United States, who concluded that 'direct self reports of happiness have considerable validity'. The present sample was of a younger group than any of the people he interviewed, but in accordance with the inverse relationship between age and happiness which he revealed, very few (2%) of the young people described themselves as 'not very happy', and the useful distinction appears to be between those who were 'very happy' and those who were 'fairly happy'.

But, in contrast with the general age trend shown by Bradburn, there was a small increase in the proportion claiming to be very happy, with increasing age. Girls more often claimed great happiness than boys.

Table 8.19 Percentage of young people who were 'very happy' by attachment, school leaving age, age and sex

School leaving age	Age	Attached			Unattached			Total		
		M	F	T	M	F	T	M	F	T
15	14-16	41	45	43	29	43	37	36	44	40
	17-20	45	43	44	39	51	47	43	48	46
	T	43	44	44	35	49	44	40	47	43
16 or over	14-16	41	46	43	31	37	35	39	44	42
	17-20	40	55	46	41	45	43	40	51	46
	T	40	50	45	37	42	40	40	47	44
	Total	41	48	45	36	46	40	40	47	44

NOTE: For bases see table R8.24

School leaving age made no difference to overall assessments of happiness. This was unexpected and again differs from Bradburn's findings, which showed the more educated to be happier than the less educated. It may be that the effects of a longer education on feelings of well-being do not appear until after the age of 20.

Most groups of the attached were more likely to say they were very happy than corresponding groups of the unattached. The exceptions were the girl early school leavers, in particular the older group, amongst whom the unattached more often said they were very happy; and the older late leaving boys who were just as likely to be very happy, whether or not they were attached.

The attached amongst the 17 to 20 year old girl early leavers, were of course a minority group and it may be that some of them went to clubs because of the relative unsatisfactoriness of other aspects of their lives, rather than because of any positive benefits they derived from membership; a possibility supported by some earlier evidence (see Tables 4.6, 8.1 and 8.7). In the case of the older late leaving boys there appears to be no explanation for the lack of difference between the two groups, which is unexpected.

Overall, social clubs included the highest proportion of very happy people. Amongst the 14 to 16 year olds, early leaving children who went to sports or social clubs, but late leavers who went to Youth Clubs were most often 'very happy'. For the older people social clubs boasted the greatest percentage of 'very happy' members amongst both early and late school leavers, and the proportion in Youth Clubs was rather low. But, in general, members of interest-centred clubs were least likely to be very happy. Perhaps this is a result of their rather poorer social relationships.

Table 8.20 Percentage of young people who were 'very happy' by type of club, school leaving age and age, (first or only club mentioned only)

School leaving age	Age	Sports club	Social club	Interest club	Youth club	Unattached
15	14-16	47	(47)	(29)	41	37
	17-20	44	47	46	35	47
	T	45	47	(38)	39	44
16 or over	14-16	41	42	42	46	35
	17-20	50	53	37	40	43
	T	46	50	40	44	40
	Total	45	48	39	42	40

NOTE: For bases see table R8.25

It cannot be said then that from the point of view of their members' happiness, Youth Clubs are doing less well on the whole than other clubs, at least as far as the younger children are concerned. But amongst early leavers, Youth Club members less often claimed to be very happy than those who used other kinds of clubs.

Bradburn showed that psychological well being has many correlates, and it would be naive to expect that an overall rating of happiness, any more than the other measures considered, was crucially influenced either by attachment or attachment to a particular type of club, although both experiences evidently play some part for some people in determining their

outlook and state of mind. But since we have shown earlier
that there is some relationship between attachment, and of
various kinds, to the measures of social integration used,
which indicates that clubs do or could affect these aspects of
young people's lives, it would seem fruitful to relate the earlier
measures to overall happiness. The reason for doing this is
that if these aspects are related to happiness, then there is
more reason to suppose that organisations which help to increase,
for example, adventurousness or social ease, are also helping
to increase happiness.

In fact, the more adventurous, on the whole, did more often
claim to be very happy, than the less adventurous, although the
differences were very small (Table 8.21). But much greater
differences were apparent for the measures of social relationships (Table 8.22). Those who found it more difficult to mix,
who perceived their parents as more restrictive, were less well
integrated with their families or were more hostile to older
people, were considerably less likely to rate themselves as
'very happy' than other young people. The greatest difference
was between the 14 to 16 year olds who were more integrated
with their families and those who were less so. And it seems
likely that, at this age, being able to rely on the support of
one's family is a more important influence on happiness than
any of the other aspects of life measured. But for the 17 to
20 year olds, being able to mix easily was equally important
to happiness. Although in both cases it is also possible to
suppose that very happy young people either generate good
relationships or are more apt to perceive relationships as good.

This measure of psychological well-being we used is crude.
Bradburn, for example, located two dimensions of happiness;

Table 8.21 Happiness related to adventurousness

(a) **Percentage of young people who were 'very happy' by attitude
towards varied experiences, age and school leaving age**

School leaving age	Age	Less keen on varied experiences	More keen on varied experiences
15	14-16	37	42
	17-20	45	46
	T	42	44
16 or over	14-16	39	43
	17-20	42	47
	T	41	45
	Total	41	45

(b) **Percentage of young people who were 'very happy' by social conservatism, age and school leaving age**

School leaving age	Age	More socially conservative	Less socially conservative
15	14–16	39	41
	17–20	47	45
	T	44	44
16 or over	14–16	38	43
	17–20	43	46
	T	40	45
	Total	42	45

(c) **Percentage of young people who were 'very happy' by interest in wider world, age and school leaving age**

School leaving age	Age	Less interested in wider world	More interested in wider world
15	14–16	38	43
	17–20	41	48
	T	40	46
16 or over	14–16	40	42
	17–20	40	47
	T	40	45
	Total	40	45

pleasurable and unpleasurable feelings, such as pride or boredom, which were unrelated to one another, but were such that overall happiness was associated with the excess of pleasurable over unpleasurable feelings. The correlates of the one type of feelings were not necessarily correlates of the other type. For example, the number of worries people had was related to unpleasurable but not to pleasurable feelings, whilst the extent of social participation was related to pleasurable but not to unpleasurable feelings. This presumably means for example that, other things being equal, a person with worries who leads an active social life may be as happy as someone with no worries, but a rather barren social life. Had we been able to devote sufficient interview time to exploring psychological well-being amongst young people, with the same degree of sophistication, it might have been possible to explain some of the relationships we found more satisfactorily.

Table 8.22 Happiness related to social integration

(a) Percentage of young people who were 'very happy' by capacity for mixing, age and school leaving age

School leaving age	Age	Finds it more difficult to mix	Finds it less difficult to mix
15	14-16	35	46
	17-20	38	51
	T	37	49
16 or over	14-16	33	49
	17-20	32	54
	T	33	52
	Total	35	51

(b) Percentage of young people who were 'very happy' by family integration, age and school leaving age

School leaving age	Age	Less well integrated	Better integrated
15	14-16	26	49
	17-20	37	51
	T	33	50
16 or over	14-16	27	50
	17-20	36	56
	T	32	53
	Total	32	52

(c) Percentage of young people, who were 'very happy' by parental restrictiveness, age and school leaving age

School leaving age	Age	Parents more restrictive	Parents less restrictive
15	14-16	33	47
	17-20	33	49
	T	33	49
16 or over	14-16	34	48
	17-20	35	48
	T	34	48
	Total	34	48

(d) Percentage of young people who were 'very happy' by attitude to older people, age and school leaving age

School leaving age	Age	More hostile	Less hostile
15	14-16	36	46
	17-20	37	51
	T	37	50
16 or over	14-16	33	48
	17-20	40	48
	T	36	48
	Total	36	48

NOTE: For bases see tables R8.29

But it seems that, whilst happiness is complex and must have many more roots than the aspects of life we considered, for young people it is at least associated with these and particularly with their perception of their relationships with other people. It follows that a club, or any other organisation or process which improves, or compensates for poor relationships is likely to be contributing to young people's happiness. This is less clearly the case for adventurousness, but on the other hand the more adventurous were less likely to complain of boredom than other young people. Consequently a club which stimulates adventurousness is likely to decrease boredom.

Table 8.23 Percentage of young people who were often bored, by adventurousness, school leaving age and age

School leaving age	Age	Less adventurous on 3 measures	Less adventurous on 2 measures	Less adventurous on 1 measure	Adventurous on all 3 measures
15	14-16	42	37	37	37
	17-20	41	33	28	27
	T	41	35	32	30
16 or over	14-16	37	29	24	20
	17-20	22	21	22	16
	T	31	26	23	18
	Total	38	31	27	22

NOTE: For bases see table R8.30

180

8.8 Summary and Discussion

From most points of view the unattached appeared to lead less satisfactory lives than the attached. More of them were bored, unenthusiastic about varied experiences, preferred the company of people they knew and had little interest in what was going on beyond their immediate experience. They were much more likely to find making friends difficult and their parents were more often worried about their social lives. More briefly they appeared to be more timid and less socially apt, but, judging by the greater prevalence of boredom amongst them and the smaller proportion who claimed to be very happy, not very satisfied with their condition.

Amongst the attached, members of youth clubs, (that is places named 'Youth Clubs') seemed to be rather less fortunate than their contemporaries. It was they who were the most bored and unadventurous, although they were no more shy than other club members. Additionally, the young people who went to youth clubs felt more restricted by their parents, were slightly more hostile to older people in general and occasioned their parents more anxiety about their behaviour than both members of other clubs and those who went to no club at all. But they were no less happy than other young people.

By contrast members of sports clubs, and more particularly of interest-centred clubs, were least often bored, most adventurous, rather less hostile to older people and least likely to worry their parents by their behaviour. On the other hand, the young people who went to interest centred groups were most likely to have difficulties in making friends, and apparently were least often dependent on their families for emotional support, and were less often very happy.

Three simple explanations of these relationships between attachment or type of club and the young people's outlooks are possible. Either attachment or belonging to a particular type of club appeals to a particular type of young person, or these experiences influence his outlook, or both processes occur. For example, someone who finds it easy to make friends may be most likely to join a club, and the experience of belonging will probably enhance his social skill. On the other hand a shy person is more likely to avoid the challenge of a group and so grow confirmed in his belief that making friends is difficult. Similarly someone with a particular interest, such as acting, will be prone to join a group which caters for his tastes, and thereby perhaps, not only increase his enthusiasm for acting but also develop a taste for related matters, like the historical background of a play or scenery painting, whilst a sociable child with no specific interest may be attracted for lack of anything else by an undifferentiated club, which in turn encourages no particular passion. Although there is little evidence from this enquiry to support one explanation rather than another, this last one seems on commonsense grounds to be the most likely.

One of the aims of this enquiry was to find out how far the Youth Service met the needs of young people. In Chapter 5 we considered their expressed desires concerning clubs, but consideration of the more inclusive concept of need suggests that, from a practical point of view, it only has meaning in relation to an end, whether it be survival, reduction of tension, a state of grace and so on. People need food, love, homes and transport in order respectively to survive, be happy, comfortable, and move about, the need in each case has no independent existence. In this chapter we have taken the end to be some degree of current satisfaction with life, and concentrated on those aspects which seemed particularly relevent to leisure time and with which the Youth Service is or might reasonably be concerned; namely interests and relationships with friends and families and the older generation. All these measures are shown to be related in some degree to either happiness or boredom.

From this point of view, and assuming an interaction between the young person's outlook and attachment, it appears that attachment in general is beneficial. Clubs probably promote interests and social ease, although they may well attract the more lively and sociable young people in the first place, just as they attract the socially and educationally privileged.

Places which include the term 'Youth Club' in their name, which presumably represent the bulk of Youth Service provision, however, probably attract on the whole young people with less interest in exploring the world beyond their own experience, but on the other hand apparently have little success in encouraging such an interest or eliminating boredom. Moreover, it seems likely that they may actually rather more than other clubs emphasise the tension between generations. However they appear to be at least as successful as other clubs in promoting sociability.

Our cautious conclusion is that whilst attachment as a whole plays a part in fulfilling the interest and social needs of young people, so named Youth Clubs are less succcessful in meeting interest needs, or, compared at least with interest centred clubs, in encouraging understanding between young people and their elders. Although they may well be tackling a greater problem by being more successful in attracting the most needy in these respects, in the same way as they are more successful in capturing the early school leavers.

Table R8.24 Bases for tables 8.1, 3, 5, 7, 9, 17 & 19 (TOTAL SAMPLE – YOUNG PEOPLE)

School leaving age	Age	Attached			Unattached			Total		
		Boys	Girls	Total	Boys	Girls	Total	Boys	Girls	Total
15	14-16	181.5	160	341.5	125	156	281	306.5	316	622.5
	17-20	289.5	191	480.5	181.5	331	512.5	471	522	993
	Total	471	351	822	306.5	487	793.5	777.5	838	1615.5
16 or over	14-16	464	425	889	85.5	151.5	237	549.5	576.5	1126
	17-20	451.5	339	790.5	133	184	317	584.5	523	1107.5
	Total	915.5	764	1679.5	218.5	335.5	554	1134	1099.5	2233.5
Total		1386.5	1115	2501.5	525	822.5	1347.5	1911.5	1937.5	3849

Table R8.25 Bases for tables 8.2, 4, 6, 8, 10, 18 & 20 (TOTAL SAMPLE – YOUNG PEOPLE)

School leaving age	Age	Type of club (1st mentioned)				Unattached
		Sports	Social	Interest-centred	Youth club	
15	14-16	75.5	38	21	166.5	281
	17-20	129.5	165	24	100	512.5
	Total	205	203	45	266.5	793.5
16 or over	14-16	229	58.5	226.5	227	237
	17-20	227	145.5	180.5	108	317
	Total	456	204	407	335	554
Total		661	407	452	601.5	1347.5

Table R8.26 Bases for tables 8.11 & 13 (PARENTS WITH ONLY ONE CHILD IN THE SAMPLE)

School leaving age	Age	Attached			Unattached			Total		
		Male	Female	Total	Male	Female	Total	Male	Female	Total
15	14-16	72.5	67.5	140	58	77.5	135.5	130.5	145	275.5
	17-20	131.5	74.5	206	86.5	132	218.5	218	206.5	424.5
	Total	204	142	346	144.5	209.5	354	348.5	351.5	700
16 or over	14-16	259.5	237	496.5	45	84	129	304.5	321	625.5
	17-20	236.5	147.5	384	59.5	77	136.5	296	224.5	520.5
	Total	496	384.5	880.5	104.5	161	265.5	600.5	545.5	1146
Total		700	526.5	1226.5	249	370.5	619.5	949	897	1846

Table R8.27 Bases for tables 8.12 & 14 (PARENTS WITH ONLY ONE CHILD IN THE SAMPLE)

School leaving age	Age	Type of club (1st mentioned)				Unattached
		Sports	Social	Interest	Youth club	
15	14–16	28.5	20	7	67	135.5
	17–20	58.5	68	15	40	218.5
	Total	87	88	22	107	354
16 or over	14–16	125.5	35	133.5	117	129
	17–20	124.5	63.5	83.5	54	136.5
	Total	250	98.5	217	171	265.5
Total		337	186.5	239	278	619.5

Table R.8.28 Bases for table 8.21

School leaving age	Age	Bases for table 8.21(a)		Bases for table 8.21(b)	
		Less keen on varied experiences	More keen on varied experiences	More socially conservative	Less socially conservative
15	14–16	225	394.5	244	375.5
	17–20	313.5	678.5	318.5	673.5
	T	538.5	1073	562.5	1049
16 or over	14–16	349	774	295.5	827.5
	17–20	302	800.5	209.5	893
	T	651	1574.5	505	1720
Total		1189.5	2647.5	1067.5	2769.5

School leaving age	Age	Bases for table 8.21(c)	
		Less interested in wider world	More interested in wider world
15	14–16	282.5	337
	17–20	339	653
	T	621.5	990
16 or over	14–16	249	874
	17–20	171.5	931
	T	420.5	1805
Total		1042	2795

Table R.8.29 Bases for table 8.22

School leaving age	Age	Bases for table 8.22(a)		Bases for table 8.22(b)	
		Finds it more difficult to mix	Finds it less difficult to mix	Less well integrated	Better integrated
15	14-16	312.5	307	238	381.5
	17-20	426.5	565.5	390.5	601.5
	T	739	872.5	628.5	983
16 or over	14-16	519	604	409	714
	17-20	431	671.5	548.5	554
	T	950	1275.5	957.5	1268
Total		1689	2148	1586	2251

School leaving age	Age	Bases for table 8.22(c)		Bases for table 8.22(d)	
		Parents more restrictive	Parents less restrictive	More hostile to older people	Less hostile to older people
15	14-16	313.5	306	330.5	289
	17-20	199.5	792.5	410	582
	T	513	1098.5	740.5	871
16 or over	14-16	513.5	609.5	441	682
	17-20	202	900.5	328	774.5
	T	715.5	1510	769	1456.5
Total		1228.5	2608.5	1509.5	2327.5

Table R.8.30 Bases for table 8.23

School leaving age	Age	Less adventurous on 3 measures	Less adventurous on 2 measures	Less adventurous on 1 measure	Adventurous on all 3 measures
15	14-16	56.5	168	246	149
	17-20	72.5	202	349.5	368
	T	129	370	595.5	517
16 or over	14-16	40.5	199	374	509.5
	17-20	27.5	129.5	341.5	604
	T	68	328.5	715.5	1113.5
Total		197	698.5	1311	1630.5

CHAPTER 9

DIFFERENCES WITHIN THE
MAIN SCHOOL LEAVING GROUPS

For the sake of simplicity the analysis has so far been mainly
concerned with differences in behaviour and attitudes between
those who leave school at 15 and those who remain after this age.
But it is not to be expected that either group is homogeneous and
indeed, as shown in chapter 2, the difference in the prevalence
of attachment between those who leave school at 16 and those who
remain until later is as great as the difference between 15 and
16 year old school leavers. In this chapter we shall briefly
examine differences within each group of school leavers to see
whether there are sections of each group who warrant particular
attention when the future development of the Youth Service is
considered. The two groups selected for closer study are firstly
the 15 year old school leavers who are the children of semi-
skilled, unskilled or unemployed workers who live in urban and
conurbational areas; and secondly the young people who gave a
school leaving age of 16 years. It was thought that information
about the first group would contribute to thinking about the
problems of urban areas; and the second group, the 16 year old
leavers, was selected because work before the main study, had
suggested that they differed in many respects from other late
school leavers, although insufficiently to justify distinguishing
them as a separate group throughout the Report. We shall not
consider all the aspects of behaviour and attitudes which were
the concern of chapters 2 to 8, but only those which appear
particularly relevant to the present problem.

9.1 Attachment

Each step down the educational or social ladder made attachment
less likely, so that 75% of all late leavers, but only 65% of the
16 year old leavers were attached. Similarly, 51% of all 15 year
old leavers were attached, but only 46% of the early leaving
children of the least skilled urban workers. Attachment was
less common amongst all groups of 16 year old leavers than
amongst the corresponding groups of all later leavers. But
within the group of early leavers, the difference was entirely
due to the lower prevalence of attachment of the younger girls
and older boys from semi and unskilled urban families.

If attachment has value, then it is clear that there is no cause
for complacency in the case of the 16 year old leavers, especially
as far as the older girls are concerned, amongst whom only

Table 9.1 Percentage of young people attached to clubs, by social and educational group, age and sex

| Age | School leaving age = 15 | | | | | | School leaving age = 16 or over | | | | | |
| | Children of semi, unskilled or unemployed urban workers | | | All 15 year old leavers | | | 16 year old leavers only | | | All leaving school at 16 or over | | |
	M	F	T	M	F	T	M	F	T	M	F	T
14-16	58	44	50	59	51	55	78	64	71	85	74	79
17-20	55	36	44	61	37	48	69	50	60	77	65	71
Total	56	39	46	60	42	51	73	57	65	81	70	75

NOTE: For bases see table R.9.17.

50% were attached. But it is equally certain that those to whom most attention should be devoted are the early leaving children of the least skilled urban workers, and whilst not neglecting the 16 year old leavers, the more detailed discussion in the following pages will be about the least privileged group.

Table R9.13   Since the proportion of the early leaving children of the least skilled who had never been attached did not differ from the proportion amongst early leavers in general, two explanations of the lower prevalence of attachment in the first group are possible: either they abandon clubs at an earlier age, perhaps before the age of 14 years, or else their attachments are more ephemeral. In the boys' case, it seems evident that the lower prevalence is due to the declining use made of clubs with increasing age within the 14-20 year range. In fact, detailed perusal of the figures shows that no considerable difference occurs until after the age of 17. With girls, the difference is already apparent in the 14 to 16 year old group. But this does not seem to be because more of the daughters of the least skilled are past members by the age of 14 years: about 22% of both this group and girl early leavers in general were past but not present members at the age of 14. The difference appeared to be due rather to the more transitory attachments of the daughters

Table 9.2 Percentage of different social and educational groups who had been attending the first or only club mentioned for varying periods. Attached 14 to 16 year olds only

| Period which has elapsed since first started attending | School leaving age = 15 | | | | | | School leaving age = 16 or over | | |
| | Children of semi, unskilled or un-employed urban workers | | | All 15 year old leavers | | | | | |
	M	F	T	M	F	T	M	F	T
4 weeks or less	(10)	(17)	13	7	9	8	7	8	7
Up to 6 months	(29)	(23)	26	26	22	24	21	27	24
Up to 1 year	(19)	(20)	20	16	22	19	16	21	18
A year or more	(41)	(40)	41	49	45	47	55	44	50

NOTE: Figures in brackets are based on less than 50 cases

188

of the least skilled. Thus 40% of the younger attached amongst
this group had been attending the first or only club mentioned for
a period of less than 6 months, whilst only 31% of all younger
girl early leavers had been attending for such a short period.
More particularly 17% of the daughters of the least skilled had
been attending for 4 weeks or less, compared with 9% of all
early leaving girls. A characteristic pattern of short dis-
continuous attachments necessarily means that fewer members
of the group will be found to be attached at any one time, even
though similar proportions (the great majority) are attached at
some time during, or before adolescence.

9.2 Attachment to Youth Clubs

'Youth Clubs' here mean, as in Chapter 2, places which the
young people regarded as Youth Clubs, mainly places with the
words 'youth club' in their name.

With the exception of one sub group, there was little difference between the four sections of the sample in the proportions
currently attached to Youth Clubs, providing further evidence that
so named Youth Clubs are equally popular with most social and
educational groups. The exception was the group of younger
girl early leavers from the least skilled urban families. But
again, since rather similar proportions of all groups were
current or past members, the explanation must lie in the briefer
period during which this group of girls remains attached to
Youth Clubs. About two thirds of all groups were current or
past members of Youth Clubs, and this indicates that Youth Clubs
are in a good position to influence young people's attitudes towards attachment, whatever their social and educational back-
grounds and prospects. As we shall underline in the next section
this is peculiarly true for the least privileged.

Table
R9.13

Table 9.3 Percentage of young people attached to what they would call Youth Clubs, by
social and educational group, age and sex

| Age | School leaving age = 15 | | | | | | School leaving age = 16 or over | | | | | |
| | Children of semi, un-skilled or unem-ployed urban workers | | | All 15 year old leavers | | | 16 year old leavers only | | | All leaving school at 16 or over | | |
	M	F	T	M	F	T	M	F	T	M	F	T
14-16	42	21	31	38	31	35	43	36	39	40	37	39
17-20	18	14	16	20	12	16	23	11	17	24	12	18
Total	28	16	22	27	19	23	32	23	28	32	26	29

Note: For bases see table R9.17

9.3 Type of club attended

Table
R9.14

Like early leavers in general, the children of the least skilled
urban workers who were attached were concentrated in sports,
social and, particularly, Youth Clubs. But considerably fewer
of them used sports clubs and far more of them attended Youth

189

Clubs than any other kind of club, although the percentage of this group using Youth Clubs was no greater than the percentage of early school leavers in general. The explanation is that the children of the least skilled were less likely than any other group to attend more than one club.

Table 9.4 Percentage of attached young people attending each type of club, by social and educational group and sex

| Type of club | School leaving age = 15 | | | | | | School leaving age = 16 or over | | | | | |
| | Children of semi, unskilled or unemployed urban workers | | | All 15 year old leavers | | | All 16 year old leavers | | | All leaving school at 16 or over | | |
	M	F	T	M	F	T	M	F	T	M	F	T
Sports	39	20	30	44	25	36	50	31	42	53	35	45
Youth Club	49	32	41	43	38	40	41	39	40	34	34	34
Social	27	32	29	27	33	30	22	37	24	17	19	18
Cultural	3	6	4	3	7	5	9	16	12	21	30	25
Students unions	-	1	-	2	2	2	6	6	6	11	14	12
Uniformed	7	4	5	6	4	5	10	7	9	12	8	10
Academic	-	-	-	-	-	-	2	1	2	13	10	12
Common rooms	1	4	2	3	3	3	7	7	7	9	9	9
Religious	3	6	4	2	5	4	4	9	6	6	12	9
Debating etc.	-	-	-	1	2	1	2	2	2	7	7	7
Film clubs	-	-	-	1	-	1	2	2	2	8	7	8

It looks therefore as if Youth Clubs are the type of club in which, if any, the least privileged are most likely to be found. Although in the case of the *daughters* of the least skilled urban workers social clubs, many of which may be commercially run, were equally patronised. But other evidence shows that whilst these girls at any one time are as likely to be found in social as in Youth Clubs, the great majority (71%) pass through Youth Clubs at sometime during their youth. And amongst those who

Table R9.15

Table 9.5 Type of club last left by past but not present members, by social and educational group and sex

| Type of club last left | School leaving age = 15 | | | | | | School leaving age - 16 or over | | |
| | Children of semi, unskilled or unemployed urban workers only | | | All 15 year old school leavers | | | | | |
	M	F	T	M	F	T	M	F	T
Youth Club	49	72	63	54	72	65	42	48	46
Uniformed organisation	14	7	10	16	6	10	21	21	21
Sports	18	5	10	13	4	8	13	6	8
Social	9	9	9	8	7	8	4	7	6
Interest-centred	6	3	4	3	6	4	10	10	10
Religious	2	4	3	2	2	2	5	3	3
Other	2	1	1	4	2	2	3	5	5

190

were past but not present members of clubs 71% had last been to a Youth Club, and 7% to a uniformed group. Thus at least 78% of past members had attended a Youth Service organisation at sometime. This is no different from the percentage of all girl early leavers who were past members, but since the daughters of the least skilled are least often attached at any one time, it indicates that the Youth Service plays a key role in determining whether attachment is perceived by them as valuable in some way or not. And as they evidently do not long remain attached it seems that on the whole the Service fails to make them feel that prolonged attachment is worthwhile.

9.4 Ideal Club activities and functions

On the whole the children of the least skilled differed little from early leavers in general about the activities they would like to pursue in clubs. The single noteworthy exception was that the older girls amongst them were more interested than any other group in domestic (including personal adornment) activities (Fig. 9.1 (a)). Compared with actual club activities which the attached amongst them experienced, the children of the least skilled wanted more active culture, more social pursuits, more entertainment and more crafts. It was particularly the older boys and all the girls who wanted more of these activities. The same groups also opted for more sport, and the girls, alone, desired more instructive activities, which were often associated with the domestic pursuits, (e.g. 'cookery classes').

The 16 year old leavers differed from all late leavers in wanting rather less instructive and cultural activities, and rather more motorised pursuits (compare Fig. 9.1 (b) and Chapter 5, Figs. 2 and 3). They wanted more sport, social and entertainment activities provided than in actual clubs, and the older children rather more often chose cultural pursuits than they actually experienced.

There were also few differences within school leaving groups in the rating of club functions. But two particularly merit attention. Firstly the younger girls amongst the children of the least skilled were more likely than any other group of girls to attach great importance to the club's providing an escape from older people. Secondly, the same group, more than any other, thought it very important that the club should provide help or advice about problems. Table R9.16

It is also worth noting that the children of the least skilled were no less enthusiastic than other groups about pursuing interests. In fact more of the younger boys amongst them than of any other group attached great importance to being able to learn new things and find new interests, although the older boys wanted to be able to do the things they were already interested in more than any other group and less often attached great importance to pursuing new interests.

191

FIG. 9.1.

Actual and ideal club activities, by age and sex

(a) Children (school leaving age = 15) of semi-skilled, unskilled or unemployed urban workers

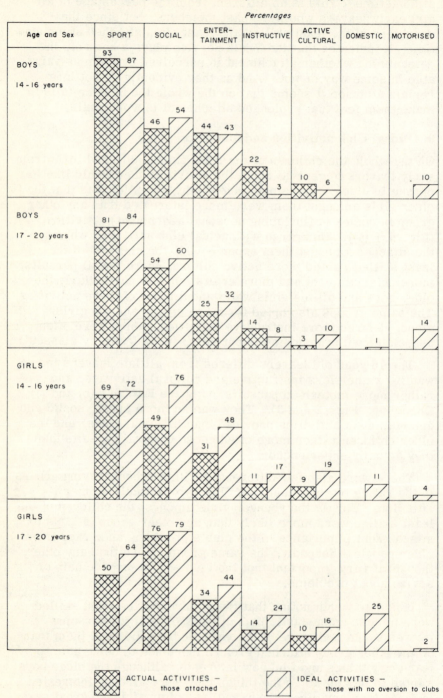

Percentages

Age and Sex	SPORT	SOCIAL	ENTER-TAINMENT	INSTRUCTIVE	ACTIVE CULTURAL	DOMESTIC	MOTORISED
BOYS 14-16 years	93 87	46 54	44 43	22 3	10 6		10
BOYS 17-20 years	81 84	54 60	25 32	14 8	3 10	1	14
GIRLS 14-16 years	69 72	49 76	31 48	11 17	9 19	11	4
GIRLS 17-20 years	50 64	76 79	34 44	14 24	10 16	25	2

ACTUAL ACTIVITIES — those attached

IDEAL ACTIVITIES — those with no aversion to clubs

FIG. 9.1. *(continued)*

Actual and ideal club activities, by age and sex

(b) All 16 year old leavers

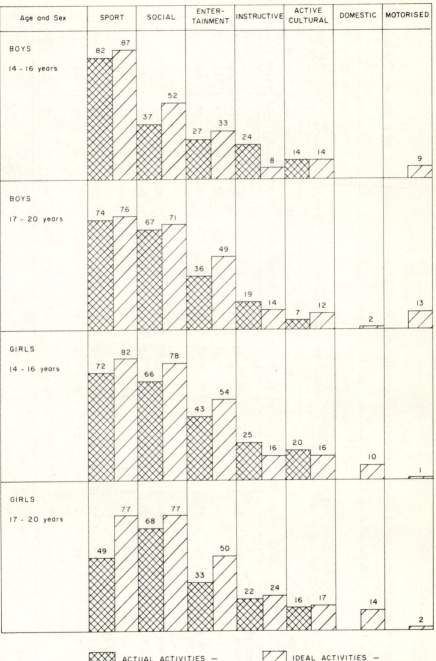

Percentages

Age and Sex	SPORT	SOCIAL	ENTER-TAINMENT	INSTRUCTIVE	ACTIVE CULTURAL	DOMESTIC	MOTORISED
BOYS 14 – 16 years	82 / 87	37 / 52	27 / 33	24 / 8	14 / 14		9
BOYS 17 – 20 years	74 / 76	67 / 71	36 / 49	19 / 14	7 / 12	2	13
GIRLS 14 – 16 years	72 / 82	66 / 78	43 / 54	25 / 16	20 / 16	10	1
GIRLS 17 – 20 years	49 / 77	68 / 77	33 / 50	22 / 24	16 / 17	14	2

ACTUAL ACTIVITIES — those attached

IDEAL ACTIVITIES — those with no aversion to clubs

193

Table 9.6 Percentage of young people saying various possible club functions were very important, by social and educational group, age and sex

A club should be a place where you can:	School leaving age = 15								School leaving age = 16							
	Children of semi, unskilled or unemployed urban workers				All 15 year old leavers				16 year old leavers				All leaving school at 16 years or over			
	M		F		M		F		M		F		M		F	
	14-16	17-20	14-16	17-20	14-16	17-20	14-16	17-20	14-16	17-20	14-16	17-20	14-16	17-20	14-16	17-20
Learn new things/ interests	76	54	67	71	69	62	68	71	67	61	70	70	68	59	70	73
Make new friends	58	58	68	72	55	64	65	73	54	62	69	73	58	62	66	74
Get on with all sorts of people	49	47	71	64	49	51	71	63	53	53	69	63	53	52	71	66
Carry on existing interests	63	68	59	61	61	63	57	62	63	61	54	57	61	59	53	59
Meet people like you	43	45	49	43	42	40	49	43	44	42	43	33	45	42	39	30
Meet old friends	34	54	28	36	36	41	28	32	36	41	33	44	38	45	35	46
Find opposite sex friends	33	42	35	32	32	42	32	31	32	39	27	22	30	39	25	21
Get help with problems	51	45	64	50	48	43	59	51	41	37	46	37	40	32	40	33
Escape from older people	43	30	43	28	44	42	30	29	36	32	33	26	31	27	30	20

194

9.5 Other differences between social or educational groups

In Chapter 8 we produced evidence to suggest that attachment may be valuable for young people in certain ways. If this is correct, then it is obviously worthwhile attempting to retain the interest of the children of the least skilled in the club membership. We also showed that the same measures used to evaluate attachment indicated that the early school leavers were in several ways less well off than late leavers. We shall now look to see whether the sections of special interest within each school leaving group differ in these respects from each group as a whole. The object is to see whether, given the evident value of attachment, it could be particularly beneficial or not for these sub groups.

(a) Boredom

Firstly, there was no difference overall in the extent of boredom between the children of the least skilled urban workers and early leavers as a whole In fact the younger members of the first group rather less often complained of boredom. On the other hand, the older boys in the first group more often reported boredom. But slightly more of the 16 year old leavers were often bored than late leavers as a whole, and the difference was particularly marked for the older girls.

Table 9.7 **Percentage of young people who said they were often bored in their spare time, by social and educational group, age and sex**

| Age | School leaving age = 15 | | | | | | School leaving age = 16 or over | | | | | |
| | Children of semi, unskilled or un- employed urban workers only | | | All 15 year old school leavers | | | 16 year old leavers only | | | All leaving school at 16 or over | | |
	M	F	T	M	F	T	M	F	T	M	F	T
14-16	22	40	32	30	44	37	25	29	27	22	26	24
17-20	28	37	33	23	36	30	20	24	22	19	18	18
Total	26	38	33	26	39	32	22	26	24	20	22	21

Note: For bases see table R9.17

(b) Adventurousness

This was also composed of measures which varied with both educational experience and attachment and might therefore be expected to vary within groups. In fact there was little difference within school leaving groups in the proportion who were less keen on varied experiences, although the older girls amongst the children of the least skilled were particularly cautious (Table 9.8). However, there were considerable differences in 'social conservatism' and 'interest in the wider world'. In the case of the early school leavers it was the sons of the least skilled who were markedly less adventurous than the early leaving boys in general, although there was little difference between the girls. But amongst later school leavers, those giving a school leaving age of 16 were, whatever sub group they belonged to, less adventurous than late leavers in general.

The implication is that whilst there is considerable scope for clubs to interest early school leavers in general in the world beyond their immediate experience, this is particularly so in the case of the sons of the least skilled. Similarly, although later leavers as a whole are already, relatively speaking, curious beyond their own horizons, clubs might usefully attempt to promote more of such interest amongst 16 year old leavers.

Table 9.8 Adventurousness, by social and educational group, age and sex

	School leaving age = 15						School leaving age = 16 or over					
a) Percentage of young people who were less keen on varied experiences	Children of semi, unskilled or unemployed urban workers			All 15 year old leavers			16 year old leavers only			All leaving school at 16 years or over		
	M	F	T	M	F	T	M	F	T	M	F	T
Aged 14-16	37	31	33	38	34	36	39	27	33	36	26	31
17-20	31	36	34	33	30	32	33	28	31	31	25	27
Total	34	34	34	35	32	33	35	28	32	34	26	29
b) Percentage of young people who were more socially conservative												
Aged 14-16	51	40	45	42	37	39	38	28	33	32	22	26
17-20	42	31	36	34	30	32	24	21	22	20	17	19
Total	45	34	39	37	33	35	30	25	27	25	20	23
c) Percentage of young people who were less interested in the wider world												
Aged 14-16	46	49	48	40	51	46	32	37	35	19	26	22
17-20	40	40	40	31	39	34	20	22	21	14	17	16
Total	43	43	43	36	42	39	25	30	28	16	21	19

Note: For bases see table R9.17

(c) Capacity for mixing

The early leaving children of the least skilled urban workers more often found mixing more difficult, than other young people. This was only true however for the 17 to 20 year olds, for, unlike any other group, the feeling of being socially inept increased with age amongst these young people. This may be

because their experiences up to the time they leave school have
been relatively unsuited to fitting them to cope with the novel
social situations they meet when they start work. But since it is
possible that attachment promotes social ease, it may be of
particular value to the children of the least skilled from this
point of view.

Table 9.9 Percentage of young people who found it more difficult to mix, by
social and educational group, age and sex

Age	School leaving age = 15						School leaving age = 16 or over					
	Children of semi, unskilled or unemployed urban workers only			All 15 year old leavers			16 year old leavers only			All leaving school at 16 or over		
	M	F	T	M	F	T	M	F	T	M	F	T
14-16	44	49	46	49	52	50	46	46	46	48	45	46
17-20	48	56	52	37	48	43	36	42	39	38	40	39
Total	46	53	51	42	49	46	40	45	42	43	42	43

Note: For bases see table R9.17

(d) Family Relationships

As shown in Chapter 8, family integration varied little with
attachment or with school leaving age, except among the older
young people. But it was considered worth examining in the
present context, since differences within school leaving groups
may suggest possible tasks for the Youth Service.

The children of the least skilled urban workers were on the
whole less well integrated with their families than early leavers
in general, and this was particularly marked for the younger
children, especially the girls, and for the older boys. It was
suggested in Chapter 8 that this measure of integration was also
in part a measure of the child's chosen independence. But this
interpretation seems less appropriate to the younger children
of the least skilled than to the older late school leavers. In the
present case it seems more likely that the less integrated were
reporting a real lack of reciprocal interest or confidence rather
than a mature independence. The parents of this group, for one
reason or another, take a relatively low practical interest in
their children, (for example in their education or choice of job),
who may well feel as a result that it is pointless to turn to their
families for advice or understanding, or, more likely, the habit
of discussion and exchange of views and advice may never have
developed.

In this case, the unusually high proportion of younger girls
amongst the children of the least skilled who are less well
integrated with their families, might explain their greater

197

Table 9.10 Percentage of young people who were less well integrated with their families, by social and educational group, age and sex

| Age | School leaving age = 15 | | | | | | School leaving age = 16 or over | | | | | |
| | Children of semi, unskilled or unemployed urban workers only | | | All 15 year old leavers | | | 16 year old leavers only | | | All leaving school at 16 years or over | | |
	M	F	T	M	F	T	M	F	T	M	F	T
14-16	46	40	43	43	34	38	37	34	35	37	35	36
17-20	54	34	43	42	37	39	51	41	47	54	45	50
Total	51	36	43	42	36	39	47	38	41	46	40	43

Note: For base see table R9.17

emphasis on the need for clubs to provide advice and help with problems. However, a check on this possibility suggested that this was not the case. For strangely enough, the least integrated least often thought it very important that clubs should provide help with problems and this was particularly marked for early school leavers. Possibly, lack of experience of talking things over with their families, makes it more difficult for these young people to seek advice from others, or indeed to conceptualise their feelings at all. For the fact that, as shown in Chapter 8, fewer of the less well integrated were 'very happy', makes it seem unlikely that they had fewer problems. But, as we suggested earlier, assigning great importance to the problem solving function of clubs is not the same as admitting to personal problems, but rather it means accepting clubs as appropriate places for providing advice. However this may be, it seems unlikely that the emphasis on the provision of advice in clubs by the early leaving children of the least skilled is related to their relatively low integration with their families.

Between 16 year old leavers and later leavers in general there where no considerable differences.

Table R9.19 There was no difference within school leaving groups in perception of parental restrictiveness, but parental anxiety about loss of control varied inversely with social or educational status, so that the children of the least skilled in urban areas had the most anxious mothers (probably with good cause) and the parents of later leavers in general were the least anxious.

Within school leaving groups, the differences were particularly marked for the younger children and for the girls. This may be another indication of the relative lack of understanding between the children of the least skilled and their parents, that is to say the parental anxiety may imply that the parent feels either uncertain of her ability to influence the child's behaviour, or of

198

Table 9.11 **Percentage of parents who were more anxious about loss of control, by social and educational group, age and sex**

THOSE WITH ONE CHILD IN SAMPLE ONLY

| Age | School leaving age = 15 | | | | | | School leaving age = 16 or over | | | | | |
| | Children of semi, unskilled or unemployed urban workers only | | | All 15 year old leavers | | | 16 year old leavers only | | | All leaving school at 16 or over | | |
	M	F	T	M	F	T	M	F	T	M	F	T
14-16	45	49	47	39	44	41	36	38	37	27	31	29
17-20	31	30	30	28	25	26	21	28	24	20	23	21
Total	36	37	37	32	33	32	28	34	31	24	27	26

Note: For bases see table R9.18

her ability to predict how the child will behave, or both. It may also reflect the genuinely greater dangers which beset these children.

(e) Happiness

Finally, there was little difference in the reports of happiness within school leaving groups. The only exception was the group of older boys from the least skilled urban families who were rather less likely to rate themselves as very happy than any other group of the same age, although the difference was small.

Table 9.12 **Percentage of young people who were 'very happy' by social and educational group, age and sex**

| Age | School leaving age = 15 | | | | | | School leaving age = 16 or over | | | | | |
| | Children of semi, unskilled or unemployed urban workers only | | | All 15 year old leavers | | | 16 year old leavers only | | | All leaving school at 16 or over | | |
	M	F	T	M	F	T	M	F	T	M	F	T
14-16	38	44	41	36	44	40	37	44	41	39	44	42
17-20	36	49	43	43	48	46	45	54	50	40	51	46
Total	37	47	42	40	47	43	42	49	46	40	47	44

Note: For base see table R9.17

In summary it appears that if attachment is valuable, more attention needs to be paid to retaining the interest of 16 year old school leavers than of those who leave school later, but that most effort should be directed at the 15 year old leavers who

199

are the children of semi, unskilled or unemployed workers living in towns and cities. This group is less likely than any other to be attending clubs and presents peculiar difficulties in addition to those described for early leavers in general. In the case of the boys, the problem is one of maintaining attachment in their late teens. Except that some of them favour more motorised activities than are provided in actual clubs there is little evidence of any specific changes which could attract them, although they favoured the general idea of interest-centred pursuits as much as any other group, and compared with other groups of older boys were unusually prone to boredom and less likely to be very happy.

The problem about the girls is that they remain in clubs for briefer periods than other groups of young people. So that attempts to retain their interest evidently need to have both an immediate and sustained appeal and to be concentrated on the 14 to 16 year olds, otherwise they will leave before they have had an opportunity to appreciate the benefits of membership. They ask for considerably more interest centred activities than are available in the clubs they actually attend, and these desired activities include more active culture and instruction as well as more domestic pursuits. They are also exceptionally inclined to require that the club should provide help with their problems. As they grow older their desire for interest centred activities remains, but the emphasis they place on domestic pursuits is greater than for any other group.

For both sons and daughters of the least skilled the organised groups which they are most likely to attend at some time are Youth Service organisations and it is therefore clear that the Youth Service is in a very good position to show them the benefits of attachment.

Table R9.13 Attachment to clubs and youth club attachment, by social and educational group, age and sex

Qs.16(c) and 19 Attachment to clubs	(a) Children (school leaving age = 15) of semi-skilled, unskilled or unemployed urban workers									(b) All 16 year old leavers								
	Boys			Girls			Total			Boys			Girls			Total		
	14-16 years	17-20 years	Total	14-16 years	17-20 years	Total	14-16 years	17-20 years	Total	14-16 years	17-20 years	Total	14-16 years	17-20 years	Total	14-16 years	17-20 years	Total
	%	%	%	%	%	%	%	%	%	%	%	%	%	%	%	%	%	%
Never attached	14	4	8	15	14	14	15	10	12	6	6	6	6	8	7	6	7	6
Past attachment	28	42	36	41	50	47	35	46	42	16	25	21	30	42	36	23	33	29
Present attachment	58	55	56	44	36	39	50	44	46	78	69	73	64	50	57	71	60	65
Q.23 Youth club attachment																		
Never attached	39	26	31	32	26	29	36	26	30	34	30	31	28	25	27	31	28	29
Past attachment	18	56	41	45	60	54	32	58	48	23	47	36	35	63	49	29	55	43
Present attachment	42	18	28	21	14	16	31	16	22	43	23	32	36	11	23	39	17	28
Total percentages	100	100	100	100	100	100	100	100	100	100	100	100	100	100	100	100	100	100
Weighted base: All young people in each category	(71)	(108)	(179)	(80)	(140)	(220)	(151)	(248)	(399)	(227.5)	(298)	(525.5)	(258.5)	(261)	(519.5)	(486)	(559)	(1045)

201

Table R9.14 Type of club, by social and educational group, age and sex

THOSE ATTACHED

Q.16(a) & (b)

Type of club	(a) Children (school leaving age = 15) of semi-skilled, unskilled or unemployed urban workers									(b) All 16 year old leavers								
	Boys			Girls			Total			Boys			Girls			Total		
	14-16 years	17-20 years	Total	14-16 years	17-20 years	Total	14-16 years	17-20 years	Total	14-16 years	17-20 years	Total	14-16 years	17-20 years	Total	14-16 years	17-20 years	Total
	%	%	%	%	%	%	%	%	%	%	%	%	%	%	%	%	%	%
Sports club	39	39	39	17	22	20	29	31	30	54	48	50	33	29	31	44	41	42
Social club	10	39	27	17	42	32	13	40	29	9	32	22	21	34	27	15	33	24
Sports and social club	5	7	6	6	10	8	5	8	7	2	9	6	1	7	3	2	8	5
Debating/current affairs society	-	-	-	-	-	-	-	-	-	2	1	2	1	2	2	2	2	2
Political societies	2	-	2	-	4	2	1	3	2	1	2	2	1	4	2	2	3	2
Cultural club	2	3	3	3	8	6	3	6	4	11	7	9	19	12	16	15	9	12
Club to do with Academic Subjects	-	-	-	-	-	-	-	-	-	3	-	2	2	1	1	3	1	2
Clubs for creative crafts	-	-	-	-	-	-	-	-	-	1	-	1	2	-	1	2	-	1
Hobbies not included elsewhere e.g. stamp collecting club, gardening club, travel club, etc.	2	2	2	3	-	1	3	1	2	4	3	3	3	-	2	3	2	3
Film society	-	-	-	-	-	-	-	-	-	2	2	2	2	-	2	2	2	2
Religious society	2	3	3	6	6	6	4	5	4	4	4	4	10	6	9	7	5	6
Uniformed Organisations	10	5	7	-	6	4	5	6	5	17	5	10	10	3	7	13	4	9
Red Cross/St. John's Ambulance Brigade																		
Youth Clubs of any kind	71	34	49	49	20	32	60	28	41	48	36	41	55	19	39	51	29	40
Chess/Bridge club	2	-	1	-	-	-	1	-	-	3	-	2	1	-	-	2	-	1
Commonroom/Library	2	-	1	-	6	4	1	3	2	6	8	7	6	8	7	6	8	7
Students Union/Assoc.	-	-	-	3	-	1	1	-	-	4	8	6	5	6	6	5	8	6
Young Farmers club	-	2	1	-	-	-	-	1	-	1	-	1	-	1	-	1	1	1
Community Centre	-	-	-	-	4	2	-	1	1	2	-	1	1	1	1	2	1	1
Other clubs not included elsewhere	2	3	3	9	4	6	5	4	4	4	10	7	4	4	4	4	8	6
Clubs for voluntary work/charities	-	-	-	-	-	-	-	-	-	-	-	-	1	2	1	1	1	1
Duke of Edinburgh Award Scheme	-	-	-	-	-	-	-	-	-	-	1	1	1	-	1	1	1	1
Total percentages	149	139	144	119	132	126	134	138	132	179	177	178	183	143	164	182	169	176
Weighted base: All young people attached to clubs in each category	(41)	(59)	(100)	(35)	(50)	(85)	(76)	(109)	(135)	(177.5)	(204.5)	(382)	(166)	(131.5)	(297.5)	(343.5)	(336)	(679.5)

202

Table R9.15 Type of club last attended by past members, by social and educational group, age and sex

Type of club last attended by past members	Children (school leaving age = 15) of semi-skilled, unskilled or unemployed urban workers only								
	Boys			Girls			Total		
	14-16 years	17-20 years	Total	14-16 years	17-20 years	Total	14-16 years	17-20 years	Total
	%	%	%	%	%	%	%	%	%
Sports	20	18	18	12	1	5	15	8	10
Social, sports and social	-	13	9	6	10	9	4	11	9
Interest-centred	20	-	6	-	4	3	8	3	4
Religious	-	2	2	6	3	4	4	3	3
Uniformed and Red Cross	20	11	14	9	6	7	13	8	10
Youth Clubs	35	56	49	67	74	72	55	67	63
Other	5	-	2	-	1	1	2	1	1
Total percentages	100	100	100	100	100	100	100	100	100
Weighted base: Those with past attachment	(20)	(45)	(65)	(33)	(70)	(103)	(53)	(115)	(168)

Table R9.16 Important club functions, by social and educational group, age and sex

Q.21

Club functions	Important	(a) Children (school leaving age = 15) of semi-skilled, unskilled or unemployed urban workers									(b) All 16 year old leavers								
		Boys			Girls			Total			Boys			Girls			Total		
		14-16 years	17-20 years	Total	14-16 years	17-20 years	Total	14-16 years	17-20 years	Total	14-16 years	17-20 years	Total	14-16 years	17-20 years	Total	14-16 years	17-20 years	Total
		%	%	%	%	%	%	%	%	%	%	%	%	%	%	%	%	%	%
1. To make new friends	Very Imp.	58	58	58	68	72	71	63	66	65	54	62	59	69	73	71	63	67	65
	Fairly Imp.	42	37	39	27	25	25	34	30	31	39	34	36	28	26	27	33	30	32
	NOT Imp.	-	4	3	5	3	4	3	4	3	6	4	5	2	2	2	2	3	4
2. Meet friends you know already	Very Imp.	34	54	46	28	36	33	31	43	38	36	41	39	33	44	38	34	42	39
	Fairly Imp.	54	37	44	48	51	50	51	45	47	51	49	50	60	48	54	56	49	52
	NOT Imp.	12	9	10	24	14	17	18	12	14	12	10	11	7	8	7	9	9	9
3. Find boy/girl friends (opp. sex)	Very Imp.	33	42	38	35	32	33	34	36	35	32	39	36	27	22	24	29	31	30
	Fairly Imp.	45	39	42	45	32	37	45	35	39	48	38	42	52	46	49	50	42	46
	NOT Imp.	21	19	20	20	34	29	20	28	25	20	22	21	22	32	26	21	26	24
4. Learn new things and find new interests	Very Imp.	76	54	64	67	71	70	71	64	67	67	61	64	70	70	70	69	65	67
	Fairly Imp.	19	40	31	27	26	26	23	32	29	28	34	31	26	27	26	27	30	29
	NOT Imp.	4	6	5	7	2	4	6	4	4	4	5	5	4	3	4	4	4	4
5. Be able to do things you are already interested in	Very Imp.	63	68	66	59	61	60	61	64	63	63	61	62	54	57	55	58	59	58
	Fairly Imp.	33	26	29	32	35	34	32	31	32	32	32	32	41	38	39	37	35	36
	NOT Imp.	4	6	5	9	4	6	7	5	6	5	7	6	5	6	5	5	6	6
6. Escape from older people	Very Imp.	43	30	36	43	28	33	43	29	34	36	32	34	33	26	29	34	29	31
	Fairly Imp.	30	36	33	32	32	32	31	34	32	40	27	32	35	33	34	37	30	33
	NOT Imp.	27	34	31	24	39	33	25	37	32	23	41	33	31	41	36	28	41	35
7. Meet people who think like you do	Very Imp.	43	45	44	49	43	45	46	44	45	44	42	43	43	33	38	44	38	41
	Fairly Imp.	37	34	35	43	40	41	40	38	39	43	39	41	42	48	45	42	44	43
	NOT Imp.	19	20	20	7	17	13	13	18	16	11	18	15	15	19	17	13	18	16
8. Get help or advice about your problems	Very Imp.	51	45	47	64	50	55	58	48	52	42	37	39	46	37	41	44	37	40
	Fairly Imp.	28	36	33	23	28	26	25	31	29	39	33	36	34	39	36	36	36	36
	NOT Imp.	21	19	20	13	21	18	17	20	19	19	29	25	20	25	23	20	27	24
9. Learn how to get on with all sorts of people	Very Imp.	49	47	48	71	64	67	61	57	58	53	53	53	69	63	66	62	58	60
	Fairly Imp.	43	40	41	24	26	25	33	32	32	35	32	33	27	30	28	30	31	31
	NOT Imp.	8	14	11	4	9	7	6	11	9	10	15	13	4	7	5	7	11	9
Weighted base: All those who were not averse to belonging to a club		(67)	(89)	(156)	(75)	(126)	(201)	(142)	(215)	(357)	(207)	(270)	(477)	(248.5)	(236.5)	(485)	(455.5)	(506.5)	(962)

Note: 'Don't know' and 'no answer' are omitted from the table so the numbers may not always add to 100%

204

Table R9.17 Bases for tables 9.1, 3, 7, 8, 9, 10 & 12 (TOTAL SAMPLE – YOUNG PEOPLE)

Age	Children of semi, unskilled or unemployed urban workers only			All 15 year old school leavers			16 year old leavers only			All leaving school at 16 or over		
	M	F	T	M	F	T	M	F	T	M	F	T
14-16	71	80	151	306.5	316	622.5	227.5	258.5	486	549.5	576.5	1126
17-20	108	140	248	471	522	993	298	261	559	584.5	523	1107.5
Total	179	220	399	777.5	838	1615.5	525.5	519.5	1045	1134	1099.5	2233.5

School leaving age = 15 spans the first two groups; *School leaving age = 16 or over* spans the last two groups.

Table R9.18 Bases for table 9.11 (PARENTS WITH ONLY ONE CHILD IN SAMPLE)

Age	Children of semi, unskilled or unployed urban workers only			All 15 year old school leavers			16 year old leavers only			All leaving school at 16 or over		
	M	F	T	M	F	T	M	F	T	M	F	T
14-16	31	37	68	130.5	145	275.5	118.5	130	248.5	304.5	321	625.5
17-20	52	57	109	218	206.5	424.5	147	109.5	256.5	296	224.5	520.5
Total	83	94	117	348.5	351.5	700	265.5	239.5	505	600.5	545.5	1146

School leaving age = 15 spans the first two groups; *School leaving age = 16 or over* spans the last two groups.

Table R9.19 Percentage of young people who felt their parents were more restrictive, by social and educational group, age and sex

Age	(a) Children (school leaving age = 15) of semi-skilled, un-skilled or un-employed urban workers			(b) All 16 year old leavers		
	Boys	Girls	Boys	Girls	Boys	Total
14-16 years	51	53	52	45	47	46
17-20 years	22	21	21	21	18	20
Total	34	32	33	31	33	32

Note: For bases see table R9.17

CHAPTER 10

DISCUSSION AND CONCLUSIONS

This enquiry had two main objectives, firstly to find out how the Youth Service and allied facilities were used and secondly to assess the extent to which these met the needs of the young people for whom they were provided. Because no single enquiry could fulfil both objectives equally well, it was designed to achieve the first aim with some degree of certainty and secondarily to provide as much information as possible relevant to the second. This means that whilst there can be little doubt that the pattern of use of facilities which is described in this Report is substantially accurate, the material on what the young people want from Youth Service type provision and the extent to which it is beneficial should be regarded with caution. It implies directions and forms for experiments rather than prescriptions for success.

10.1 Use of the Youth Service and Allied Provision

93% of the young people have attended a club, society or similar group at sometime before they are 21, and most of them (65%) are attached at any one time, but the least educationally and socially privileged are considerably less likely to be attached than other young people. Specifically girls, early school leavers and the children of manual workers, particularly of the unskilled, are least often attached to clubs and so on. This is not because they are much less likely ever to have been attached, but because they much more often drop out in their mid-teens or earlier. Moreover, such other evidence as exists suggests that this pattern has prevailed at least since the late 1940's.

The Youth Service, in so far as it is represented by what the young people regarded as Youth Clubs is, by contrast, much more successful in attracting the less privileged, almost as much as their more fortunate contemporaries. About 70% of 14 to 20 year olds evidently use Youth Clubs at some time during or before adolescence, although only a minority (26%) attend such clubs at any one time, and the decline in use with age is much more abrupt than for clubs generally. So that although the Youth Service officially caters for the 14 to 20 year age range, it evidently engages the loyalty of very few indeed after the age of 17 years. At this point, the people who leave school at 16 years or over, who are most likely to hold multiple memberships in the first place, mostly remain attached to some clubs. But the early leaving girls in particular embark on what, from other studies, appears to be a life time habit of unattachment.

Thus, much of the concern in recent years about the Youth Service and the unattached seems to have been misplaced. Most young people *do* use clubs, and although only a minority participate in the Youth Service at any one time, the great majority are involved for a period of their youth. So that if attachment is valuable, attention should be focussed on those who are prone to leave all such organisations in their mid-teens.

Those who attend clubs mostly go to Sports clubs, followed in frequency by Youth clubs, then social clubs and least frequently to what we have termed interest-centred clubs, for example amateur dramatic societies, groups concerned with academic subjects and music societies. Amongst the younger early school leavers, Youth Clubs were patronised more than any other kind of club. The commonest activities pursued in clubs are sport, social activities, like talking and dancing, and entertainment such as listening to tapes and records. Helping to run the organisation and active culture like singing and acting are mainly undertaken by late school leavers. In fact, although the order of popularity of type of club and activity is more or less the same for each group, the later school leavers are considerably more likely to use clubs to pursue interests, age for age, than early leavers who concentrate on physical recreation and being sociable.

Voluntary community service and non-vocational residential courses, which we were also asked to examine, largely attract those who are concurrently attached to clubs. In the former case this seems to be mainly because opportunities to participate are largely available through school, at a time when attachment is at a peak, rather than because it appeals peculiarly to late school leavers. In both cases about a third or less of 14 to 20 year olds had ever been involved. And neither voluntary service nor residential courses can be regarded as providing an alternative facility to those who do not use clubs.

10.2 The extent to which the Youth Service and allied facilities meet the needs of young people

It was suggested in Chapter 8 that from a practical viewpoint the concept of need has meaning only in relation to ends, and before going on to discuss the relationship between provision and need it is as well to be clear about what is meant by this suggestion.

Psychological theories and lists of needs, whatever their theoretical status, are of little practical value in considering the effectiveness of services in meeting needs. This is because, as Goldthorpe and his colleagues argue in a different context, 'What is in fact of major interest is the variation in the ways in which groups differently located in the social structure actually experience and attempt to meet the needs which at a different

207

level of analysis may be attributed to them all' (Goldthorpe et al, 1968, P.178). Consequently it seems more useful to ask people about their desires, preferences and expectations than to turn to psychological theory for help. But this approach is obviously unsatisfactory when there is reason to believe that the people concerned are either unaware of or unable to express what to an informed observer appears to be a need. To take one extreme example; an injured and unconscious man is unaware of his need for medical aid. In such cases the informed observer has to determine need other than by reference to psychological theory or to the individual concerned. In doing so he is likely to assume an end; in this particular example the end will presumably be the survival of the injured man. The 'needs' are then the require-ments for achieving the end.

But expressed desires also imply ends. People want interesting work, more leisure, houses or money and so on because they believe these goods will contribute to more or less specific aspects of their sense of well being.

Normal, healthy young people may be aware of many of their more particular needs. But on the other hand, apart from variations in articulateness, it is likely that within extremes of depressing and exhilerating experiences, most people will, for many reasons be unaware of the more general conditions which promote or inhibit their sense of well being; an end which we suggest below seemed appropriate in the present case. To determine such conditions or needs one approach is to examine the young people's experience in areas of their lives which seem likely to be related to their feeling of satisfaction; a range of areas limited in the present study by the condition of relevence to Youth Service provision. And if, as proved to be the case, these experiences are related to their sense of well being, then such experiences can reasonably be termed needs.

The ends considered in this Enquiry were of two kinds: the first was the specific one of enjoyment of a club, and in this case we assessed the related needs by eliciting the young people's desires, their conscious and expressed needs. This enabled us to compare actual with desired provision and to show how these differed. In turn this yielded ideas about how the Youth Service might be developed to give greater satisfaction to those who already use it and thus, hopefully, to retain their attachment, and at the same time to attract at least some of those who currently do not.

These findings will be discussed in Section 3, but presumably future action to attract greater numbers of young people to the Youth Service and similar provision will depend at least upon the belief of those responsible that success will benefit the young people involved if not society as a whole. The question then becomes one of whether the attached young people were in some sense better off than their unattached contemporaries and whether if so this could be attributed in any way to their being attached. Thus the second kind of end was the satisfaction of the young people's lives; specifically, their overall happiness or freedom from boredom in their spare time. And the needs considered were certain aspects of their lives which appeared to be related to these conditions and which might be the concern of the Youth Service. In practice, we sought to discover whether the attached were more adventurous, found it easier to make friends, and had better relations with the older generation, as well as whether they were actually happier and less often bored than the unattached. This approach made it possible to show both the relationship between attachment and psychological well-being and some of the processes which might contribute to the relationship.

Although in many cases the differences between early and late school leavers were at least as great as differences between the attached and unattached, within each group the attached appeared to be more fortunate than the unattached. Fewer of them were bored, and more were adventurous, socially confident and very happy. Moreover the attached had more frequent contacts with friends and were more active in their spare time. But there was no difference between the two groups in their relationships with the older generation.

But satisfaction in this sense was related not only to attachment, but to the type of club the attached young people used, and in this respect places named "Youth Clubs" did not always come out well. Within most age and school leaving age groups, more of the Youth Club members were bored, unadventurous and apparently in conflict with the older generation than members of sports and particularly interest-centred groups. But Youth Club members were at least as socially confident as other attached young people.

The relationships, however, throw no light on the mechanisms involved. Does attachment appeal most to the happy, adventurous and socially confident or does attachment make them so? Similarly; are Youth Clubs most successful in attracting the most bored, unadventurous and antagonistic young people, or are they least successful in improving these aspects of their lives? In the absence of other kinds of investigation, specifically longitudinal studies, it is impossible to answer this question. In order to do so it would be necessary to know at least; whether the young people who join clubs, and those who join Youth Clubs, differ or not from their peers in their proclivity to boredom, and so on, at the time they join; as well as, the experiences provided by clubs, including those which are offered but rejected. The limited evidence presented and common sense suggests an interaction between the child and the experience of attachment. The possession of social skills, for example, will be conducive to club membership which in turn will be likely to enhance such skills. In the same way, people who join Youth Clubs rather than sports or interest-centred groups are, according to their own recollections, less likely to do so because of a particular interest, but once in the club they are less likely than others to be involved in an interest-centred activity. For what it is worth, our *impression* from the reasons young people gave for leaving clubs is that Youth Clubs were less likely than other kinds to encourage interests. Fairly typical examples of explanations for leaving a Youth Club were; 'there were no activities there, just listening to records and drinking coffee', and 'apart from table tennis and listening to records, there wasn't anything else going'.

If it were known, then, that the greater adventurousness, social confidence and so on of the attached, *resulted from* their use of clubs, then it could be said that attachment, and particularly of certain kinds, met at least some of the needs of young people. However whilst the demonstrated relationships are consistent with such an interpretation, they allow us to say no more than that attachment may act in this way. But if there is, prima facie, evidence that attachment, particularly of certain kinds, is beneficial to young people, it seems worth considering how its possible benefits could be extended.

Before going on to discuss this question however, it is useful to review briefly the evidence and suggestions from this enquiry in conjunction with those from other studies, of any wider benefits of adolescent attachment. We were able to examine only some aspects of the quality of the young people's lives at the time of interview. But it is possible that in the long run developing the habit of attachment may have benefits for people which are not especially evident in adolescence. For example, in later life membership of voluntary organisations is probably one of the most effective means open to most individuals of influencing the quality of their own and their family's environment, whether it be for instance through a Parent Teacher Association, a consumers' group a Trade Union or a sports club, which simply ensures that adequate facilities for watching and playing games are available. And certainly there is evidence that the adult member of a voluntary organisation, as opposed to the non-member, is more likely to be the "Democratic Citizen", (Almond & Verba, 1963, P.310), '[who not only thinks] he can participate [but] thinks that others ought to participate as well. Furthermore he does not merely think he can take a part in politics: he is more likely to *be* more active. And, perhaps most significant of all, [he] is also likely to be the more satisfied and loyal citizen'. (Op Cit. P.257).

If, as seems likely, from the evidence presented and quoted here, the habit of attachment or non-attachment is established in mid adolescence, then those who drop out at this time are possibly foregoing future benefits for themselves and for society as a whole. If a participatory democracy, in which every individual is involved in some way in influencing the decisions which affect him in important respects, is worth aiming for, then cultivating the habit of attachment may well be one way of working towards it.

10.3 How can the benefits of attachment be extended?

If attachment is valuable, then there are various indications of the way in which the benefits might be extended. Firstly it is evident that the greatest scope for expansion exists amongst older early school leavers. This is particularly true of the girls, of whom only a little over a third belonged to clubs. Thus the question of how to attract the unattached is largely one of how to attract the older early school leavers and especially the girls amongst them; or, more economically, how to prevent the younger members of the group from becoming unattached.

Secondly, it is probable that there is a considerable inertia in the habit of non-attachment or of becoming unattached. This is because the habit is common to most members of this group, so that few of them will have friends or relations who use clubs and therefore non-attachment will appear to them to be a natural condition. This likelihood, together with the fact that most young people pay their first visit to a club in the company of friends, suggests that the most successful appeals to join or remain in clubs will often be made to groups of friends and acquaintances rather than to individuals.

Thirdly, apart from the effects of habit, there are indications that attachment may be a less satisfying experience for the early school leavers than for their more educated contemporaries. They evidently join clubs with less positive expectations of their provision, they tend overwhelmingly to join undifferentiated types of clubs like Youth and Social clubs, rather than sports and particularly interest-centred groups, and inside clubs they are much less likely to experience organisational or interest-centred activities. Perhaps this is because they prefer the less demanding and less structured occupations like table tennis, dancing and chatting. And the fact that the early leavers, especially the girls, more than other groups favoured com-mercial provision lends some support to this possibility. However, in assessing possible functions of clubs, this group as much as any other emphasised the importance of being able to pursue interests. It seems that to some extent, they are thinking of different kinds of interests than the late school leavers. For, whilst favouring more instructive and active cultural activities than the attached amongst them experienced in actual clubs, the unattached girls also wanted more provision for domestic pursuits, like cookery and dressmaking sessions, and opportunities to learn about practical interior design, baby care and personal adornment. The early leaving boys, on the other hand, were interested in more motorised sports and engine maintenance. All these subjects are of a kind which could be extended, of course, to develop consumer consciousness in the widest sense, if it is considered that the Youth Service should play a part in promoting "participation". But it should be emphasised that the young people's requirements of clubs imply a shift in emphasis of activities in Youth Clubs and not the radical substitution of one type of provision for another. For all groups, sports of one kind or another, and social occupations were the most popular requirements, but it seems that a mixture of indoor sports in particular and dancing and chatting alone have ephemeral attractions only. If the loyalty of more early school leavers is to be retained and their leisure lives to be made more enjoyable then the introduction of more interest-centred activities at some stage, seems to be important.

But, as was suggested in Chapter 5, the fact that the young people said they wanted these activities is no guarantee that they will adopt them when the opportunities to do so are provided. They may be mistaken in their beliefs, or they may only respond if opportunities are presented in particular ways. On these questions, a study of this kind can offer little guidance. Only practical experiments in which activities and modes of presentation are more or less systematically varied can provide answers.

Although Youth Clubs failed to hold young people after their mid-teens, they were, compared with other kinds of clubs, particularly good at attracting the younger early school leavers in the first place. Consequently they would seem to be the key to extending and improving the quality of attachment amongst this group. This does not mean to say that individual Youth Clubs should seek to retain their members throughout their teens: on the contrary, the indications are that the young people prefer narrower age groupings. But rather that, if places like Youth Clubs, but with a more limited age range than 14 to 20 years, can capture the interest of the younger early leavers they may, through practical links with other groups catering for roughly the 18 to 25 or 30 year groups, be in a better position than other sorts of clubs to induce the habit and develop the benefits of attachment amongst the least socially privileged.

It would appear simpler to retain the attachment of the younger children rather than to attempt the reattachment of older teenagers who no longer attend clubs. Once the young people leave school and clubs they are likely to be scattered. Many of them will have jobs where there are few other young people, and even if it were ever to be possible to place or recruit youth workers in most of the coffee bars, pubs, dance halls and so on, where young people congregate, about a third of the unattached evidently rarely get together with friends, and 17% are married or engaged, both of which situations probably mean that they are seldom to be found in such places.

It is important to acknowledge that this Report in no way deals with all the recent questions and suggestions raised about the Youth Service, because no single enquiry could do so. The criteria for submitting specific problems to examination were not only their importance and relevence, but also their amenability to study by the method used. Two questions in particular which have been much discussed are not examined here. Both concern the wider question of the proper role of the Youth Service and the first is part of the debate on the function of the service as promoter of the active or participant society. Specifically it is about the organisation of clubs; to what extent the members do, can or want to control or influence the organisation and what it provides. This is a question much better tackled by club-centred studies and experiments. The second question is about club-centred versus 'detached' work. Increasingly the Youth Service's emphasis on club-centred facilities is being questioned, and imaginative ideas developed about youth work carried out in places where young people gather outside clubs. It is evident that throughout this Report we have been mainly concerned with the club-based facilities, or, more precisely, with organised groups. The reason for this is again a practical one. In so far as the new ideas have been put into practice, their very nature precludes investigation of their prevalence and effects on a national scale. However, this enquiry has demonstrated the wide use and apparent value of organised groups to young people, which indicate that, whatever the need for other kinds of youth work, organised groups which are available during their leisure time have an important part to play in young people's lives. Moreover, as suggested above, it is likely that however many detached workers there are, a fair proportion of young people will be inaccessible to them in the present situation. Thus, important though the role of the detached worker may be amongst gregarious delinquescent or 'alienated' youth, we would suggest that for the great majority of the unattached the main problem is one of increasing the attractions and value of organised groups for them *before they become* unattached.

As we pointed out at the beginning of this chapter, the material in this Report offers no certain means of developing the Youth Service in such a way that it will hold and help the majority of young people who would otherwise become the un-attached. But we believe the findings summarised here and discussed in more detail in the main body of the Report suggest directions for experimental studies which might be undertaken in clubs or areas to establish specifically what kinds of provision will have the greatest value. 'Experiment' of course does not mean the introduction of loosely defined innovations whose effects are assessed from the impressions of the innovators. Such procedures may have their own value, but to determine with some certainty the range of facilities and the modes of presenting them which will have specific desired effects and can therefore be usefully introduced on a large scale involves monitoring changes by recognised research methods. We would hope that at least some such projects will result from the present Report.

APPENDIX 1

THE SAMPLE DESIGN

1. Sample population

The enquiry was concerned with two populations; young people
aged 14-20 years inclusive living in England and Wales and
parents of these young people. The survey was carried out in
two phases. Half the sample was to be contacted in the summer
and the other half in the winter. For the purposes of this
report no distinction is made between the two phases unless
otherwise stated.

2. Sampling frame

There was no national sampling frame from which the names
and addresses of young people in the relevant age group could be
obtained. As the 1966 Sample Census figures indicate that the
members of the population were on average likely to be found
at less than one third of all occupied dwellings, it was decided
to draw a representative random sample of addresses from the
Electoral Registers, and to identify eligible young people by
means of a postal sift.

3. Primary sampling units

The selected primary units were 100 local authority areas distributed throughout England and Wales according to the percentage
distribution of population. (See Table I).

4. Sample size

The aim was to achieve interviews with 3,500 14-20 year olds,
and the relevant number of parents. The first problem therefore was to estimate the number of addresses which would have
to be sifted to produce this number of interviews. The three
relevant factors to be considered were,

    (a) the proportion of addresses likely to contain 14-20 year
          olds.
    (b) the likely response to the postal sift.
    (c) the likely response to interview amongst those responding
          to the postal enquiry.

The calculations used to obtain the target numbers were as follows:

(a) allowing for a 90% response to interview from those replying to the postal sift, a set interview sample of 3,885 young persons would be needed to achieve interviews with 3,500.

(b) the pilot study preceding the main enquiry indicated that approximately one responding address in four produces on average one 14-20 year old. The postal sift was therefore required to yield replies from about 15,540 addresses.

(c) the pilot survey indicated that the response rate to the postal sift would be in the region of 85%. Therefore, the sample size of addresses for the sift would have to be set at about 18,275. This was subsequently rounded up to 18,400 which meant that for each phase 92 addresses would be sampled from each of the 100 primary units.

Table I Distribution of 100 areas according to the distribution of population* by standard region, and within region by type of area derived from the Registrar General's Annual Estimates of population, 1967

Region	Conur-bations	Urban	Semi-rural	Truly rural †	Total
North	2	3	1	1	7
Yorkshire and Humberside	4	5	1	-	10
North West	8	5	1	-	14
East Midlands	-	4	2	-	6
West Midlands	5	3	2	-	10
East Anglia	-	2	1	1	4
South East	16	13	6	-	35
South West	-	5	2	1	8
Wales (South East)	-	3	1	-	4
Wales (remainder)	-	1	-	1	2
Total	35	44	17	4	100

*Derived from the Registrar General's Annual Estimate of Population, 1967
†The probability of selection of the truly-rural area in East Anglia and the one Northern Region was deliberately increased to provide sufficient information about these areas for analysis

5. Sample design

A four-stage multi-stratified sample design was used. The local authorities in England and Wales were divided into standard regions (taken from the Registrar General's Revised Standard Regions), and within the regions stratified according to whether they were conurbations, urban areas, semi-rural or truly-rural areas. The distinction between semi-rural, truly-rural and urban areas was made on the grounds of density. Semi-rural areas had a population density greater than 0·25 persons per acre or were contiguous with an urban area having a population greater than 25,000. Truly-rural areas had a population density of less than 0·25 persons per acre.[1] Urban districts[2] are in most cases compact townships having larger populations than rural districts, but administering a much smaller area. The conurbations[2] are areas of urban development formed by an aggregation of entire local authority areas.

Stage I

Within the strata the local authorities were arranged in descending order of size (Registrar General's Annual Estimates of Population 1967) and 100 areas were selected with probability proportional to population size in each area.

Stage II

Four wards were selected from each of the selected conurbations and urban districts with probability proportional to size (number of electors), with one exception. This exception was Birmingham which has a population of over a million, and in this case eight wards were selected. In rural areas where the population is often widely dispersed two groups of contiguous parishes were selected from each local authority, again with probability proportional to size.

Stage III

Within each selected ward or group of parishes a systematic random sample of 42 addresses was drawn from the Electoral Registers. The same number of addresses was drawn from each local authority area, except Birmingham for which the number was doubled because of its size. (See Stage II above). Institutions and commercial premises were excluded from the sample because of the lack of information about these residences.

Stage IV

Each selected address was sent a simple questionnaire as described below. From the completed returns the names and addresses of all eligible young people were extracted and used for the interviewing stage.

6. The Postal Sift

To each selected address a simple questionnaire was sent. This was addressed to "the occupier" of the address, and was

---

[1] Rural areas are listed in Registrar General's Annual Estimates of Population. Division into semi—and truly rural made by Sampling Branch.
[2] As listed in Registrar General's Annual Estimates of Population.

accompanied by a short explanatory letter. It asked the occupier to fill in the names, dates of birth and sex of each occupant aged between 10 and 25, if any, and return the form marked "none" if there were no such occupants. An age range wider than the required range was used because previous experience had shown that sifts produced deficient numbers, by comparison with census figures, towards the limits of a specified range. The initial letter was followed where necessary by up to two reminders over a period of 5 weeks.

Because institutions had been excluded from the samples of addresses, "occupiers" were asked to include on the questionnaire those people in the age range who were away from home for training or educational purposes. This was an attempt to cover people who were living in boarding schools, students, nurses or other hostels, particularly important because of the relatively high proportion of this age group who live in institutions. Those in military establishments however, were excluded.

From the returned postal forms the names and addresses of all eligible young people were extracted. Interviewers then called at each of the resulting addresses and interviewed as far as possible all those eligible young persons at the address, and one parent of each young person, except when the young person was married or living away from home other than for educational or training purposes.

Table II

Postal sift set and achieved Sample		
	No.	%
Set Sample Addresses	18,400	100
Achieved Sample		
Total addresses returning questionnaire	17,143	93.2
Total addresses producing usable information	16,948	92.1
Addresses containing one or more		
14-20 year olds	3,395	18.4
Number of 14-20 year olds identified	4,734	
†Number found eligible by interviewers	4,566	100
*Number interviewed	3,942	86.3
†Number found eligible at coding stage	3,916	85.8

†Ineligibility was mostly due to errors on the postal return, so that on checking, the young person failed to qualify for inclusion in the sample due to his age or residence. The remaining cases were young people who could not be usefully interviewed because of mental or physical handicap.
*394 of eligible young people refused interview.
230 of eligible young people were not contacted.

APPENDIX 2

THE QUESTIONNAIRES

S.437/Y   <u>YOUTH SERVICE SURVEY - 1. YOUNG PERSON</u>

		area			address	Y.P. digit	parent digit
Serial Number:							

Interviewer's Name ....

Auth. no. ....

Date of interview:

Day	Month	Year
		1969

(i) Whether any adult interviewed/ to be interviewed about this young person:

Adult has already been interviewed 1

Adult still to be interviewed 2

No adult to be interviewed (SPECIFY REASON) 3

....

....

....

(ii) Whether anyone other than informant present for half or more of the interview:

No, only informant present 1

One or both parents present 2

Other relative present 3

Others (specify) 4

....

(iii) REASONS FOR NON-CONTACT AND NOTES ON DISCREPANCIES BETWEEN SITUATION FOUND AT INTERVIEW AND DETAILS SHOWN ON ADDRESS LIST.

W	C

(iv) Sex of young person

Male 1

Female 2

(v) Age last birthday

14 or under 1

15 2

16 3

17 4

18 5

19 6

20 or over 7

(vi) Date of birth

GIVE IN FIGURES

INTERVIEW ONLY
IF BORN BETWEEN
2.11.48 AND 1.11.55
INCLUSIVE

INTERVIEW ONLY
IF BORN BETWEEN
2.6.48 AND 1.6.55
INCLUSIVE

(vii) Marital status

Single 1

Engaged 2

Married 3

Widowed/Divorced/
    Separated 4

(viii) Residence

Lives in parental home for 4 days a week or more .. . 1

Lives in parental home for less than 4 days a week . 2

220

1. I'd like to start by asking a little about yourself. Would you
   tell me first what you are doing now. Are you:

PRIORITY
CODE

RUNNING
PROMPT

In a full-time paid job (include
  self-employed) .... 1 ask(a)

Studying full-time .... 2 ask(b)

On a sandwich course - currently in a job .... 3 ask(a)

          - currently in college ..... 4 ask(b)

Or doing something else .... 5 ask(c)
                    over
                    page

(a) <u>IF IN PAID JOB OR SANDWICH STUDENT AT WORK (1), (3)</u>

 OCCUPATION:

 INDUSTRY:

<u>GO TO Q.2</u>

(b) <u>IF STUDYING FULL-TIME OR SANDWICH STUDENT AT COLLEGE (2), (4)</u>

 Are you:

RUNNING
PROMPT

At school* .... 1 Go to
             Q.2

College .... 2 ask(i)

or At a University ...... 3 Go to
             Q.2

Other (specify) 4
................'.....
....

> *PROBE 'Is that a
> school which takes
> pupils under the
> age of 15?' If 'no'
> COUNT AS COLLEGE

 (i) <u>If at a college (2) to (b)</u>

  What kind of college are you at?

  Technical college/Polytechnic/Commercial College/
   College of Further Education 1

  College of Art/Music/Drama 2

  College of Education 3

  Other (specify) 4

  ....

<u>GO TO Q.2</u>

Q.1 (continued)

(c) <u>IF DOING SOMETHING ELSE (5) TO MAIN</u>

What are you doing now?

PRIORITY
CODE

Looking after nouse/family (and not working or
  studying full-time) 1

Waiting to start job for which he (she) has been
  accepted 2

Waiting to take up place at college/university for
  which he (she) has been accepted (but not in
  temporary full-time paid job) 3

Unemployed, looking for work 4

Other (specify) 5

....

....

....

2. (a) What kind of school are you at (did you last go to)?

PROMPT AS NECESSARY

*PROBE 'Did the school take any pupils under the age of 15?' IF NOT, DO NOT COUNT AS SCHOOL BUT ASK ABOUT PREVIOUS SCHOOL	

Secondary Modern 0

Comprehensive school, incl. bilateral or
  multilateral schools 1

State Grammar 2

Technical School* 3

Independent/Direct Grant* 4

Schools abroad* 5

Other types of school* (specify) 6

(b) Is it (was it) at the time you left a
boys (girls) school or a mixed school?

Boys only 1

Girls only 2

Mixed 3

(c) Are you (were you) a day pupil or a
boarder (for most of the time you were
at school)?

Day pupil 5

Boarder 6

THOSE AT SCHOOL NOW ASK Q.3 OTHERS GO TO Q.4

222

DNA, NO LONGER AT SCHOOL ....A go to Q4

3. What do you hope to do when you leave school:

RUNNING PROMPT
- Get a job ....1 ask(a)
- Become a full-time student ......2 ask(b)
- Or do something else? ....3 ask(c)

(a) HOPES TO GET A JOB (1)

What kind of job are you hoping to do?

D.K. haven't decided 0

GO TO Q.4

(b) HOPES TO BECOME A FULL-TIME STUDENT (2)

What kind of educational institute do you hope to go to?

D.K. haven't decided 0

Technical college/Polytechnic/commercial college 1

Art/Music/Drama college/school 2

College of Education 3

University 4

Other (specify) 5

....

GO TO Q.4

(c) HOPES TO DO SOMETHING ELSE (3) TO MAIN

What are you thinking of doing

(GIRLS ONLY) get married 1

4. At what age are you expecting to
   (did you) leave school?

At 15 or under 1

At 16 2

At 17 3

At 18 or over 4

Over 15 but exact age not known ..... 5 USE CARD
                                          A2 FOR
                                          Q.5

AVOID USING THIS CODE IF POSSIBLE   D.K. 6

DNA. DON'T KNOW WHEN WILL LEAVE SCHOOL ...... A GO TO
                                                  Q.6

5. Here are some reasons which other people of round your age have given
   for (leaving school when they did) (staying on at school until 17/18)

INFORMANT STILL AT SCHOOL	WILL LEAVE AT AGE 16 OR UNDER – SHOW CARD A1
	WILL LEAVE AT AGE 17 OR OVER – SHOW CARD A2
INFORMANT NO LONGER AT SCHOOL	LEFT AT AGE 16 OR UNDER – SHOW CARD A3
	LEFT AT AGE 17 OR OVER – SHOW CARD A4

(a) Please pick out any reasons which apply to you. RECORD IN COL. (a)

(b) Can you say for each of the reasons you have mentioned whether it was very
    important, fairly important or not important at all in making you decide
    to leave (stay on at school). PROMPT REASONS GIVEN AND RECORD ANSWERS
    IN COL. (b)

DO NOT PROMPT	(a)	(b)		
CARDS A1 AND A3 (if leaving/left at 16 or under)	Applies	Very important	Fairly important	Not important
1. On the whole I dislike(d) school	1	1	2	3
2. I want(ed) to earn money of my own	2	1	2	3
3. Most of my friends are (were leaving)	3	1	2	3
4. I can (thought I could) get a better job by leaving then	4	1	2	3
5. I'm not (wasn't) much good at school work	5	1	2	3
6. My parents want(ed) me to leave then	6	1	2	3
7. I want(ed) to leave school then to go on to college	7	1	2	3
8. No one can (could) stay longer at my school	8	1	2	3
9. For as long as I can remember I've (I'd) expected to leave school at 15 or 16	9	1	2	3
CARDS A2 and A4 (If staying/stayed on until 17 or over)				
1. On the whole I enjoy(ed) school	1	1	2	3
2. I wouldn't (didn't) feel ready to earn my own living at 15 or 16	2	1	2	3
3. Most of my friends are (were) staying on until 17 or 18	3	1	2	3
4. I can (thought I could) get a better job by staying till then	4	1	2	3
5. I am (was) quite good at school work	5	1	2	3
6. My parents want(ed) me to stay on at school	6	1	2	3
7. I want(ed) to stay on to go to college or university	7	1	2	3
8. For as long as I can remember I've (I'd) expected to stay at school until I was 17 or 18	8	1	2	3

5. (continued)

O <u>ASK ALL</u>
   Was any other reason important in making you decide to
   leave (stay on at) school?

                                    Yes (specify below) 1

                                    No. 2

6. So far we have been talking about (your job and) your education, but thinking about things in general - work and play - what are your main interests?

RECORD UP TO THREE FIRST MENTIONED   None ....0 go to
                                                                                 Q.3

   (1) ....

   (2) ....

   (3) ....

7. ASK FOR EACH MAIN INTEREST MENTIONED:
O How did you first come to be interested in ....(main interest)

     PROBE FULLY   DNA No main interest mentioned, or none for
                                  which question makes sense, e.g. TV,
        1st main interest (specify) courting, seeing friends, my family ....A go to Q8
(1)..............................   DNA 0

        2nd main interest (specify)
(2) ....   DNA 0

        3rd main interest (specify)
(3) ....   DNA 0

226

8. (Now can we talk about your spare-time) What sort of things do you usually do in your spare-time at present:

PROMPT (i) - (V)

(i) When you are with your friends?

(ii) When you are on your own? PROMPT AS NECESSARY 'I don't just mean exciting things or going out'

227

8. (continued)

    (iii) When you are with your boy (girl) friend (opp. sex) (if
           you have one) /husband/wife (and children)?

                             Has no boy/girl friend/husband/wife 0

    (iv) With your family (parents/brother/sisters)? PROMPT AS
          NECESSARY 'I don't just mean exciting things but anything at all
          you do with them in your spare time'

    (v)   Are there any other things you do in your spare time that you
          haven't already mentioned?

228

9. Is there anything you would like to do in your spare-time and can't for some reason?

Yes .... 1 ask
                  (a)&(b)
No 2

If yes (1)
(a) What is it that you'd like to do?   NUMBER ACTIVITIES MENTIONED

(b) And what makes it difficult to ...... (ACTIVITY)? NUMBER DIFFICULTIES TO CORRESPOND WITH ACTIVITIES

10. Do you usually enjoy your spare time   Usually enjoys spare time 1
0   or do you often get bored?   Often gets bored 2

11. On the whole who do you most enjoy spending your spare time with?

RUNNING
PROMPT

Your family (parents, brothers, sisters) 1

Your friends 2

(Your boy/girl friend/husband/
    wife (and children)) 3

Or on your own 4

Family and friends equally 5

Other (specify) 6

....

229

12. Now I'd like to go on to talk some more about friends:

MORE THAN ONE COL MAY BE RINGED

(a) Where did you meet most of your present friends in the first place?

DO NOT PROMPT

```
+--------------------------------+
| IF SAYS 'Grew up with          |
| them' PROBE 'did they          |
| live nearby or did you         |
| meet them at school or         |
| what?'                         |
+--------------------------------+
```

At school 1

At work 2

At college/university 3

In the neighbourhood 4

At youth club/scouts/guides 5

Other (specify) 6

....

....

Has no friends ....8 Go to Q.14

(b) During the past week on how many days have you seen any of your friends to talk to ?

(INCLUDE SEEING AT SCHOOL, COLLEGE OR WORK)

DO NOT PROMPT

CODE HIGHEST NO.MENTIONED FOR (b), (c) & (d)

Not at all 0

Once 1

2 days 2

3 " 3

4 " 4

5 " 5

6 " 6

7 " 7

(c) On how many days have you got together with friends in the past week to do things like going out together or visiting each other's homes?

DO NOT PROMPT

Not at all 0

Once 1

2 days 2

3 days 3

4 " 5

5 " 5

6 " 6

7 " 7

(d) About how many close friends would you say you have?

DO NOT PROMPT

None 1

1 2

2-3...................3

4-5 4

More than 5 5

230

                              DNA. Married/not living in parental home ..... A Go to
                                                                               Q.16

UNMARRIED INFORMANTS LIVING IN PARENTAL HOME FOR 4 DAYS A
WEEK OR MORE
                                   DNA has no friends ..... B Go to
                                                                   Q.14

13. Do your parents like you to bring your friends home or not?

                       Yes, like friends brought home 1
                       No, don't like friends brought home 2
                       They don't mind 3
                       Other answers (specify) 4

<table>
<tr><td rowspan="9">UNMARRIED INFORMANTS LIVING IN PARENTAL HOME (FOR AT LEAST 4 DAYS/ WEEK)</td><td colspan="4">14. Do your parents make any rules   DNA Married/not living or say anything about: in parental home .... A Go to Q.16</td></tr>
</table>

14. Do your parents make any rules   DNA Married/not living
    or say anything about: in parental home .... A Go to
                                                                          Q.16

    INDIVIDUAL PROMPT

	Yes	No	DNA
(1) Who you go out with	...1	...2	...3
(2) The time you come in at night	...4	...5	...6
(3) How you dress	...1	...2	
(4) Helping about the house and garden	...3	...4	
(5) Your homework or studies (if you have any)	...5	...6	...7
(6) The way you spend your money	...1	...2	...3
(7) Or the time you go to bed	...4	...5	

15. Do you think parents should have a say in these things
    (PROMPT LIST IN Q.14 IF NECESSARY) for people of your
    age, or do you think you should decide entirely for
    yourself? (DO NOT PROMPT)

                      Parents should have a say 1
                      Young person should decide 2
                      Parents should have a say but
                         young person should decide 3
                      Other (specify) 4

PP	PA
1	2

231

16. One of the things we are interested in is the things people belong
or go to like clubs and so on, so can you tell me:

(a) THOSE AT WORK/SCHOOL/COLLEGE/UNIVERSITY

                              DNA. Not at school/college/university/work ....A go to
                                                           (b)

                                                            ASK (ii)
(i) Are there any clubs or societies run by or attached   Yes ...|....1 & (iii)
     to your school (college/place of work) which you
     could go to if you wan'ed to?   No ...|....2 go to
                                                        (iii)

(ii) What clubs and societies are there? RECORD AT A BELOW
      THEN ASK (iii)

(iii) Is there anywhere attached to your school (college/   Yes ...|....3 ASK (iv)
      place of work) you can go to after school (college/
      work) for social activities or just to talk to   No ...|....4 Go to
      friends?   (v)

(iv) Where is that? RECORD AT A BELOW THEN ASK (V) IF APPLICABLE

                                                       RECORD
(v) THOSE AT SCHOOL (COLLEGE/UNIVERSITY) ONLY (OTHERS GO TO(vi))Yes ...|....5 AT A &
    Is there a school council (Students union or association)   ASK (vi)
                                                 No ...|....6

      IF YES TO (i), (iii) OR (V) (codes 1, 3 or 5)
(vi) (Which of these things) do you actually go to ....(club etc)
      PROMPT LIST AT A BELOW IF NECESSARY, AND RING CCDES IN COL.B

A	B		Off. use
Name of club/society etc or description of place	Goes	Does not go	
1..	1	2	
2..	1	2	
3..	1	2	
4..	1	2	
5..	1	2	
6..	1	2	
7..	1	2	
8..	1	2	

16. (Continued)

(b) <u>TO ALL</u>

Do you go along to any (other) clubs, societies or other groups, things like football teams, political groups, drama clubs, scouts/guides or church or social groups for example?

Yes 1

LIST BELOW

No 2

Name or description of club etc.	Off. use	Name or description of club etc.	Off. use
1.	......	6.	......
2.	......	7.	......
3.	......	8.	......
4.	......	9.	......
5.	......	10.	......

(c) So could I just check, altogether you go to .... (sum of (a) and (b)) organisations.

RECORD TOTAL NO. OF CLUBS ETC. INFORMANT GOES TO ie ALL THOSE CODED 1 IN COLUMN B, AT PART (a), PLUS ALL THOSE LISTED AT (b).

IF INFORMANT NOW OR LATER RECALLS ANOTHER CLUB HE GOES TO, RECORD AT (a) OR (b) AS APPROPRIATE

233

IF BELONGS TO ANY CLUB ETC.

DNA GOES TO NO CLUB ETC. ...... A GO **TO**

Q.19

17. THOSE WHO GO TO MORE THAN 3 CLUBS ETC. ASK (a) OTHERS GO TO (b)

(a) Of the (ORGANISATIONS) you go to which 3 do you most enjoy?

DNA attends 3 or less clubs ...... B GO TO
(b)

RECORD NAMES
THEN ASK (b) OF
THESE 3 ONLY

1. ....

2. ....

3. ....

(b) ASK (i)-(viii) FOR EACH CLUB ATTENDED OR EACH CLUB LISTED AT (a)
Now thinking of ...... (CLUB ATTENDED) Could you tell me:

NAME OF FIRST CLUB	Off. use	NAME OF SECOND CLUB	Off. use	NAME OF THIRD CLUB	Off. use
1.		2.		3.	
(i) What do you do there?					
O (ii) What made you decide to go along to ..... in the first place?					

234

Q.17(b) (continued)

NAME OF FIRST CLUB	Off. use	NAME OF SECOND CLUB	Off. use	NAME OF THIRD CLUB	Off. use
1.		2.		3.	

(iii) Did you go alone the first time or with someone else?

IF WENT WITH SOMEONE ELSE PROMPT 'Did you go':	Went alone 1
	With 1 or 2
	   friends 2
	In a group 3
	With a
	   relative 4
	Or with some-
	   one else 5
		Went alone ...1
		With 1 or 2
		   friends 2
		In a group 3
		With a
		   relative 4
		Or with some-
		   one else ...5
			Went alone ...1
			With 1 or 2
			   friends 2
			In a group ...3
			With a
			   relative ...4
			Or with some
			   -one else ..5

(iv) Is it for boys/males/girls/females only or is it mixed?

Boys/males only ....1 Girls/females only ....2 Mixed 3	Boys/males only ....1 Girls/females only ....2 Mixed 3	Boys/males only ......1 Girls/females only ...2 Mixed 3

(v) What ages are the other people who go?

TRY TO OBTAIN A RANGE WITH AN UPPER AND LOWER LIMIT

LOWER LIMIT .... UPPER LIMIT	LOWER LIMIT .... UPPER LIMIT	LOWER LIMIT .... UPPER LIMIT ....

(vi) About how often do you go there?

PROMPT
More than once a week 1
About once a week 2
Less than once a week
  but at least once a
  month 3
Or less than once a
  month 4
	PROMPT
	More than once a week 1
	About once a week 2
	Less than once a week
	  but at least once a
	  month 3
	Or less than once a
	  month 4
		PROMPT
		More than once a week ...1
		About once a week 2
		Less than once a week
		  but at least once a
		  month 3
		Or less than once a
		  month 4

(vii) And about how long is it since you started going there?

4 weeks or less ....1 Up to six months ......2 Up to a year ....3 A year or more 4	4 weeks or less ......1 Up to six months ....2 Up to a year ....3 A year or more 4	4 weeks or less .....1 Up to six months ....2 Up to a year ....3 A year or more 4

(viii) How long is it since you last went there?

A week or less ....1 Up to 4 weeks ....2 Up to 3 months ....3 3 months or more 4	A week or less ....1 Up to 4 weeks ....2 Up to 3 months ......3 3 months or more 4	A week or less ....1 Up to 4 weeks ....2 Up to 3 months ......3 3 months or more 4

DNA/does not go to any club ....|. A GO TO
Q.19

THOSE WHO GO TO AT LEAST ONE CLUB ETC.

18. (a) Do you hold a position of responsibility, like
committee member or secretary in (any of) the ...
(organisation(s)) ... you go to?

Yes ....|. 1 ask(i)

No ....|. 2

THOSE WHO
GO TO
A CLUB ETC.

    (i) If yes (1)

       What position(s) do you hold?

(b) Did you help to start (any of) the (organisation(s))
you go to now?

Yes ....|. 1

No ....|. 2

TO ALL

19. Have you ever in the past been to any club or
group which you no longer go to?

Yes ....|. 1 ask(a)

No ....|. 2

(a) If yes (1)

    (i) Which of these was the one you stopped going to most
recently? RECORD NAME OF CLUB ETC. OR DESCRIPTION OF GROUP

    ....

0 (ii) Why did you stop going there?

(iii) How long is it since you last went to ... (CLUB ETC.)

1 week or less ....|. 1

Up to 4 weeks ....|. 2

Up to 3 months ....|. 3

3 months or more ......|. 4

236

20. Can you imagine for a moment a club or centre of <u>any kind</u> that you
    would really enjoy going to <u>nowadays</u>.

                        DNA Wouldn't want to go to any club etc. .... O GO TO
                                                                            Q.22

    (a) What sort of things would you like to be able to do there?
    O

    (b) What sort of place would it be? (PROMPT ONLY IF NECESSARY - 'I
    O   mean what sort of building, furniture and equipment would you
        like it to have?')

                                                        Prompt used ..... O

237

Q.20 (continued)

    (c) (Thinking still of a club you would enjoy going to now) What ages
        would you want the other people who went there to be?
        (TRY TO OBTAIN A RANGE WITH AN UPPER AND LOWER LIMIT)

lower limit	upper limit

    (d) Would you want this place to be for boys (males/girls/females)
        only or mixed?

Males only	1
Females only	2
Mixed	3

    (e) How do you think it should be run, by the members themselves
        or by someone older? (DO NOT PROMPT)

DNA desired club is for all ages	A GO TO(f)
By the members	1
By an older person	2
By the members with older person in charge ..	3
Other (specify)	4

        ....

        ....

    (f) And how often would you like it to be open, even if you didn't
        go every time? (DO NOT PROMPT)

CODE HIGHEST
NO.MENTIONED

Every night (7 nights a week)	1
6 nights a week	2
5 nights a week	3
4 nights a week	4
3 nights a week	5
2 nights (weekdays or unspecified)	6
1 night a week	7
Weekends only	8
All the time (incl. daytime)	9
Other (specify)	10

        ....

21. I'm going to read out a list of things some people have said are important in a club or centre they enjoy going to and I'd like to know how you feel about each thing.

Do you think it is <u>very</u> important, <u>fairly</u> important or <u>not</u> important that it should be a place where you can:

PROMPT LIST - HAND CARD B TO INFORMANT	Very important	Fairly important	Not important	D.K.
1. Make new friends	1	2	3	4
2. Meet friends you know already	1	2	3	4
3. Find boy/girl friends (opp. sex)	1	2	3	4
4. Learn new things and find new interests	1	2	3	4
5. Be able to do the things you are already interested in	1	2	3	4
6. Escape from older people	1	2	3	4
7. Meet people who think like you do	1	2	3	4
8. Get help or advice about your problems	1	2	3	4
9. Learn how to get on with all sorts of people	1	2	3	4

22. Now, can you think of other sorts of places you might go to, like coffee bars, night clubs, dance halls, and so on. In general would you expect to enjoy yourself more or less at a commercially run place than at one of the other kinds of clubs and places we were talking about?

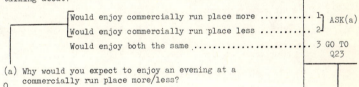

Would enjoy commercially run place more .... 1 ⎤ ASK(a)
Would enjoy commercially run place less .... 2 ⎦
Would enjoy both the same .... 3 GO TO Q23

(a) Why would you expect to enjoy an evening at a commercially run place more/less?
0

23. (Can I just check) would you call any of the places you (go to now or) have ever been to a Youth Club?

Yes .... 1 ask(a)

No 2

DK 3

    (a) IF HAS EVER BEEN TO A YOUTH CLUB (1)

        Would you call any of the places you go to now a youth club?
    OR You said that one of the places you go to now is a youth club, is that right?

Yes 4

No 5

DK 6

24. Here is a list of things which some people have said about Youth Clubs, and I'd like you to say for each remark whether or not you agree with it.

    (From what you know or have heard)
    Do you agree or disagree that at
    youth clubs you will:

PROBE IF NECESSARY 'On the whole'

	Agree	Neither/ DK	Disagree	Clubs differ
1. Find the people there are friendly	1	2	3	4
2. See fights and violence	1	2	3	4
3. Be bored	1	2	3	4
4. Be able to please yourself what you do there	1	2	3	4
5. Be bossed around	1	2	3	4
6. Have lots of interesting things to do	1	2	3	4
7. Feel obliged to go regularly	1	2	3	4
8. Find too many younger people there	1	2	3	4
9. Be treated as an adult	1	2	3	4
10. Feel lonely and out of it	1	2	3	4

ADMINISTER SELF-COMPLETION SCHEDULE SECTION BY SECTION.

INTRODUCE BRIEFLY USING INSTRUCTIONS AT HEAD OF EACH SECTION.

25. Have you ever done any unpaid voluntary work - like looking after handicapped children, visiting old people or helping in a work camp?

Yes .... 1 ask (a)-(c)

No 2

No, but would like to 3

IF YES (1) ASK (a) - (c)

(a) What have you actually done?

(1) ....

(2) ....

(3) ....

(4) ....

(b) ASK FOR EACH TYPE OF WORK

How did you find out about ... (work done) in the first place?

(1)

(2)

(3)

(4)

(c) ASK FOR ALL CONTINUOUS WORK (i.e. not flag selling, fund raising marches). Are you still doing this (any of these things)?

Yes 1

No .... 2 ASK(i)

0 (i) Why did you stop doing this kind of work?

IF SAYS 'No time' PROBE

241

26.
0

Have you ever been away from home on a residential course of any
kind? for example a course in mountaineering, music, an outward
bound school or just on how to get on with other people.

Yes .... 1 ASK(a)
and(b)

No 2

If yes (1) ASK FOR EACH

(a) What kind of course was it?

(1) ....

(2) ....

(3) ....

(4) ....

(5) ....

(b) Who organised this course?

(RECORD ORGANISATION, NOT PERSON)	COURSES			
	1	2	3	4
School	1	1	1	1
College	2	2	2	2
Club* (including school and college clubs)	3	3	3	3
Work ,.................................	4	4	4	4
Scouts/guides/cadets	5	5	5	5
Other (specify)	6	6	6	6
....				
....				

* CHECK 'CLUB' IS NOT NAME OF
  COMMERCIAL TRAVEL AGENCY

27. INTRODUCE ALONG THE LINES OF:
   What people read and hear about often influences their opinions
   or the things they do, so can I just ask:

   (a) Do you usually read a daily   Usually reads daily newspaper .... 1 ask(i)
       newspaper, at least twice a   Does not usually read daily
       week or not?   newspaper 2

       (i) If yes (1)   CODE ALL
                                                                       THAT APPLY
           What daily paper do   Daily Mirror 1
           you usually read?   Daily Express 2
                                                  Daily Mail 3
                                                  Daily Telegraph 4
                                                  Daily Sketch 5
                                                  The Guardian 6
                                                  The Times 7
                                                  The Sun 8
                                                  Other (specify) 9

                                                  ....

   (b) Do you usually read a Sunday
       newspaper - at least once a   Usually reads Sunday newspaper .... 1 ask(i)
       fortnight?   Does not usually read Sunday
                                                newspaper 2

       (i) If yes (1)   CODE ALL
                                                                       THAT APPLY
           What Sunday paper do   News of the World ... 1
           you usually read?   The People 2
                                                  Sunday Mirror 3
                                                  Sunday Express 4
                                                  Sunday Times 5
                                                  Sunday Telegraph ... 6
                                                  The Observer 7
                                                  Other (specify) 8

                                                  ....

---

28. (Now thinking of radio and TV) Do you watch   Yes 1
    or listen to the news fairly regularly - I   No 2
    mean 4 times a week, or more?

---

29. Do you regularly watch or listen to documentary or
    current affairs programmes like Panorama, This Week, Yes 1
    24 Hours, Ten O'clock or the World at One? (REGULARLY No 2
    MEANS AT LEAST ONE OF THEM ONCE A FORTNIGHT)

---

30. What kind of news and so on do you find most interesting?
O   RECORD NEGATIVE AS WELL AS POSITIVE ANSWERS e.g. 'Not foreign news'
    PROBE VAGUE ANSWERS e.g. 'World News', 'Home news', 'all news'.

31. Can we return for a moment to
your education (and job) to
clear up one or two points I
didn't ask about earlier; have
you ever taken any CSE or GCE
O or A level exams?

IF 'YES',SPECIFY WHICH:		CODE ALL TAKEN
CSE	1	ASK A
GCE O level	2	ASK B
GCE A level	3	ASK C
		THEN D OF ALL
None of these but other exam mentioned	4	
None of these	5	GO TO TOP OF P.27

A. If has taken CSE
    (i) What subjects have you taken in CSE? RECORD IN COL.(1) BELOW
    ASK FOR EACH SUBJECT TAKEN
    (ii) What grades did you get in this subject? RECORD IN COL.(2) BELOW

B. If has taken GCE O level
    What subjects have you passed at O level? RECORD IN COLS.(1) & (3) BELOW

C. If has taken GCE A level
    (i) What subjects have you passed at A level? RECORD IN COLS. (1) & (4)
    (ii) Did you take any A levels and pass at O level? RECORD IN COLS. (1)
                                            & (3) IF NOT ALREADY RECORDED

D. ASK FOR EACH EXAM SUBJECT RECORDED:
    Did you work for ..... at school or elsewhere?
    (i) If elsewhere
        Did you study for .... full-time after leaving school, RECORD ANSWERS
        part-time or in some other way?   IN COL. (5)

(1)	OFF. USE	(2) CSE GRADE		(3) GCE O pass	(4) GCE A pass	(5) Has studied for:			
SUBJECT		Grade 1	Other Grades			At school	Full-time after school	Part-time after school	Other
....		1	2	3	4	5	6	7	8
....		1	2	3	4	5	6	7	8
....		1	2	3	4	5	6	7	8
....		1	2	3	4	5	6	7	8
....		1	2	3	4	5	6	7	8
....		1	2	3	4	5	6	7	8
....		1	2	3	4	5	6	7	8
....		1	2	3	4	5	6	7	8
....		1	2	3	4	5	6	7	8
....		1	2	3	4	5	6	7	8
....		1	2	3	4	5	6	7	8
....		1	2	3	4	5	6	7	8
....		1	2	3	4	5	6	7	8
....		1	2	3	4	5	6	7	8
....		1	2	3	4	5	6	7	8

244

32. Since leaving school have you taken or are you taking any of the following kinds of courses: PROMPT LIST AND HAND CARD C TO INFORMANT. RECORD ANSWERS AT A

DNA, still at school .... A GO TO Q.42 P.30

If 'yes' to any
(i) Are you taking any of these kinds of courses at present?
   REPEAT PROMPT AND RECORD ANSWER AT B
(ii) Were you taking any of them a year ago - that is last .... (state month a year ago) RECORD ANSWER AT C

INDIVIDUAL PROMPT AS NECESSARY	A Ever taken		B Taking at present		C Was taking a year ago	
	Yes	No	Yes	No	Yes	No
A full-time course	1	2	3	4	5	6
A sandwich course	1	2	3	4	5	6
A part-time course you attend(ed) during the day time only	1	2	3	4	5	6
A part-time course you attend(ed) during some days and evenings	1	2	3	4	5	6
Or a course you attend(ed) in the evenings only	1	2	3	4	5	6
Other course (specify)	1	2	3	4	5	6
....						

THOSE AT COLLEGE/UNIVERSITY OR ANSWERED 'YES' TO Q.32 MAIN (COL.A)

DNA No further education ... A GO TO Y FOOT OF PAGE

33. (a) Which examinations if any are you (were you) studying for? RECORD BELOW.

(b) Have you completed this course, are you still studying or have you given up the course. RECORD BELOW.

THOSE WHO HAVE HAD SOME FURTHER EDUCATION

	(a) Exams studied/ studying for	(b) Course completed	Still studying	Course given up
No examination	01	3	4	5
City and Guilds	02	3	4	5
R.S.A.	03	3	4	5
Degree/Dip.Tech./C.N.A.A.	04	3	4	5
G.C.E. 'A' level	05	3	4	5
G.C.E. 'O' level	06	3	4	5
C.S.E.	07	3	4	5
H.N.C./H.N.D.	08	3	4	5
O.N.C./O.N.D.	09	3	4	5
Other (specify)	10	3	4	5
....		3	4	5
....		3	4	5

Y — THOSE AT COLLEGE/UNIVERSITY FULL TIME GO TO Q.41 P.29
OTHERS ASK Qs. 34-42.

34. Are you serving or have you ever started to serve an
    apprenticeship?

    Yes .... 1 ask(a)

    No 2

      (a) <u>If yes (1)</u>
         Are you:

               PROMPT   serving an apprenticeship now... 1
               AS   have you completed an
               NECESSARY   apprenticeship 2
                           or did you start one and give
                           it up 3

35. How many hours did you work last
    week, including overtime if you
    did any?

    Number of hours

    INCLUDE LUNCH HOURS AS WORK

36. Were you on shift work last week?

    Yes 1

    No 2

THOSE IN FULL-TIME JOB NOW

37. How much did you earn last week
    (month) including overtime, if any,
    but <u>after</u> deductions for tax,
    national insurance (and other
    compulsory deductions)

    Amount earned

£	s.	d.

    Amount was for week 1

    fortnight 2

    month 3

    Other (specify) 4

    ....

    D.K. amount 5

38. Is that what you:

    RUNNING
    PROMPT

    Usually earn each week (month etc.) 1

    More than you usually earn 2

    Or less 3

    Varies 4

    D.K. 5

39. Do you normally have holidays
    with pay in your present job?

Yes 1

No 2

DK 3

40. (a) Do you receive any of the following benefits from
    your present employer?

CODE ALL
THAT APPLY

PROMPT

Luncheon vouchers .... 1 ask(i)

Free travel .... 2 ⌉

A travel allowance, car allowance or
petrol allowance when you are not
travelling on your employers business ... 3 ⌋

ask
(ii)

Free or subsidised housing or
accommodation 4

None 5

DK 6

THOSE IN A
FULL-TIME
JOB NOW

(i) If receives luncheon vouchers (1)

What is the value of each voucher

s.	d.

(ii) If receives free travel or travel/car/petrol
allowance (2), (3)

Do you (travel free on) (receive a travel/car/
petrol allowance for) every journey you go on?

Yes 1

No 2

(b) Is there anything else which you receive in addition
to your wages or salary from your employer for which
you make no payment?

Yes (specify) 1

No 2

41. (Apart from your present job) how many full-time paid jobs have you
    had since leaving school, not counting holiday jobs? I mean jobs
    with different employers?

ENTER NO. OF JOBS HERE ⟶

TO ALL

42. Is there anything else you'd like to say about spare-time provision
0   for people like you, or about your needs?

(sects.(ix)-(xvi) to be completed only for informants for whom no adult has been/is to be interviewed. Others record duration of interview at (xvii)

(ix) A. Household composition

PERSON NO.	RELATIONSHIP TO INFORMANT	OFF. USE	SEX		AGE LAST BIRTHDAY	MARITAL STATUS			WORKING STATUS		
			M	F		M	S	W/D/S	Full time	Part time	Not working
1	Informant		1	2		1	2	3	5	6	7
2			1	2		1	2	3	5	6	7
3			1	2		1	2	3	5	6	7
4			1	2		1	2	3	5	6	7
5			1	2		1	2	3	5	6	7
6			1	2		1	2	3	5	6	7
7			1	2		1	2	3	5	6	7
8			1	2		1	2	3	5	6	7
9			1	2		1	2	3	5	6	7
10			1	2		1	2	3	5	6	7
11			1	2		1	2	3	5	6	7
12			1	2		1	2	3	5	6	7
13			1	2		1	2	3	5	6	7
14			1	2		1	2	3	5	6	7
15			1	2		1	2	3	5	6	7

B.   Head of household is (Record PERSON NO. FROM A) ─────→ [   ]

(x) If informant lives in an institution, record type.

Informant does not live in an
   institution 1

School 2

Students hostel/works hostel/hall of
   residence 3

Nurses home 4

Military establishment 5

Hotel/Boarding house 6

Other (specify) 7

(xi) Number of bedrooms household has - (include bedsitter) whether used or not

RECORD NUMBER IN BOX ────→ [OFF USE]

(xii) Country or origin of informant's parents –

	Mother	Father
U.K. including N.Ireland, Ch. Is., I.O.M.	...1	...1
Eire (S.Ireland)	...2	...2
Other (specify)		
Mother	...3	
Father		...3

(xiii) Occupation of informant's father | Off. use

Occupation:

Industry:

IF FATHER HAS RETIRED OR DIED ETC. NOTE AND RECORD LAST OCCUPATION

IF INFORMANT IS A MARRIED WOMAN
(xiv) Occupation of informant's husband

Occupation:

Industry:

(xvi) Informant's brothers and sisters, including step and adoptive brothers and sisters.

RECORD IN BIRTH ORDER AND INCLUDE INFORMANT IN APPROPRIATE POSITION

No. of brothers & sisters in family, including informant	First name or initials	Sex M F	Age last birthday	Off. use
1	....	...1..2..	....	
2	....	...1..2..	....	
3	....	...1..2..	....	
4	....	...1..2..	....	
5	....	...1..2..	....	
6	....	...1..2..	....	
7	....	...1..2..	....	
8	....	...1..2..	....	
9	....	...1..2..	....	
10	....	..1..2..	....	
11	....	...1..2..	....	
12	....	...1..2..	....	
13	....	...1..2..	....	
14	....	...1..2..	....	
15	....	...1..2..	....	

(xv) Age at which parents completed full-time education

	Father	Mother
14 and under	...1	...1
15 but under 16	...2	...2
16 but under 17	...3	...3
17 but under 18	...4	...4
18 and over	...5	...5
D.K.	...6	...6

RECORD FOR ALL

(xvii) Length of interview

Less than ½ of an hour	1
½ but less than 1 hour	2
1 hour but less than 1¼ hours	3
1¼ hours but less than 1½ hours	4
1½ hours but less than 2 hours	5
2 hours or longer	6

250

S 437/P

		area	address	parent digit

Serial No.

Interviewer's name ....

	Day	Month	Year
Auth. No. .... Date of interview .. | | | 1969

(i) The informant is ... (RECORD RELATIONSHIP AT A BELOW) ... of following child(ren)
(RECORD IN B BELOW)

A. Relationship of informant to sample child(ren)				Sex		B. Sample child(ren)			Off.use	
Natural mother	Foster or adoptive mother	Natural father	Other (specify)	M	F	Christian name	Y.P. ident. digit	Parent ident. digit	Y.P. int.	Y.P. not int.
1...	..2......	...3.....	..4................	.5..	.6.	....	....	....	..7..	..8
1...	..2......	...3.....	..4................	.5..	.6.	....	....	....	..7..	..8
1...	..2......	...3.....	..4................	.5..	.6.	....	....	....	..7..	..8
1...	..2......	...3.....	..4................	.5..	.6.	....	....	....	..7..	..8
1...	..2......	...3.....	..4................	.5..	.6.	....	....	....	..7..	..8
1...	..2......	...3.....	..4................	.5..	.6.	....	....	....	..7..	..8
1...	..2......	...3.....	..4................	.5..	.6.	....	....	....	..7..	..8

(ii) If no interview obtained with parent or parent substitute of young people listed
at (i) give full explanation here.

(iii) Whether anyone other than informant present for half or more of interview

No, only informant present 1
Spouse present 2
One or more sample children present 3
Other 4

1. A. First of all would you tell me the first
names or initials of the children in this
family?

RING NUMBER IN A BELOW

THEN COMPLETE HOUSEHOLD BOX BELOW.

> THIS REFERS TO ALL CHILDREN WHO
> ARE ALIVE NOW, WHETHER OR NOT
> THEY ARE LIVING AT HOME.

A Ring total no. of children in family	B First names or initials	C Sex M F	D Age last birthday	E Date of birth	F Living: Here Away	G Whether in sample Yes No	H What doing: RECORD FOR SAMPLE CHILDREN ONLY F/time Educ. Job Other	Off. use
1		1 2			1 2	3 4	5 6 7	
2		1 2			1 2	3 4	5 6 7	
3		1 2			1 2	3 4	5 6 7	
4		1 2			1 2	3 4	5 6 7	
5		1 2			1 2	3 4	5 6 7	
6		1 2			1 2	3 4	5 6 7	
7		1 2			1 2	3 4	5 6 7	
8		1 2			1 2	3 4	5 6 7	
9		1 2			1 2	3 4	5 6 7	
10		1 2			1 2	3 4	5 6 7	
11		1 2			1 2	3 4	5 6 7	
12		1 2			1 2	3 4	5 6 7	
13		1 2			1 2	3 4	5 6 7	
14		1 2			1 2	3 4	5 6 7	
15		1 2			1 2	3 4	5 6 7	
Off.use								

IF LISTED CHILDREN INCLUDE ANY NOT IN SAMPLE, SAY

'Now I'd like to talk to you about ...... (NAME ALL CHILDREN IN SAMPLE)'
AND EXPLAIN WHY THE INTERVIEW IS CONCERNED ONLY WITH THOSE IN THE SAMPLE.

2. I would like to start by asking you some questions about the kind of places there are round here* where young people of ..... (NAME THOSE IN SAMPLE) .... age(s) can go to:

What sort of places are there for young people round here*?

RECORD ALL BELOW IN (A) THEN PROMPT

> *CLARIFY IF NECESSARY 'Within easy reach'

---

(1) PROMPT ...... Is there anything you would call a youth club that .... (THOSE IN SAMPLE) .... could go to (apart from .... (MENTION THOSE INFORMANT HAS CALLED A YOUTH CLUB))

   RECORD IN (A) AND CODE '1' (COL.B) FOR THESE AND ANY ALREADY MENTIONED

(2) PROMPT ...... Are there any other clubs or societies you haven't already mentioned like a sports club or social centre, drama group (or scouts or guides) that ...... (THOSE IN SAMPLE) could go to?

   RECORD IN (A) ANY NOT ALREADY MENTIONED

(3) PROMPT ...... Are there any other places where young people of .... (THOSE IN SAMPLE) .... age(s) go much — like bowling alleys (night clubs) cinemas (or pubs)?

   RECORD IN (A) (TYPE OF PLACE ONLY) ANY NOT ALREADY MENTIONED

(A)	(B) youth club	Off. use	(A)	(B) youth club	Off. use
1.	1		9.	1	
2.	1		10.	1	
3.	1		11.	1	
4.	1		12.	1	
5.	1		13.	1	
6.	1		14.	1	
7.	1		15.	1	
8.	1		16.	1	

3. Are any of the things you have mentioned places
you'd rather your son (daughter/children) did <u>not</u>
go to? (PROMPT LIST AT Q.2 IF NECESSARY)

Yes .... 1 ask(a)
                  and(b)
No/don't mind .... 2 ⎤ GO TO
D.K. .... 3 ⎦ Q.4

<u>IF YES (1)</u>

(a) Which places would you rather he (she/they) didn't go to?

O (b) Why would you rather he (she/they) didn't go there?

(a) PLACE	Off. use	(b) REASON	Off. use

4. So on the whole would you say there are plenty of things provided for young people like (SAMPLE CHILDREN) round here or not?

Plenty/enough provided 1
Not enough/much .... 2 ⎤ ask(a)
Nothing provided .... 3 ⎦
D.K. 4
Other (specify) 5

....

(a) <u>If not enough/nothing provided (2) or (3)</u>

What (else) would you like to see provided? (for sample children)

5. How does (do) (SAMPLE CHILD(REN)) usually spend his (her/their) spare time? (LIST ACTIVITIES)

Watching T.V. 1

....
....
....
....
....
....
....
....
....
....
....
....

6. Now I'd like to ask you to think for a moment about a good club or
    centre of any kind for young people like .... (NAME THOSE IN SAMPLE)

    (a) What sort of things would you like them (those in sample) to be
    O   able to do there?

                                    Informant/children wouldn't want club .... 1 GO TO
                                                                                  Q.7

    (b) What sort of place should it be? (PROMPT ONLY IF NECESSARY - I
    O   mean what sort of building, furniture and equipment do you think
        it should have?)

                                                           Prompt used .... O

    (c) (Thinking still of a good club for young people like ....) what
        ages do you think the club or centre should be for?

                                                    LOWER LIMIT ....
        (TRY TO OBTAIN ONE OR MORE RANGES WITH
        UPPER AND LOWER LIMITS. CHECK THAT RANGES   UPPER LIMIT ....
        INCLUDE AGES OF SAMPLE CHILDREN)

                                                    LOWER LIMIT ....

                                                    UPPER LIMIT ....

    (d) Do you think it should be for
        both sexes or one sex only?   Mixed sex 1

                                                    Boys/Girls only 2

                                                    Don't mind 3

                                                    D.K. 4

                                                    Other (specify) 5

                                                    ....

256

6. (continued)

(e) How do you think it should be run, by the members themselves or someone older?

DNA desired club is for all ages	. A GO TO(f)
Young people	. 1
Someone older	. 2
By young people and older person (include'with older person in charge')	. 3
Other (specify)	. 4
....	

(f) And how often do you think it should be open even if they didn't have to go each time it was open?

	CODE HIGHEST NO.MENTIONED
Every night (7 nights a week)	. 1
6 nights a week	. 2
5 nights a week	. 3
4 nights a week	. 4
3 nights a week	. 5
2 nights a week	. 6
1 night a week	. 7
Weekends only	. 8
All the time (incl. day time)	. 9
Other (specify)	.10
....	

(g) Should there be someone there to whom young people could talk about their personal problems or don't you think it would be the right place for that?

Should be someone	. 1
Not the right place	. 2
D.K.	. 3
Other (specify)	. 4
....	

7. (Can we talk now about Youth Clubs in particular)

(a) Have you (or your husband) ever visited a youth club*?

Yes (informant or spouse)	. 1
No/don't remember/D.K.	. 2

*'youth club' means anything informant would call a youth club

(b) Have you (or your husband) ever met or spoken to a Youth leader or Youth worker?

Yes	. 1
No/don't remember/D.K.	. 2

(c) Have (either of) you ever taken part in the running of a youth club?

Yes	. 1
No/don't remember/D.K.	. 2

(d) Did you (or your husband) ever go to anything you would call a youth club when you were younger?

Yes	. 1
No/don't remember/D.K.	. 2

8. Could I read out some things which some people have said about youth clubs. Would you say, in each case, whether you, yourself, agree or disagree with the remark. PROBE AS NECESSARY 'On the whole do you agree or disagree that':

PROMPT LIST	Agree	Can't say D.K.	Disagree	Clubs differ
(a) Youth clubs are good for helping young people to find new interests	1	2	3	4
(b) Youth clubs are full of the wrong type of people	1	2	3	4
(c) Fights and violence are common in youth clubs	1	2	3	4
(d) Youth clubs are good for the shy young person	1	2	3	4
(e) Youth clubs have nothing for the young person with serious interests	1	2	3	4
(f) Parents know their children are safe when they are at a youth club	1	2	3	4
(g) Youth clubs are good for helping young people to make the right kind of friends	1	2	3	4
(h) Only young people who don't know what to do with themselves go to youth clubs	1	2	3	4
(i) A useful thing about youth clubs is that they keep young people off the streets	1	2	3	4

9. In some districts young people do voluntary unpaid work like visiting old people, helping to look after handicapped children or helping in work camps.

   Have any of the young people in your family done this kind of thing at all?

   Yes .... 1 ask(a)
   No 2
   No, but would like them to 3
   D.K. 4

   (a) If yes (1) What have they done?

10. Are you (would you be) in favour of members of your family doing this kind of voluntary work or not?

   Yes 6
   No 7
   D.K. 8

258

<table>
<tr><td>Qs. 11-26 ARE TO BE ASKED
ABOUT EACH Y.P. IN SAMPLE
WHO COMES UNDER THIS ADULT
AND LIVES AT THIS ADDRESS</td><td>Address
Serial No.</td><td></td><td></td><td></td><td></td><td></td><td></td></tr>
</table>

FOR EACH QUESTION ASK FIRST ABOUT ELDEST CHILD IN SAMPLE, THEN SAY SOMETHING
LIKE: 'And how about .... (NEXT ELDEST IN SAMPLE) .....' AND REPEAT QUESTION,
UNTIL YOU HAVE ANSWERS FOR EVERY CHILD IN SAMPLE.

INTRODUCE AS NECESSARY ALONG THE LINES OF 'I'd like to ask the next few questions
about ..... (SAMPLE CHILDREN) in turn'.

11. Does ... (SAMPLE CHILD) spend
    most of his (her) spare time at | LAST TWO DIGITS OF Y.Ps SER.NO.
    home or is he (she) mostly out | Y.Ps INITIALS OR NAMES
    at this time of year?

    DNA lives away from home 4 days a week
        or more .... A....A....A....A....A GO TO Q.13
    Mostly at home .... 1....1....1....1....1
    Half and half .... 2....2....2....2....2
    Mostly out .... 3....3....3....3....3
    Other (specify) .... 4....4....4....4....4

LAST 2 DIGITS OF SER. NO.

12. How do you feel about the amount of time
    he (she) spends at home:

                    ┌ Are you quite happy .... 1.....1.....1.....1.....1
    RUNNING   │ Do you wish he (she) would spend
    PROMPT   │   more time at home .... 2.....2.....2.....2.....2
                    │ Or would you like to see him (her) go
                    └   out more? .... 3.....3.....3.....3.....3

                      Other answer (specify) .... 4.....4.....4.....4.....4

13. Would you say he (she) meets enough of the kind of people you like him (her) to mix with or not?

	LAST TWO DIGITS OF Y.Ps SER.NO.								
	Y.Ps INITIALS OR NAME								

Yes, enough ....1.....|....1.....|....1.....|....1.....|....1
No, not enough ....2.....|....2.....|....2.....|....2.....|....2
Don't mind who he (she) mixes with ......3.....|....3.....|....3.....|....3.....|....3
Other (specify) ....4.....|....4.....|....4.....|....4.....|....4

LAST 2 DIGITS OF SER. NO.

14. On the whole is ...... the sort of person who makes friends easily or not?

Yes makes friends easily ....1.....|....1.....|....1.....|....1.....|....1
Doesn't make friends easily ....2.....|....2.....|....2.....|....2.....|....2
D.K. ....3.....|....3.....|....3.....|....3.....|....3
Other (specify) ....4.....|....4.....|....4.....|....4.....|....4

15. What about his (her) friends - do you know most of them, some of them or none of them?

Has no friends at all ....1.....|....1.....|....1.....|....1.....|....1 GO TO Q.18
Knows most ....2.....|....2.....|....2.....|....2.....|....2
Knows some ....3.....|....3.....|....3.....|....3.....|....3
Knows none ....4.....|....4.....|....4.....|....4.....|....4
Other answer (specify) ....5.....|....5.....|....5.....|....5.....|....5

260

16. Do you (would you) like him (her) to bring friends home or not?

LAST TWO DIGITS OF Y.Ps SER. NO.						
Y.Ps INITIALS OR NAME						

Likes friends brought home - no
    reservations ....1.....1.....1.....1.....1
No doesn't like friends brought home .....2.....2.....2.....2.....2
Don't mind ....3.....3.....3.....3.....3
Other answer (specify) ....4.....4.....4.....4.....4

LAST 2 DIGITS OF SER.NO

17. Do you prefer him (her) to mix mainly with people:

RUNNING PROMPT

Of his (her) own age ....1.....1.....1.....1.....1
Older than him (her) self ....2.....2.....2.....2.....2
Younger than him (her) self ....3.....3.....3.....3.....3
Or with people of all ages ....4.....4.....4.....4.....4
Don't mind, it's up to him (her) ....5.....5.....5.....5.....5
Other (specify) ....6.....6.....6.....6.....6

18. Do you ever have to say anything to him (her) nowadays about ......

	LAST TWO DIGITS OF Y.Ps SER. NO.							
	Y.Ps INITIALS OR NAME							

PROMPT

(1) The time he (she) comes in at night

DNA, does not go out at night ....0......0......0......0......0
Yes ....1......1......1......1......1
No ....2......2......2......2......2
It's up to him (her) ....3......3......3......3......3

(2) How he (she) dresses

Yes ....5......5......5......5......5
No ....6......6......6......6......6
It's up to him (her) ....7......7......7......7......7

(3) Who he (she) goes out with

DNA, goes out with no-one ....0......0......0......0......0
Yes ....1......1......1......1......1
No ....2......2......2......2......2
It's up to him (her) ....3......3......3......3......3

(4) Helping about the house and garden

Yes ....5......5......5......5......5
No ....6......6......6......6......6
It's up to him (her) ....7......7......7......7......7

(5) His (her) homework or studies if he (she) has any

DNA, has no homework ....0......0......0......0......0
Yes ....1......1......1......1......1
No ....2......2......2......2......2
It's up to him (her) ....3......3......3......3......3

(6) The way he (she) spends his (her) money

DNA, has no money of own ....5......5......5......5......5
Yes ....6......6......6......6......6
No ....7......7......7......7......7
It's up to him (her) ....8......8......8......8......8

(7) The time he (she) goes to bed

Yes ....1......1......1......1......1
No ....2......2......2......2......2
It's up to him (her).....3......3......3......3......3

262

19. (May I just check) is ... now:

	LAST TWO DIGITS OF Y.Ps SER. NO.							
	Y.Ps INITIALS OR NAME							

*INCLUDE SANDWICH COURSE AS AT COLLEGE (2)

‡INCLUDE TRAINING ON JOB E.G. NURSING AS JOB

PROMPT

At school ....1......1......1......1.....1
At college/university or other F.E. institution*) ....2......2......2......2.....2
In a job*‡ ....3......3......3......3.....3
Other (specify) ....4......4......4......4.....4

LAST 2 DIGITS OF SER. NO.								

FOR Y.Ps AT SCHOOL ASK Qs. 20-23 OTHERS GO TO Q.24

20. At what age does .... want to leave school?

DNA. Y.P. not at school ....A......A......A......A.....A
15 or under ....1......1......1......1......1
16 ....2......2......2......2......2
17 or over ....3......3......3......3......3
Over 15 but exact age not decided ...4......4......4......4......4
D.K. ....5......5......5......5......5

21. Have you discussed with .... when he (she) should leave school or have you left it entirely to her (him)

YOUNG PEOPLE STILL AT SCHOOL

Have discussed ....1......1......1......1.......1
Have discussed but left (final) decision to him (her) ....2......2......2......2......2

LAST 2 DIGITS OF SER. NO.

Have not discussed (yet) ....3......3......3......3.......3
Other (specify) ....4......4......4......4......4

263

			LAST TWO DIGITS OF Y.Ps SER. NO.						
			Y.Ps INITIALS OR NAME						

22.0 What does .... want to do when he (she) leaves school – take a job or go to college or what?

		Take a job	...1...	...1...	...1...	...1...	...1		
		Go to college (university/other full-time F.E.)	...2...	...2...	...2...	...2...	...2		
LAST 2 DIGITS OF SER. NO.		D.K.	...3...	...3...	...3...	...3...	...3		
		Other (specify)	...4...	...4...	...4...	...4...	...4		

23. Is that what you want him (her) to do or not?

		DNA, D.K. what wants to do	...A...	...A...	...A...	...A...	...A	GO TO Q.27	
		Yes, want him (her) to do this ..	...1...	...1...	...1...	...1...	...1		
		No, would like him (her) to do something different	...2...	...2...	...2...	...2...	...2		
		Don't mind what he (she) does ...	...3...	...3...	...3...	...3...	...3		
		Other (specify)	...4...	...4...	...4...	...4...	...4		

IF ALL SAMPLE Y.Ps AT SCHOOL GO TO Q.27 OTHERS ASK Qs. 24-26.

264

	LAST TWO DIGITS OF Y.Ps SER. NO.						

24. At what age did ....   Y.Ps INITIALS
    leave school?   OR NAME

DNA, Y.P. still at school ....A	...A	...A	...A	...A
15 or under 1	...1	...1	...1	...1
16 2	...2	...2	...2	...2
17 or over 3	...3	...3	...3	...3

25. Did you discuss with ... when he
    (she) should leave school at all,
    or did you leave it entirely to
    him (her)

Discussed leaving 1	...1	...1	...1	...1
Discussed but left (final) decision to him (her) 2	...2	...2	...2	...2
Did not discuss 3	...3	...3	...3	...3
Can't remember 4	...4	...4	...4	...4
Other (specify) 5	...5	...5	...5	...5

LAST 2 DIGITS OF SER. NO.

YOUNG PEOPLE WHO HAVE LEFT SCHOOL

26. You said that he (she) is ...
    (SPECIFY PRESENT OR PROSPECTIVE
    JOB, F.E. STATUS)* ... Is that
    what you wanted him (her) to do or
    not?

*IF YOU DO NOT ALREADY KNOW WHAT Y.Ps
JOB IS, ASK HERE 'You said that ... is
in a job, what does he actually do?'
.... THEN ASK Q.26 'Is that what you
wanted ......'

DNA. No job/F.E. position at present ....A	...A	...A	...A	...A
Yes, wanted him (her) to do this ...1	...1	...1	...1	...1
No, would like him (her) to do something different 2	...2	...2	...2	...2
Don't mind 3	...3	...3	...3	...3
Other (specify) 4	...4	...4	...4	...4

265

TO ALL

27. Some parents worry about the way their children spend their spare time. I would like to read you some things that parents have said about this. Thinking about .... (specify those in sample) would you tell me whether you ever feel this about him (her/any of them) now?

    (CODE 1 IF WORRIES ABOUT ANY CHILD IN SAMPLE)

PROMPT LIST	Sometimes feels this	Does not feel this	D.K.
(1) I wish there were more for him (her) to do round here	1	2	3
(2) I wish he (she) had more friends	1	2	3
(3) I am sometimes afraid he (she) might get into trouble	1	2	3
(4) I worry in case he (she) is in an accident	1	2	3
(5) I worry in case he (she) tries taking drugs	1	2	3
(6) I am anxious in case he (she) is attacked	1	2	3
(7) I worry about him (her) (trying) drinking	1	2	3

28. Some parents say they wish there was somewhere they could go for advice or help about teenagers' problems. Do you ever feel you would like advice about your son (daughter/children)?

    (PROMPT IF NECESSARY - 'I mean ... (THOSE IN SAMPLE)')

    Yes .... 1 ask(a)

    No 2

    D.K. 3

    (a) If yes (1):

    O What have you felt you would like advice about?

       (CHECK THAT EACH PROBLEM MENTIONED OCCURRED WITHIN THE LAST 2 YEARS)

INTRODUCE ALONG THE LINES OF: 'So far we have been talking about your son
(daughter/children)'s spare time activities and so on ......'

29. A. Can I ask you now about the things you do in your spare time (when you
have any) what sort of things do you do?   RECORD BELOW

Informant	Off.use
Watches T.V.	1
....	
....	
....	
....	
....	
....	
....	

IF INFORMANT'S SPOUSE IS LIVING IN THE HOME:

B. What about your husband (wife), what sort of things does he (she) do in his
spare time?   RECORD BELOW

SPOUSE	Off.use
DNA, no spouse	0
Watches T.V.	1
....	
....	
....	
....	
....	
....	
....	

267

	Informant	Spouse

30. (I know you must be busy but) do you belong to any clubs or societies of any kind, or take part in any other local activities or associations?

THEN SAY 'What about your husband (wife), does he (she) ... (REPEAT QUESTION)'

	Informant	Spouse
DNA, no spouse	....	0
Yes	1 ask(a)	1 ask(a)
No	2	2
D.K.	3	3

(a) If yes (1): What do you (does he/she) do or belong to?

INFORMANT:

SPOUSE:

---

31. Do you do any unpaid voluntary work - things like taking meals to old people, helping with handicapped children or discharged prisoners? THEN SAY 'What about your husband (wife) does he (she) ... (REPEAT QUESTION)'

	Informant	Spouse
DNA, no spouse	....	0
Yes	1 ask(a)	1 ask(a)
No	2	2
No, but would like to	3	3
D.K.	4	4

(a) If yes (1): What kind of work do you (does he/she) actually do?

INFORMANT:

SPOUSE:

268

32. (a) How would you describe the kind of upbringing you yourself
         had - would you say that it was:

                                    ┌ Very strict 1
                        RUNNING   │ Fairly strict 2
                        PROMPT   └ Or pretty free on the whole? 3

     (b) Is this the kind of upbringing you are trying (have tried) to
         give your family or not?

                              Yes, with no reservations .... 1 Go to
                                                                       Q.33
                              No, or some reservations .... 2 ask(i)

         (i) If no, or some reservations (2):
         0   What kind of upbringing are you trying (have you tried)
             to give them?

33. IF SPOUSE LIVING IN HOME   DNA, no spouse living in home .... 0 Go to
                                                                            Q.34

     (a) What about your husband (wife) - as far as you know was his (her)
         upbringing:
                                    ┌ Very strict 1
                        RUNNING   │ Fairly strict 2
                        PROMPT   └ Or pretty free on the whole 3

     (b) And what kind of upbringing does he (she) want the children
     0   to have?

                              Same as informant wants for
                                  child......................... 1
                              Not concerned/leaves it all to
                                  wife/husband 2
                              Other (specify) 3

269

34. INTRODUCE ALONG THE LINES OF:

The things people read and hear may influence their views on some of
the sorts of things we have been talking about so can I ask ....

Do you (or your husband/wife) usually read a daily newspaper, I mean
at least twice a week?

Yes .... 1 ask(a)

No 2

(a) _If yes (1)_:

What daily newspapers do you (or your husband/wife) usually
read?

	RING ALL THAT APPLY
Daily Mirror	1
Daily Express	2
Daily Mail	3
Daily Telegraph	4
Daily Sketch	5
The Guardian	6
The Times	7
The Sun	8
Other (specify)	9
....	

35. Do you (or your husband/wife) usually read a Sunday newspaper - at
least once a fortnight?

Yes .... 1 ask(a)

No 2

(a) _If yes (1)_:

What Sunday papers do you (or your husband) usually read?

	RING ALL THAT APPLY
News of the World	1
The People	2
Sunday Mirror	3
Sunday Express	4
Sunday Times	5
Sunday Telegraph	6
The Observer	7
Other (specify)	8
....	

36. (Now thinking of radio and TV) Do you (or your husband/wife) watch or listen to the news fairly regularly - I mean 4 times a week or more?

          Yes, informant or spouse does 1

          No, neither does 2

37. Do you (or your husband) regularly watch documentary programmes or programmes about current affairs like Panorama, This Week, 24 Hours, Ten O'clock or the World at One?

REGULARLY MEANS AT LEAST ONE OF THEM ONCE A FORTNIGHT

          Yes, informant or spouse does 1

          No, neither does 2

38. What kind of news and so on do you find most interesting?

O RECORD NEGATIVE AS WELL AS POSITIVE ANSWERS e.g. 'Not foreign news'.

   PROBE VAGUE ANSWERS e.g. 'World news', 'Home news', 'All news'.

CLASSIFICATION SECTION

(iv) <u>Household Composition</u> For children of informant - use information from Q.1

Person No.	Relationship to H.O.H.	Sex M F	Age last birthday	Marital Status M S W/D/S	Employment Status Full time	Part time	Not working
1 ..... H.O.H.	.1..2.	....	.1....2.....3...	..5......6......7		
2	.1..2.	....	.1....2.....3...	..5......6......7		
3	.1..2.	....	.1....2.....3.	..5......6......7		
4	.1..2.	....	.1....2.....3...	..5......6......7		
5	.1..2.	....	.1....2.....3...	..5......6......7		
6	.1..2.	....	.1....2.....3...	..5......6......7		
7	.1..2.	....	.1....2.....3...	..5......6......7		
8	.1..2.	....	.1....2.....3...	..5......6......7		
9	.1..2.	....	.1....2.....3...	..5......6......7		
10	.1..2.	....	.1....2.....3...	..5......6......7		
11	.1..2.	....	.1....2.....3...	..5......6......7		
12	.1..2.	....	.1....2.....3...	..5......6......7		
13	.1..2.	....	.1....2.....3...	..5......6......7		
14	.1..2.	....	.1....2.....3...	..5......6......7		
15	.1..2.	....	.1....2.....3...	..5......6......7		

(v) <u>Type of Dwelling</u>

Whole house - detached 1

- semi-detached (inc.prefab) 2

- terrace 3

Flat/Maisonette - self contained 4

Rooms 5

Caravan 6

Other ...... SPECIFY 7

(vi) <u>Ownership of Dwelling</u>

Owned by household or being bought 1

Rented 2

Rent free 3

(vii) <u>Number of bedrooms</u>

(include unused bedrooms and bedsitters)

household has ⟶ ☐

O F F U S E

(viii) Countries of birth of informant and spouse

	Informant	Spouse
U.K.	...1	1
Eire (Southern Ireland)	...2	2
Other (specify)		
Informant	...3	
....		
Spouse		3
....		
D.K.		4

272

	Informant	Spouse

(ix) Type of school informant and spouse last attended

1. Secondary Modern/Elementary/Junior Secondary/Non-grammar
   church school/All-age school/Village school ....01.......01

2. Comprehensive school, incl. Bilateral or Multilateral
   schools ....02.......02

3. Central/Intermediate/Higher Grade school ....03.......03

4. State Grammar/Technical Grammar/County High or Senior
   Secondary School ....04.......04

5. Technical school ....05.......05

6. Independent/Direct Grant school ....06.......06

7. All schools abroad, incl. Eire (up to and including
   age 18) ....07.......07

8. Don't know type of school ....08.......08

9. Other types of school (specify) ....09.......09

    INFORMANT ....

    SPOUSE   ....

(x) Age at which informant and spouse completed full-time continuous education

    14 and under ....1.......1

    15 but under 16 ....2.......2

    16 but under 17 ....3.......3

IGNORE GAPS OF ANY LENGTH
DUE TO ILLNESS AND OF 3
MONTHS OR LESS FOR ANY OTHER
REASON

    17 but under 18 ....4.......4

    18 and over ....5.......5

    D.K. ....6.......6

(xi) Qualifications obtained by informant and spouse

CODE ALL THAT APPLY

None ....0.. 0

University degree/higher degree (including full medical
   training) membership of a professional institute, full
   professional qualification 1 1

Higher National Certificate or Diploma, Teachers
   Certificate ....2.......2

Intermediate professional qualification, S.R.N., G.C.E.
   A level, Higher School Certificate, Intermediate
   (Arts/Science) ....3.......3

Ordinary National Certificate or Diploma ....4.......4

G.C.E. O level, matriculation, General School Certificate,
   City & Guilds, R.S.A., Forces Educational Certificates,
   commercial or trade certificate/diploma ....5.......5

Apprenticeship ....6.......6

D.K. ....7.......7

Other (specify) ....8.......8

    INFORMANT ....

    SPOUSE   ....

			Informant	Spouse
(xii)	Whether informant and spouse have ever attended an evening course for at least one term.			
	(Include all who have attended any evening course for at least one term, whether course was recreational or academic)	Yes ....1..........1		
		No ....…2.........…2		

(xiii) <u>Occupation of Y.Ps father (or father substitute)</u>

Occupation (DESCRIBE FULLY):

ALWAYS REQUIRED.
IF UNEMPLOYED, NOT IN HOUSEHOLD
OR DECEASED, GIVE LAST JOB.

i

Industry:

ii

<u>COMPLETE (a) and (b) BELOW ALSO</u>

(a) Self-employed or employee?

Self-employed 1

Employee 2

IF MANAGER

(b) Number of employees

DNA Not manager (etc.) or self-employed .... A

(xiv) <u>Income of Y.Ps father (or father substitute Otherwise H.O.H.)</u> <u>after</u> deductions for tax, national insurance, etc.

SHOW CARD

Annual	Last week	
Up to £260	– Up to £5	01
Over £260 – £520	– Over £5 to £10	02
Over £520 – £780	– Over £10 to £15	03
Over £780 – £1040	– Over £15 to £20	04
Over £1040 – £1300	– Over £20 to £25	05
Over £1300 – £1560	– Over £25 to £30	06
Over £1560 – £1820	– Over £30 to £35	07
Over £1820 – £2340	– Over £35 to £45	08
Over £2340 – £2860	– Over £45 to £55	09
Over £2860 – £3380	– Over £55 to £65	10
Over £3380	– Over £65	11
	D.K.	12
	Refusal	13

(xv)

Duration of Interview

Less than three quarters of an hour 1

$\frac{3}{4}$ but less than 1 hour 2

1 hour but less than 1$\frac{1}{4}$ hours 3

1$\frac{1}{4}$ hours but less than 1$\frac{1}{2}$ hours 4

1$\frac{1}{2}$ hours but less than 2 hours 5

2 hours or longer 6

274

S.437/YPQ

<u>Confidential</u>

GOVERNMENT SOCIAL SURVEY

Self-Completion Questionnaire

YOUTH SERVICE ENQUIRY

PP	PA
1	2

TO BE COMPLETED BY INFORMANT

We would like to know your opinions on a number of things that young people have said. Below and on the next two pages you will find a series of statements made by young people the same age as you. All you have to do is to tell us whether or not you agree with these statements.

To the right of each statement you will see five numbers. At the top of each page the numbers are marked as follows:-

STRONGLY AGREE	AGREE ON THE WHOLE	DISAGREE ON THE WHOLE	STRONGLY DISAGREE	UNCERTAIN
1	2	3	4	5

These numbers enable you to tell us what you think about each statement. Just ring the number which best shows how much you agree or disagree with each statement.

	STRONGLY AGREE	AGREE ON THE WHOLE	DISAGREE ON THE WHOLE	STRONGLY DISAGREE	UNCERTAIN
1. As far as holidays are concerned I would like to explore a completely different place each year	1	2	3	4	5
2. Older people irritate me with things they say.	1	2	3	4	5
3. I'm not what you call a good mixer.	1	2	3	4	5
4. I prefer to do the things I know about rather than learn completely new things.	1	2	3	4	5
5. I'd like to have the opportunity to get to know a foreign country really well.	1	2	3	4	5
6. I would like to make friends with people who have different outlooks and interests from me.	1	2	3	4	5
7. I like to hear about what's going on in the world.	1	2	3	4	5

276

	STRONGLY AGREE	AGREE ON THE WHOLE	DISAGREE ON THE WHOLE	STRONGLY DISAGREE	UNCERTAIN
8. I hate going to new places like a club, unless I have friends with me.	1	2	3	4	5
9. I like to know that home is always in the background.	1	2	3	4	5
10. I prefer to stay where I know people rather than go to new places.	1	2	3	4	5
11. Sometimes I'd rather do things on my own than with friends.	1	2	3	4	5
12. I would always ask my parents' advice before I took a really big decision.	1	2	3	4	5
13. I find it easy to talk to other people when I first meet them.	1	2	3	4	5
14. Older people often say one thing and do another.	1	2	3	4	5
15. You get in a rut meeting the same people every week.	1	2	3	4	5
16. You usually reject your parents' advice at my age.	1	2	3	4	5
17. People don't seem to be interested in what I have to say.	1	2	3	4	5
18. I don't mind what I do in my spare time as long as I'm with friends.	1	2	3	4	5
19. My parents realise that I need more freedom at my age.	1	2	3	4	5
20. I find it easy to make new friends.	1	2	3	4	5
21. My parents quite understand that I can make up my own mind about things.	1	2	3	4	5

	STRONGLY AGREE	AGREE ON THE WHOLE	DISAGREE ON THE WHOLE	STRONGLY DISAGREE	UNCERTAIN
22. The older generation go on about young people so much that it makes me sick.	1	2	3	4	5
23. I sometimes feel my parents are a bit too strict.	1	2	3	4	5
24. As a family, we are always discussing things together.	1	2	3	4	5
25. Parents understand you more than anyone else does.	1	2	3	4	5
26. I'm rather a shy person in fact.	1	2	3	4	5
27. I like to spend my spare time with the same group of people.	1	2	3	4	5
28. My parents are always interested to know what I've been doing.	1	2	3	4	5
29. I like to have all sorts of different friends.	1	2	3	4	5
30. Older people often blame young people for things that aren't really young people's fault.	1	2	3	4	5
31. Whatever age you are, older people seem to treat you like a child.	1	2	3	4	5

Section II

Taking all things together, how would you say
things are nowadays, would you say you're very
happy, fairly happy or not very happy?

	Put a tick in the box that applies to you
Very happy	
Fairly happy	
Not very happy	

Section III

In your opinion what sort of people go to youth clubs? Below are some ways in which people can be described printed like this:-

LIVELY   1   2   3   4   5   DULL

What we want you to do is to tell us whether you think that people who go to youth clubs are on the whole very like the word on the left, rather like the word on the left and so on right through to very like the word on the right. So if you think that on the whole people who go to youth clubs are quite lively you should ring number 2 like this:-

LIVELY   1 (2) 3   4   5   DULL

If you thought they were very dull, of course you would ring number 5. Please go through the list quickly and don't stop to think too much.

PEOPLE WHO GO TO YOUTH CLUBS ARE:

i	ROUGH	1	2	3	4	5	WELL-BEHAVED
ii	SENSIBLE	1	2	3	4	5	SILLY
iii	CHILDISE	1	2	3	4	5	MATURE
iv	LIVELY	1	2	3	4	5	DULL
v	PEOPLE WHO THINK FOR THEMSELVES	1	2	3	4	5	PEOPLE WHO FOLLOW THE CROWD
vi	LONELY	1	2	3	4	5	POPULAR
vii	BEHIND THE TIMES	1	2	3	4	5	UP TO DATE
viii	FRIENDLY	1	2	3	4	5	UNFRIENDLY

279

Now we would like to know your views about the sort of people you think usually run clubs for young people - either from your own experience or from what you have heard.

Below are some ways in which other people have described those who run clubs for young people and we would like you to say whether you strongly agree, agree on the whole, disagree on the whole or strongly disagree with each description. Just ring the number in the box which most represents what you think.

PEOPLE WHO RUN CLUBS FOR YOUNG PEOPLE ARE USUALLY:	Strongly agree	Agree on the whole	Disagree on the whole	Strongly disagree	Uncertain
(i) DULL	1	2	3	4	5
(ii) SYMPATHETIC	1	2	3	4	5
(iii) INTERESTED IN YOUNG PEOPLE'S IDEAS	1	2	3	4	5
(iv) BOSSY	1	2	3	4	5
(v) FULL OF GOOD SENSE	1	2	3	4	5
(vi) TRYING TO PUSH THEIR IDEAS ON TO YOU	1	2	3	4	5
(vii) YOUNG	1	2	3	4	5
(viii) BEHIND THE TIMES	1	2	3	4	5

APPENDIX 3

EXAMPLES OF THREE MAIN TYPES OF CLUB

1. Sports Clubs

School swimming club
School table tennis club
Go Kart club
Works netball club
Athletics club (organised by work mates)
Wolves supporters club
Football team formed by group of friends
School fishing club
Volley ball team, attached to sports centre stadium
School rambling club
Old boys rugby club
Dover Colts (youth team which trains players for adult team)
Snooker club
Estate cricket club
School canoeing club
Badminton club, affiliated to Youth Club
Bank squash club

2. Social Clubs

Polish club (discotheque)
Avengers dancing club
Social club attached to hospital
School 'Umbrella Society'
Top Twenty club (work based)
Ballroom dancing club
Working mens club
Queensway social club
British Legion
Recreational Institute run by council
Boot Trade Association social club
Church based social club
United Services club
Civil Servants club (with discotheque and dancing)
Casino club dancehall
Trent Bus Co. social club
University Bar club
Inland Revenue social club
Mecca Dancing
British Rail Staff Association club
School Discotheque

3. Interest-Centred Clubs

Folk club
Choral society
Young Conservatives
Blues club
Photographic society
Welsh Nationalists
Debating society
Drama society
Geography society
Jazz club
Model Racing Car club
Art and Craft club
New music society
Church choir
Chess club
Corfe Mullen Band
Folk dancing society

APPENDIX 4

THE FACTOR ANALYSES AND CONSTRUCTION OF INDICES

The original intention was to construct indices which would measure the salience to the young people of three areas of their lives, and the satisfactoriness of their experiences within each area. The areas selected were: interests, friends and family relationships. Thus we hoped to be able to find out, for example, to what extent friends were a dominant influence on important decisions in the young people's lives and how well they were able to make friendships. This approach was suggested by early exploratory work which indicated that some young people's lives largely centred on and were influenced by their friends, others by their parents, and yet others by their own interests.

In the event the items used to construct these indices did not always coalesce into the groups we had envisaged, so that the analysis presented in Chapter 8 took a rather different form from that forseen. This was no doubt because it was not possible within the timetable set to conduct enough pilot trials to produce satisfactory measures of all these concepts.

The factor analyses were carried out with a computer programme based on that devised by H. H. Harman and modified by C.E.I.R. (UK) Ltd. and the computing section of the Social Survey. The results given are an orthogonal rotated solution using H. F. Kaiser's varimax criterion.

For each factor analysis alternative solutions produced by different numbers of rotations were provided. Thus, for example the results for the first analysis described below were rotated 5, 6 and 7 times. The optimal solution was then selected; that is, the solution which produced the maximum number of meaningful factors; or if no new meaningful factors were yielded by the higher number of rotations, the factors from the rotation which provided the highest loadings.

5 factor analyses were carried out as follows:-

(1) *Young People's Attitudes*

No. of items included	31	[This analysis covered areas 2)
No. of rotations	5, 6 & 7	to 4) below, but less extensively.
Solution selected	6	All the items came from Sect.1
Number of meaningful factors	6	of the Self-Completion Question-
Number of factors used	3	naire]

(2) *Friends*
No. of items included	24
No. of rotations	3, 4 & 5
Solution selected	5
Number of meaningful factors	3
Number of factors used	-

(3) *Interests*
No. of items included	16
No. of rotations	2, 3 & 4
Solution selected	3
Number of meaningful factors	3
Number of factors used	1

(4) *Family Relationships*
No. of items included	26
No. of rotations	4, 5 & 6
Solution selected	4
Number of meaningful factors	4
Number of factors used	3

(5) *Parental Anxieties*
No. of items included	13
No. of rotations	2, 3 & 4
Solution selected	3
No. of meaningful factors	3
No. of factors used	2

The resulting factors were checked for internal consistency and edited by calculating the Alpha Coefficient for each (see McKennel – Use of Coefficient Alpha).

The edited items were then dichotomised, so that about 50% of the sample fell on to each side of the dividing line where more than two responses to the question were possible. Each of the two sectors was allotted the number 0 or 1 according to the sign of the factor loading and each individual was then given the score of 0 or 1 according to which side of the division his answer fell. The measures used in Chapter 8 were then composed by totalling the number of items in the factor for which the individual received a score of 1. Thus in a 5 item measure 6 final scores are possible, ranging from a score of 1 on no item, to a score of 1 on all 5 items. These scores have the advantage over factor scores that they can be used in other studies, by employing identical items, without replication of the factor analysis itself.

After examination of the results of cross tabulating the measures with other relevant variables it was decided to dichotomise each measure so that half the scores fell on each side of the dividing line. Where the number of scores was uneven the division was made next to the mid-point on the side which maximised differences between sub-groups.

The variables which had the highest loadings on each factor are listed below under the area to which they belong. Following this is a list of all the variables and loadings in the 5 factor analyses arranged under the analysis involved.

A. Friends

1. *Capacity for mixing*   *Loading*

Self completion section 1

Q.20.	I find it easy to make new friends	.70
26.	I'm rather a shy person, in fact	-.62
3.	I'm not what you call a good mixer	-.61
13.	I find it easy to talk to other people when I first meet them	.49
8.	I hate going to new places, like a club, unless I have friends with me	-.40

Alpha coefficient = .71

2. *Social Conservatism*

Self completion section 1

Q.27.	I like to spend my spare time with the same group of people	-.46
18.	I don't mind what I do in my spare time, as long as I'm with friends	-.45
10.	I prefer to stay where I know people rather than go to new places	-.47
4.	I prefer to do the things I know about rather than learn completely new things	-.42

Alpha coefficient = .53

B. Interests

1. *Attitudes towards varied experiences*   *Loading*

Self completion section 1

5.	I'd like to have the opportunity to get to know another country really well	.49
6.	I'd like to make friends with people who have different attitudes and interests from myself	.44
29.	I like to have all sorts of different friends	.38
1.	As far as holidays are concerned I'd like to explore a different place each year	.30

Alpha coefficient = .50

2. *Interest in wider world*

S.C.7.	I like to hear what's going on in the world	.47
Q.29.	Regularly watches documentary/current affairs programmes	.44
Q.30.	Limited interest in the news	-.42
Q.27a.	Usually reads daily newpaper	.23
Q. 5.	Stayed on or left school to get a better education	.39

Alpha coefficient = .51

C. Family Relationships and attitudes towards older generation

1. *Perceived parental restrictiveness/permissiveness*   *Loading*

S.C.21.	My parents quite understand that I can make up my own mind about things	.59
S.C.19.	My parents realise I need more freedom at my age	.57
S.C.23.	I sometimes feel my parents are a bit too strict	-.40
Q.15.	Y.P. feels he should decide (about how to behave)	.27
Q.14.	No. of items parents make rules about	-.21

Alpha coefficient = .78

285

2. Family integration

S.C.24.	As a family we are always discussing things together	-.61
S.C.28.	My parents are always interested to know what I've been doing	-.46
S.C.12.	I would always ask my parent's advice before taking a really big decision	-.45
S.C.25.	Parents understand you more than anyone else does	-.45
Q.11.	Most enjoys spending spare time with family	-.37

Alpha coefficient = .78

3. Attitudes towards older people   *Loading*

Self completion section 1

22.	The older generation go on so much about young people that it makes me sick	-.70
2.	Older people irritate me with the things they say	-.57
30.	Older people often blame young people for things that aren't really their fault	-.55
31.	Whatever age you are, older people treat you like a child	-.55
14.	Older people often say one thing and do another	-.55
16.	You usually reject your parents advice at my age	-.34

Alpha coefficient = .74

D. Parental Anxieties

1. Anxiety about fullness of Social Life   *Loading*

Parent's Schedule

Q.27(2).	Parent wishes Y.P. had more friends	-.62
Q.13.	Parent thinks at least one of children doesn't meet enough of kind of people she likes him to mix with	-.62
Q.27(1)	Parent wished there was more for Y.P. to do round here	-.38
Q.14.	Parent thinks at least one of children doesn't make friends easily	-.33
Q.12.	Parent not happy about time Y.P. spends at home	-.53

Alpha coefficient = .65

2. Anxiety about anti-social activity/loss of control

Q.27(7).	Worries about Y.P. drinking	.53
Q.27(3).	Afraid Y.P. may get into trouble	.52
Q.27(5).	Worries in case Y.P. takes drugs	.47
Q.18.	No of items parent has to say anything about	.37
Q.28.	Would like advice about Y.P.	.31
Q.27(6)	Anxious in case Y.P. attacked	.26

Alpha coefficient = .61

Comparison of the above list of measures with the following details of factor analyses shows that not all the factors considered meaningful were used. Meaningful factors were not used: if they were very similar to other factors composed of more items, or of items having higher loadings; or if their composition made them appear to be of doubtful value.

Variables included in the factor analyses and their factor loadings

1. Young People's Attitudes

F1 Attitudes towards older people (not used)
F2 Capacity for mixing
F3 Parental restrictiveness (not used)
F4 Social conservatism
F5 Family integration (not used)
F6 Attitudes towards varied experiences

	Factor Loadings					
Variables	1	2	3	4	5	6
1. As far as holidays are concerned I would like to explore a completely different place each year	-0.15	0.06	-0.17	0.00	0.00	0.3
2. Older people irritate me with things they say	-0.57	-0.05	0.10	-0.1	0.16	-0.09
3. I'm not what you call a good mixer	-0.04	-0.62	0.07	0.01	0.00	-0.06
4. I prefer to do the things I know rather than learn completely new things	-0.12	-0.11	-0.01	-0.42	0.04	-0.18
5. I'd like to have the opportunity to get to know a foreign country really well	-0.03	0.04	-0.03	0.14	0.12	0.49
6. I would like to make friends with people who have different outlooks and interests from me	0.05	0.15	0.09	0.07	-0.13	0.44
7. I like to hear about what's going on in the world	0.02	0.02	-0.12	-0.01	-0.05	0.30
8. I hate going to new places like a club unless I have friends with me	-0.13	-0.42	0.11	-0.27	-0.03	-0.03
9. I like to feel that home is always in the background	-0.02	-0.04	-0.11	-0.15	-0.25	-0.06
10. I prefer to stay where I know people rather than go to new places	-0.04	-0.31	0.06	-0.47	0.10	-0.25
11. Sometimes I'd rather do things on my own than with friends	-0.02	-0.14	-0.05	0.29	0.02	0.04
12. I would always ask my parents' advice before I took a really big decision	0.14	-0.05	-0.03	-0.03	-0.46	0.08
13. I find it easy to talk to other people when I first meet them	-0.11	0.47	-0.09	0.01	-0.03	0.1
14. Older people often say one thing and do another	-0.53	0.07	-0.02	0.01	0.09	-0.03
15. You get in a rut meeting the same people every week	-0.18	-0.11	-0.00	0.1	0.15	0.13
16. You usually reject your parents' advice at my age	-0.34	0.03	0.21	0.03	0.24	-0.03
17. People don't seem to be interested in what I have to say	-0.26	-0.19	0.09	-0.15	0.21	-0.08

Variables	Factor Loadings					
	1	2	3	4	5	6
18. I don't mind what I do in my spare time as long as I'm with friends	-0.22	0.11	-0.04	-0.45	-0.04	0.07
19. My parents realise that I need more freedom at my age	0.05	0.07	-0.56	0.04	-0.07	0.09
20. I find it easy to make new friends	-0.07	0.69	-0.03	-0.08	-0.07	0.12
21. My parents quite understand that I can make up my own mind about things	0.09	0.07	-0.63	-0.05	-0.2	0.11
22. The older generation go on so much about young people that it makes me sick	-0.7	-0.01	0.06	-0.08	0.09	0.04
23. I sometimes feel that my parents are a bit too strict	-0.2	-0.04	0.49	0.01	0.16	0.01
24. As a family we are always discussing things together	0.17	0.10	-0.25	0.11	-0.58	0.08
25. Parents understand you more than anyone else does	0.15	0.04	-0.27	-0.08	-0.46	0.00
26. I'm rather a shy person in fact	-0.09	-0.63	-0.05	-0.06	-0.06	-0.02
27. I like to spend my spare time with the same group of people	-0.05	-0.17	-0.07	-0.46	0.03	-0.01
28. My parents are always interested to know what I've been doing	0.06	0.01	-0.01	0.06	-0.51	0.03
29. I like to have all sorts of different friends	-0.11	0.33	0.09	0.13	-0.18	0.38
30. Older people often blame young people for things that aren't really young people's fault	0.55	0.00	0.07	-0.01	-0.02	0.18
31. Whatever age you are older people seem to treat you like a child	-0.55	-0.05	0.14	-0.19	0.08	0.05

2. Friends

F1   Ease of making friends
F2   Salience of friends
F3   Importance of clubs for meeting people   } not used
F4   Desire for variety of friends
F5   ?

Variables	Factor loadings				
	1	2	3	4	5
1. I'm not what you call a good mixer	-0.61	0.08	0.13	0.12	0.12
2. I would like to make friends with people who have different outlooks and interests from me	0.22	0.06	-0.04	0.40	-0.08
3. I hate going to a new place like a club unless I am with friends	-0.4	-0.16	0.02	-0.01	0.19
4. Sometimes I'd rather do things on my own than with friends	-0.09	0.26	0.00	-0.07	0.11
5. I find it easy to talk to other people when I first meet them	0.49	-0.03	-0.03	0.1	0.06

Variables	Factor Loadings				
	1	2	3	4	5
6. You get in a rut meeting the same people every week	0.01	0.05	0.03	0.06	0.37
7. People don't seem to be interested in what I have to say	-0.19	-0.14	0.03	-0.04	0.28
8. I don't mind what I do in my spare time so long as I'm with friends	0.04	-0.54	-0.02	0.11	0.11
9. I find it easy to make new friends	0.7	-0.17	-0.11	0.05	-0.04
10. I'm rather a shy person in fact	-0.6	-0.03	0.14	0.07	0.07
11. I like to spend my time with the same group of people	-0.25	-0.47	-0.02	-0.07	-0.04
12. I like to have all sorts of different friends	0.38	0.08	0.05	0.34	0.05
13. Friends important in deciding when to leave school	-0.03	-0.18	-0.05	0.08	0.00
14. First became interested in something because of friends	-0.01	-0.10	-0.06	-0.05	-0.13
15. Most enjoys spending spare time with friends	0.01	-0.29	0.02	-0.02	-0.08
16. No. of times got together with friends	-0.12	0.35	0.1	0.11	0.18
17. No. of close friends	-0.18	0.11	0.12	-0.11	0.24
18. Parent feels Y.P. meets enough of the kind of people she would like Y.P. to mix with	0.05	-0.09	0.01	0.42	-0.04
19. Parent thinks Y.P. makes friends easily	-0.08	-0.01	-0.04	0.14	0.06
20. Parent wishes Y.P. had more friends	0.00	-0.25	0.01	-0.04	0.14
21. Important that club should be place to meet new people	-0.07	-0.01	0.08	0.43	0.07
22. Important that club should be a place to meet friends you know already	-0.05	0.00	0.60	-0.02	0.06
23. Important that club should be a place to meet people who think like you do	-0.26	0.03	0.32	0.02	0.05
24. Important that club should be a place where you learn how to get on with all sorts of people	-0.12	0.08	0.61	0.04	0.09

3. Interests

F1 Attitude towards new experiences (not used)
F2 Interest in wider world
F3 Attitude towards varied experiences (not used)

Variables	Factor loadings		
	1	2	3
1. As far as holidays are concerned I'd like to explore a completely different place each year	-0.04	0.08	-0.31
2. I prefer to do the things I know about already rather than learn completely new things	0.45	-0.24	0.06
3. I'd like to have the opportunity to get to know a foreign country really well	-0.14	0.19	-0.4
4. I would like to make friends with people who have different outlooks and interests from me	-0.16	0.16	-0.45
5. I like to hear about what's going on in the world	0.04	0.46	-0.15

Variables	Factor Loadings		
	1	2	3
6. I hate going to new places like a club unless I have friends with me	0.45	0.03	0.08
7. I prefer to stay where I know people rather than go to new places	0.55	-0.11	0.18
8. I like to have all different sorts of friends	-0.23	0.05	-0.42
9. Stayed on/left school to get a better job/ education/ go to college	-0.16	0.39	-0.00
10. Usually enjoys spare time	-0.23	0.23	0.02
11. Usually reads daily newspaper	-0.07	0.22	-0.11
12. Regularly watches or listens to documentary/ current affairs programmes	-0.08	0.45	-0.05
13. Limited interest in news	-0.02	-0.42	0.06
14. Disliked school	0.09	0.02	0.1
15. Clubs should be places where you can learn new things and find new interests	0.02	-0.05	-0.27
16. Clubs should be places where you can do things you are already interested in	0.00	0.04	-0.08

4. Family Relationships

F1 Attitude towards older people
F2 Parental domination (not used)
F3 Parental restrictiveness
F4 Family integration

Variables	Factor loadings			
	1	2	3	4
1. Older people irritate me with things they say	0.53	-0.09	-0.05	0.26
2. I like to know that home is always in the background	0.01	-0.06	0.16	-0.15
3. I would always ask my parents' advice before taking a really big decision	-0.11	-0.12	0.04	-0.45
4. Older people often say one thing and do another	0.51	-0.00	0.08	0.16
5. You usually reject your parents' advice at my age	0.32	-0.08	-0.17	0.26
6. My parents realise that I need more freedom at my age	0.08	0.13	0.57	-0.07
7. My parents quite understand I can make up my own mind about things	-0.11	0.17	0.59	-0.22
8. The older generation go on about Y.P. so much it makes me sick	0.72	-0.02	0.01	0.16
9. I sometimes feel my parents are a bit too strict	0.21	-0.28	-0.40	0.18
10. As a family we are always discussing things together	-0.13	0.00	0.26	-0.61
11. Parents understand you more than anyone else does	-0.13	0.00	0.27	-0.45
12. My parents are always interested to know what I've been doing	-0.03	-0.17	0.11	-0.46
13. Older people often blame Y.P. for things that aren't Y.P.'s fault	0.57	0.01	0.01	0.04

290

Variables	Factor loadings			
	1	2	3	4
14. Whatever age you are older people seem to treat you like a child	0.57	-0.04	-0.13	0.09
15. Parents important in decision when to leave school	-0.01	-0.04	-0.02	-0.02
16. Became interested in something because of parents	-0.06	-0.09	-0.09	-0.16
17. Inadequate leisure activities with family	0.12	0.15	0.05	0.31
18. Most enjoys spending spare time with family	-0.12	0.08	-0.07	-0.37
19. Parents like friends brought home	-0.06	0.02	0.08	-0.23
20. Parents make rules on who Y.P. goes out with	0.12	-0.53	-0.12	-0.11
21. Parents make rules on how Y.P. dresses	0.07	-0.62	-0.05	-0.06
22. Parents make rules about how Y.P. spends his money	0.07	0.14	-0.05	-0.09
23. No. of things parents make rules about (code 1 = 7)	0.08	-0.82	-0.21	-0.01
24. Y.P. feels he should decide about things at Q'4	0.11	0.23	0.27	0.15
25. Parent not discussed with Y.P. when to leave school	-0.05	0.27	-0.05	0.04
26. Parent is trying to bring up family strictly	-0.04	0.02	-0.05	0.00

5. Parental Anxieties

F1 Anxiety about child's social life
F2 Anxiety about loss of control
F3 Anxiety about harm befalling child (not used)

Variables	Factor loadings		
	1	2	3
1. Parent not happy about the amount of time Y.P. spends at home	-0.53	0.07	-0.1
2. Parent thinks Y.P. does not meet enough of the kind of people parent likes him to mix with	-0.62	0.14	0.08
3. Parent thinks Y.P. does not make friends easily	-0.33	0.00	-0.01
4. No. of things parent has to say anything about to Y.P. (Q18) Code 1 = 7 items	-0.1	0.37	-0.07
5. Parent wants Y.P. to do job Y.P. wants to do	-0.08	0.11	-0.05
6. Parent wishes there was more for Y.P. to do round here	-0.38	0.08	-0.09
7. Parent wishes Y.P. had more friends	-0.62	0.07	0.03
8. Parent sometimes afraid Y.P. might get into trouble	-0.01	0.52	-0.1
9. Parent worries in case Y.P. is in an accident	-0.01	0.12	-0.41
10. Parent worries in case Y.P. tries taking drugs	-0.03	0.47	-0.19
11. Parent worries in case Y.P. is attacked	-0.06	0.26	-0.41
12. Parent worries about Y.P. (trying) drinking	-0.02	0.53	-0.23
13. Parent feels she would like advice about children	-0.25	0.31	0.06

REFERENCES

Almond G.A., Verba S. (1963) The Civic Culture; Political Altitudes & Democracy in Five Nations. Princeton University Press. Princeton, New Jersey, 1963.

Bradburn N.M. (1969) The Structure of Psychological Well-Being. National Opinion Research Centre Monographs in Social Research No. 15. Aldine Publishing Co., Chicago, 1969.

Department of Education & Science (1969) Youth & Community Work in the 70s; proposals by the Youth Service Development Council. H.M.S.O., London, 1969.

Department of Education & Science (1970) Statistics of Education 1969; Vol. 1. Schools. H.M.S.O.,London, 1970.

Goldthorpe J.H., Lockwood D., Bechhofer F., Platt J., The affluent worker; industrial attitudes and behaviour. Cambridge University Press, Cambridge, 1968.

Harris M. (1959). Further Education; a Survey carried out for the Central Advisory Council for Education (England). SS.271 Central Office of Information. September 1959.*

Horton M. (1967). Management of Local Government, Vol. 3. The Local Government Elector. H.M.S.O., London, 1967.

Katz E., Lazarsfeld P.F. (1960) Personal Influence; the part played by people in the flow of mass communications. A report of the Bureau of Applied Social Research, Columbia University. The Free Press, Glencoe, Illinois, 1960.

McKennell A.C. Use of Coefficient Alpha in Constructing Attitude & Similar Scales. M139 in the Methodological Series of the Social Survey Division of the Office of Population Censuses & Surveys.*

Morton-Williams R., Finch S. (1968) Young School Leavers; Schools Councils Enquiry 1. H.M.S.O., London, 1968.

Sillitoe K. (1969) Planning for Leisure, H.M.S.O., London, 1969.

Ward J. (1948) Children out of School — The Social Survey-New Series No. 110, June 1948.*

Wilkins L.T. (1951) The Employment of Adolescents. The Social Survey-Report No. 148(1), January 1951.*

*Available at the Social Survey Division of the Office of Population Censuses & Surveys, Atlantic House, Holborn Viaduct, London E.C.2.

Printed in England for Her Majesty's Stationery Office
by Hobbs the Printers Ltd., Southampton
(283) Dd503809 1,750 4/72 G3313